EPIC AND TRAGIC STRUCTURE IN PARADISE LOST

EPIC AND TRAGIC STRUCTURE IN PARADISE LOST

John M. Steadman

The University of Chicago Press
Chicago and London

JOHN M. STEADMAN has been a research associate
at the Huntington Library and editor of the
Huntington Library Quarterly since 1962. He is
also professor of English at the University of
California at Riverside. Among his publications
are *Milton and the Renaissance Hero; Milton's
Epic Characters: Image and Idol; The Myth of
Asia; Disembodied Laughter: Troilus and the
Apotheosis Tradition;* and *The Lamb and the
Elephant: Ideal Imitation and the Context of
Renaissance Allegory.*

Portions of chapter 1 are reprinted from John
Steadman, "Milton and Renaissance Epic
Theory," in *Medieval Epic to the "Epic Theater"
of Brecht,* ed. R. P. Armato and J. M. Spalek,
University of Southern California Studies in
Comparative Literature, 1 (1968): 109–24, copy-
right © 1968 by the University of Southern
California.

The University of Chicago Press, Chicago 60637
The University of Chicago Press, Ltd., London

© 1976 by The University of Chicago
All rights reserved. Published 1976
Printed in the United States of America
80 79 78 77 76   9 8 7 6 5 4 3 2 1

Library of Congress Cataloging in Publication Data

Steadman, John M
 Epic and tragic structure in Paradise lost.

 Includes bibliographical references and index.
  1. Milton, John, 1608–1674. Paradise lost.
I. Title.
PR3562.S64   821'.4   75-43234
ISBN 0-226-77134-2

CONTENTS

PREFACE

Aristotle, *Poetics,*
trans.
Ingram Bywater

The first essential, the life and soul,
... of Tragedy is the Plot.
The proper construction of the
Fable or Plot, ... that is at once
the first and most important thing
in Tragedy.

Paradise Lost is a poem of multiple structures. For all its painstaking concern for unity—in action, in time and place, and perhaps in *moralitas*—it is, in significant respects, a polymorph. This does not, to be sure, compromise its integrity—that "organic" unity so highly esteemed by the biologist and metaphysician turned dramatic critic, "master of those who know." For the poetic organism, like the living organism, is a synthesis or hierarchy of subsidiary structures: parts of a larger whole. Recent critics have, with justice, emphasized the parodic structure of Milton's epic: the tissue of types and antitypes, ideas and eidola; the secondary or tertiary imitations of persons and actions within a poem that is itself conceived and executed as the imitation of an action. With equal justice, they have stressed the patterns resulting from the elaboration of analogies or from the juxtaposition of contraries, isolated the poem's metaphorical and linguistic structures and its mythical and allegorical patterns, defined its thematic structure—ethical or psychological or theological—or emphasized its variety in unity as a poetic heterocosm, a "vast design" modeled deliberately on the order of the visible and invisible universe. Several critics have investigated geometrical or arithmetical structures of Milton's epic, its linear or circular patterns, the logical organization of its similes, its affinities with the five-act structure of tragedy and Davenant's unfinished epic on Gondibert, the patterning of particular books or blocks of books. Some have examined in detail the poet's technique of linking past and future with present events, compared his narrative method with classical or Renaissance exemplars, and composed running commentaries on the action of his poem. Some have found inspiration in depth psychology, reading sermons in stones and case histories in the deployment of a shield and a spear. Others have borrowed the structuralist techniques perfected by anthropologists and philologists. In the strictest sense, these methods serve primarily to elicit unsuspected patterns through comparison and contrast with related works and motifs rather than to elucidate overt patterns within the poem itself.

All these approaches are valid; and many of them are, in fact, indispensable. Nevertheless, just as every endeavor to uncover undetected layers of meaning may obscure the poet's principal and less recondite intent, so the concern with subtler, symbolic structures can easily distort the more elementary and basic pattern of the plot. To emphasize the latter does not compromise the value and validity of other structural analyses, but it may, to some extent, serve as a complement, if not as a corrective.

A comprehensive analysis of the subsidiary forms in Milton's poem lies beyond the scope of this book. Instead, I shall be concerned primarily with the plot as "idea" or formal cause of the epic poem, examining the three principal parts of the epic or tragic fable—reversal, recognition, and "scene of suffering"—against the background of Renaissance critical theory.

Since all three of these elements (*peripeteia, anagnorisis, pathos*) are common to epic and tragedy,[1] I shall reconsider the interrelationship between epic and tragic effect—reinterpreting *Paradise Lost* not only against the background of Renaissance poetic theory but also through comparison with *Samson Agonistes*. In centering this study specifically on three major elements in the epic or tragic plot, I have necessarily deferred such problems as character, thought, and style (*ethos, dianoia, lexis*) for more detailed discussion in a separate monograph.

Of the eight chapters in this book, the first reexamines Milton's knowledge of Italian epic theory. The second reconsiders his assimilation of other literary modes—comic, satiric, pastoral, and tragic—to the conventions of heroic poetry. The third chapter concerns the interrelationship between the epic and the tragic illustrious. The next four chapters reassess his treatment of *peripeteia, anagnorisis,* and *pathos* (reversal, recognition, "scene of suffering") against the background of Renaissance critical theory. The final chapter explores the interrelationships between theological and poetic conceptions of the marvelous and their bearing on epic and tragic affects.

ACKNOWLEDGMENTS

Portions of this study originally appeared in somewhat different form under the following titles and are reprinted by kind permission of the editors: "Milton and Renaissance Epic Theory," in *Medieval Epic to the "Epic Theater" of Brecht*, ed. R. P. Armato and J. M. Spalek, University of Southern California Studies in Comparative Literature, 1 (1968): 109–24; "*Paradise Lost* and the 'Tragic Illustrious,'" *Anglia* 78 (1960): 302–16; "Peripeteia in Milton's Epic Fable," *Anglia* 81 (1963): 429–52; "Recognition in the Fable of *Paradise Lost*," *Studia Neophilologica* 31 (1959): 159–73; "Miracle and the Epic Marvellous in *Paradise Lost*," *Archiv für das Studium der neueren Sprachen und Literaturen* 198 (1961): 289–303.

A HUMANISTIC EPIC

MILTON'S DEBT TO ITALIAN CRITICISM

1 What did "John Milton Englishman" (Joannes Miltonius Anglus—as he styled himself)[1] owe to Italian poetics? What light can sixteenth-century Italian theory throw on seventeenth-century England and its poetry? How far can Renaissance criticism aid and direct the Milton critic today?

Such questions as these belong (one suspects) rather to rhetoric than to scholarship, for one does not really expect to answer them. They do not, in fact, lend themselves very readily to definitive answers. But we shall not look for final answers to these queries. Instead, we shall try to clarify a few of the problems they involve and the challenges they present to the contemporary scholar. The problems, it appears, are altogether too many; the facts appallingly few.

At the outset we are confronted by a paradox. Milton has been called many things—regicide and Fifth Monarchist, Puritan and sensualist, Satanist and theocrat; egoist, heretic, Cyclops, antifeminist, syphilitic, and albino. But he has rarely, if ever, been called an "Italianate Englishman." Nevertheless such an epithet admirably fits his literary tastes and critical orientation, which were prevailingly classical and Italian. Moreover, to a considerable extent he tended to see the classics themselves through Italian eyes.

For Milton's specific debts to particular Italian critics we have little substantial proof—little evidence that can establish certainties instead of conjectures. On the other hand, we possess a considerable body of evidence for arguing probabilities.

1

Milton's extensive reading in Italian history and poetry is common knowledge. So is the identity of some of the particular poets and historians he consulted—Dante, Petrarch, Boccaccio; Ariosto, Boiardo, Pulci; Tasso, Della Casa, Boccalini; Machiavelli, Guicciardini, and many others. In numerous instances one can, in fact, identify the particular editions he consulted. He read Dante, for instance, in a volume containing Daniello's commentary.[2]

These are clearly "facts," but when we try to estimate their significance we are once again in the realm of conjecture. Even though we can identify particular works that Milton read, we can rarely be sure that he owed a specific detail to a particular author rather than to other representatives of the same tradition. Even in the case of works that Milton obviously knew, it is usually safer to stress his indebtedness to a tradition or a movement than to try to pinpoint individual "sources."

When we turn from Italian poets and historians to Italian critics, our evidence is still less conclusive, and we must perforce treat it with even greater caution. Though we know many of the major poets he read, the identity of the critics he consulted remains largely a matter of conjecture. These range from near certainties to remote possibilities.

Among the near certainties we may rank Tasso, Mazzoni, and Castelvetro, for Milton himself recommends them as authorities on poetic theory. (Though it is conceivable that he could have based his judgment on their reputation rather than on direct experience, this scarcely seems likely in view of all that we know of him as a scholar and as a man; he was rarely willing to accept another's verdict uncritically.) We may assume, therefore, that he had read at least one of the principal treatises of each of these three writers—that he had seen Castelvetro's translation and exposition of Aristotle's *Poetics;* the first volume of Mazzoni's *Defence* of the *Divine Comedy* and perhaps his shorter *Discourse* on the same poem; and (most important of all for an epic poet) Tasso's *Discourses on the Heroic Poem* or his earlier *Discourses on the Art of Poetry.* To these treatises we may add Tasso's "Allegory of the *Jerusalem Delivered,"* which Milton could easily have encountered in many Italian editions of this poem as well as in Fairfax's English translation.

That Milton had read several or all of these works is a virtual certainty. They seem, therefore, to be the logical point of departure for examining his debt to Italian criticism.

It seems equally certain that he must have consulted other works, but when we attempt to identify these we are once more in the realm of conjecture. His own remarks on poetics are widely scattered and sometimes inconsistent; they reveal change and development. Modern scholarship has accordingly been forced to rely largely on analogy in attempting to relate them to the continental tradition. Minturno and Scaliger, Muzio and Varchi, Trissino and Vellutello, Alessandro and Francesco Piccolomini, and the Dutch critics Heinsius and Vossius have all (at one time or another) been regarded as possible sources for his doctrines. There are, moreover, suggestive parallels even in the brief critical epistles that Italian poets frequently prefixed to their poetry; Valvasone's preface to the *Angeleida* appears to foreshadow Milton's insistence that the poet may be a "better teacher" than Aquinas.[3]

Milton's resemblances to these authors are also "facts," but they do not, as a rule, establish his indebtedness to the works in question or even demonstrate that he had read them. Though such analogies are essential for an understanding of his own epic theory and its general relationship to the Renaissance critical tradition, they hardly provide sufficient grounds for identifying Milton's actual sources.

When we examine his indebtedness to particular critics, then, as opposed to his *general* debt to Italian poetic theory, we are again left, on the whole, with possibilities rather than certainties. The vital questions—what particular authors influenced him, what specific doctrines he owed to one critic rather than another—can rarely be answered with finality.

Though Milton showed surprisingly little interest in evolving a systematic poetics for himself, he nevertheless displayed a lifelong interest in several of the crucial issues raised by the Italian critics. These were for the most part problems of immediate practical (and indeed personal) concern—questions that were of vital importance for the epic and tragedy he was planning. Before he could seriously embark on a major work, he first had to settle to his own satisfaction the central issues of technique: the definition and distinction of genres, the "laws" that governed each literary species, the problem of the unities and (in particular) the question of unity or multiplicity of action, the structure or "economy" of the plot, decorum in character and style, the relative merits of rhymed and blank verse, the moral or psychological "effects" of poetry and its subservience to national and religious ends. All these issues had been warmly debated by Renaissance theorists, but his own attitude toward them seems to have been (on the whole) practical rather than theoretical. In approaching the complex and often contradictory body of Italian criticism, he was not primarily seeking the elements of a comprehensive poetic theory; he was looking for the particular principles that might guide him in planning and composing his own poetry in accordance with the "laws" of epic, lyric, or tragedy.

If this was what he was looking for, one would expect him to treat his sources with considerable freedom, picking and choosing exactly what suited his immediate purpose as a dedicated poet, a confirmed Protestant, and an incorrigible Englishman. One would expect him to be as eclectic—and as individual—in his poetics as in his politics and his theology.

In speculating on Milton's poetics, therefore, it is expedient to bear in mind the motto that a British bibliographer habitually kept before him on his desk: "A house built of hypotheses must be of one storey." Since Milton left no systematic poetics for us, we should show a decent reluctance to invent one for him. For at best we can achieve a hypothesis, at worst a mare's nest.

Though an effective controversialist, Milton was not primarily a theorist. In most areas of life (from religion downward) he distrusted theory; and the immediate motivation of most of his prose writings was (in the best sense of the word) practical. They were oriented toward civil, domestic, or religious ends; and for the most part they were composed in response to specific issues that were likewise civil, domestic, or religious. As a prose writer he was essentially an "engaged" artist. The fact that he often reasons from first principles or from final causes should not blind us to the equally significant fact that the bent of his arguments is usually toward the contemporary situation (toward particular ills he wishes to remove or specific goals he wants his church or country to achieve) and that he hopes for eventual, if not immediate, practical results. His writings on grammar, logic, and education; his works on British history and Christian doctrine; and even his emendations to the text of Euripides and his additions to Stephanus's Latin dictionary—these are all, in varying degrees, oriented toward practical and utilitarian ends. They bear a definable relationship to his career as a schoolmaster, his early plans for a poem on British history, or his abiding concern for toleration and peace in the English church and state.

As his *Art of Logic* demonstrates, Milton could (and did) take a ready-made, systematic work like Ramus's *Dialectica* and both expound and amplify it with the aid of other authorities (Aristotle, Cicero, Downham, and others). It is conceivable that he could have done the same with Aristotle's *Poetics*, drawing on the various and often contradictory opinons of the Italian "commentators." But the task would have been infinitely more difficult, and he never attempted it. In all likelihood he never even considered doing so. For he was far less interested in evolving a coherent and comprehensive epic theory than in solving the particular issues he inevitably had to face in composing a heroic poem himself. It was (he knew) as a practicing poet that he had to earn his "immortality of fame," not as a poetic theorist.

Our second question—the degree to which Italian theory affected not merely his poetics but his actual poetry—is equally a stumbling block. Perhaps the safest way to approach it is to ask precisely what he was looking for in Italian criticism. "Practical guidance for composing his own poetry," I have already suggested. But this explanation is hardly enough. We must also inquire why he turned primarily to Italy; and to this query his own remarks suggest the right answer. In his own words, Italy was "the lodging-place of *humanitas*," the school of classical humanism and indeed "of all the arts of civilization."[4]

From the Italians, accordingly, he sought guidance to the understanding of the ancients and to making the most effective use of the literary models they had left. From the Italians he looked for help in determining how and what to imitate in classical poetry and how to bridge most effectively the inevitable gulf between ancients and moderns. Italy was not only (in his eyes) the cradle of the Renaissance; it had not only led the way in perfecting the knowledge of the classical tongues and restoring the texts of classical authors. It had also gone much further than most other nations in assimilating the doctrines and examples left by the ancients, in adapting the principles of classical civilization to contemporary needs, and in accommodating them to the history and doctrines of Christendom, the social and political values of modern Europe, and the grammatical, syntactical, and prosodic limitations of the vernacular tongues.

It is hardly surprising, therefore, that he associates Renaissance Italians with the ancients as the chief authorities on the art of poetry. With Aristotle's *Poetics* and Horace's *Ars Poetica* he couples "the Italian commentaries of Castelvetro, Tasso, Mazzoni, and others" for the principles of poetic theory—"that sublime art which ... teaches what the laws are of a true epic poem, what of a dramatic, what of a lyric, what decorum is (which is the grand masterpiece to observe)."[5] For the structure or "modeling" of his single tragedy (*Samson Agonistes*), he follows "the Antients and Italians ..., as of much more authority and fame." In the preface to *Paradise Lost* he justifies his preference for blank verse rather than rhyme by appealing not merely to classical poets (Homer and Vergil) but also to modern "Italian and Spanish poets of prime note."

Like most other Renaissance writers, he regarded poetry as a conscious discipline—an "organic art" like rhetoric and logic, with characteristic "rules" and "laws" of its own. Like many of his contemporaries, moreover, he looked to Aristotle for the most authoritative statement of these laws. Inevitably he encountered the problem of interpreting these "rules"—of ascertaining what Aristotle probably meant, and of applying his dicta specifically to Renaissance epic and drama. On crucial points the *Poetics* was often ambiguous; moreover, since its principal emphasis fell on tragedy, it did not offer clear guidelines to the heroic poet. These the Renaissance theorists had to evolve for themselves, piecing them together out of Aristotle's cursory observations on the epic or developing them by inference and analogy from his fuller discussion of tragedy.

Milton turned to the Italian critics, then, much as a modern reader might resort to Bywater or Butcher or Else—for alternative readings and interpretations of Aristotle. He consulted them as standard authorities. He would hardly have expected a completely reliable interpretation from a single commentator, any more than a modern reader would expect an absolutely perfect reading from a single Aristotelian scholar today. Nor would he have anticipated any great unanimity of opinion among them, any more than we should look for widespread agreement among critics or scholars in our own century. Though the Italian commentators disagreed on many of the fundamental issues raised by the *Poetics*, they were not more divided than twentieth-century scholarship on (let us say) the interpretation of Chaucer or Shakespeare. Their diversity would hardly have impaired Aristotle's authority in Milton's eyes, but it

did very definitely leave him considerable freedom to interpret the
"laws" of the *Poetics* according to his own judgment.
In this respect the range and variety of critical opinion were
distinct assets. The tendency of many Renaissance commentators
to insist on Aristotle's legislative authority could easily have led to
sterility and rigidity; several generations later it indeed came close
to paralyzing critical originality. Renaissance poetics preserved its
vitality, however, largely through its variety of viewpoints and its
constant modifications of doctrine—through the inherent tensions
that resulted from the conflict between the commentators' exaggerated respect for a single authority and their excessive individual-
ism in interpreting him. Their diverse and sometimes contradictory
views paradoxically gave Aristotle's "laws" a surprising degree of
fluidity. Despite his pronounced respect for the "rules" of epic and
tragedy as promulgated by Aristotle and amplified by the Italians,
Milton found adequate scope for asserting his own judgment and
exercising his own independence of mind.

We should not forget, however, that he was looking for models
and exemplars as well as for theoretical doctrines. For the principles
that influenced his art, he was indebted to poets as much as (and
perhaps more than) to critics. This dual indebtedness further com-
plicates the already perplexed issue of sources and influences, for it
is not always possible to determine whether Milton owed a particular concept to a critical treatise or to an actual poem. In his
observations on education he repeatedly stressed the superiority of
example to precept, and elsewhere his own remarks suggest that he
formed his tastes—and modeled his poems—largely on the *example*
of the ancients and (in a lesser degree) on that of their Renaissance
imitators. Though theory assisted him in making the most judicious
use of the precedents set by earlier poets, we should avoid over-
stressing its influence on his poetry.

What insights can these sixteenth-century commentaries offer the
modern critic? As legislative criticism they are outmoded; they
belong largely to the history of ideas. In other respects, however,
they still possess practical value for the critic today. In the first
place, they can protect him against one of the easiest anachronisms
of contemporary scholarship—the tendency to project twentieth-
century interpretations of ancients backward into the Renaissance,
comparing or contrasting cinquecento poets with classical writers

whose works they saw through eyes very different from ours. One
has only to read Landino on Vergil, Spondanus on Homer, or
Castelvetro's interpretation of *peripeteia* to realize the gulf betwen
sixteenth-century readings of the classics and our own. The cinquecento commentaries can, in part at least, restore to us the Homer
and Vergil and Aristotle that Milton and Tasso knew.

In the second place, they can provide a critical terminology that
has greater *historical* relevance to Renaissance authors than the
vocabulary we generally use today. Admittedly there is great variety in the technical idiom of sixteenth-century poetics. The major
critics frequently differed in the distinctions they made and the
classifications they followed, and their terminology naturally reflected these differences. Nevertheless their principal terms were
usually based on Aristotle, and on these they tended to agree. Even
allowing for different translations of the *Poetics*, there remains a
substantial technical vocabulary that most cinquecento commentators possessed in common. This can be of undeniable value to the
modern scholar.

One is not, of course, arguing that the critic should set the clock
back or discard the vocabularies of other generations and schools—
the terminology of romantics and Victorians, imagists and symbol-
ists, Freudians and Jungians, or the New Critics and their succes-
sors. These have thrown, and will doubtless continue to throw,
considerable light on many aspects of Milton's poetry. In certain
respects, however, these vocabularies are anachronistic, and in
applying their terms to *Paradise Lost* one runs the risk of obscuring
instead of clarifying the actual issues as they once existed for the
poet. In such cases a return to Renaissance terminology can be a
healthful corrective.

Take, for instance, the problem of the hero of *Paradise Lost*. For
Dryden it was Satan; for Addison (who nevertheless deplored the
search for a "hero" as something that Milton had never intended) it
was the Son. More probably, however, it is Adam: the "Man"
whose "First Disobedience" and "loss of Eden" are specifically cited
in the first lines of the proposition and constitute the subject,
argument, and principal action of the poem. In the language
of Renaissance poetics, Adam would be the "primary hero" or
"epic person" of *Paradise Lost*, just as Christ would be the
"epic person" of *Paradise Regained* and Samson the "tragic person"
of *Samson Agonistes*. (In Christ and Satan, Milton has transformed

the conventional epic "machines" into archetypes of true and false heroic virtue, embodying spiritual and carnal, Christian and secular ideals of heroism. Neither, however, is the "epic person" or "primary hero" of the poem.)

There is no real problem here, and perhaps neither Dryden nor his contemporaries would have raised the question had they been as familiar with Italian poetics as with French poetic theory. Like Milton, they regarded the art of poetry as a set of "laws" and "rules," and they too venerated Aristotle and Horace as basic authorities. Nevertheless, for the sixteenth-century "Italian commentaries" Milton had extolled, they substituted the seventeenth-century *Poetics* of a French clergyman, Le Bossu.

A similar problem has arisen, in recent years, in regard to the relationship between history and poetic invention, or between literal and fictive statement in *Paradise Lost*. One scholar, for example has argued that Milton seriously "believed that he was adding historic details" to Genesis. Such a view not only overlooks Aristotle's fundamental distinction between poetry and history, but also ignores the nature of poetic imitation as his Renaissance commentators conceived it. Tasso insisted that the poet ought to base his argument on a real historical event and then proceed to elaborate it in accordance with the rules of poetic imitation. In fact he argued (though with reservations) that a subject remote in time or place would give the writer greater freedom to feign or imitate. For Milton's nephew, Edward Phillips, the doctrine of imitation (mimesis) similarly implied the poet's license to invent or feign.[6] In basing his argument on history, Milton condemned the "feigned" arguments of other epics; yet he never surrendered his traditional right to feign or invent details and episodes—such as the scene at Hellgate, Satan's apprehension by the angelic guard, or the celestial scales in which Jehovah weighs the sequels of parting or of fight. The poet surely did not regard these as "historic details" that Moses had unaccountably overlooked. Nor can he have believed that his heavenly muse was seriously delivering a new astronomical doctrine. (If this was what she really proposed to tell him about the origin of the constellation Libra, he would doubtless have suspected diabolical rather than celestial inspiration.)

A third critical battle has been waged over the "subject" or "thesis" of *Paradise Lost*. The contestants have, on the whole, tended to blur the distinction between the poetic and logical senses of "argument" and to assume all too readily that Milton's "great Argument"—the "argument of the Poem"—is none other than the vindication of "Eternal Providence" and the justification of God's ways to men. Actually his argument is the subject announced in his proposition or (in a somewhat narrower sense) the events summarized at the beginning of each book. Both of these senses are conventional, and in this context they are strictly literary rather than logical or rhetorical. Milton's argument is the fall of man, just as Vergil's argument (according to several Italian critics) is Aeneas's arrival in Italy and just as Homer's arguments are Achilles' wrath and Odysseus's *nostos* or homecoming.

Several decades ago Waldock called attention to the vast amount of controversy generated by a single issue—the *theme* of Milton's epic.[7] More recently G. A. Wilkes devoted a timely and valuable monograph to this problem. Few scholars will challenge the latter's contention that "the intent of *Paradise Lost* is to assert eternal providence, to show how it operates to bring forth good from evil." They may, however, hesitate before agreeing that "this and no other" is "the thesis that Milton must demonstrate." Denying that *Paradise Lost* is "a treatment of the fall of man, aiming to show that obedience to God is the highest of all virtues," Wilkes looks for an alternative "formula." The poem, in his opinion, is a "treatment of the operation of Providence, traced through the celestial cycle from the revolt of the angels to the Last Judgment." Other critics have advanced the same interpretation in different words. The subject of *Paradise Lost*, in their view, is not the fall of man, but his redemption.

The chief difficulty with such interpretations is that they confuse Milton's subject with his purpose. Or, in Aristotelian terms, they tend to mix up formal, material, and final causes indiscriminately. The material contents of the poem are indeed derived from the "celestial cycle" (or rather from scripture as amplified by exegetical and poetic tradition). The "essential form" or idea of *Paradise Lost* is, however, to be found primarily in the plot or fable—"the soul of the poem," as Aristotle called it. The final cause, or purpose, is of a different order. When Wilkes asserts that the "purpose is to justify the workings of Providence to mankind," he may be oversimplifying the author's intent, but he is nonetheless echoing the best evidence we have of the poet's purpose—his own words. On the other hand, when the same scholar substitutes a "treatment . . . of Providence" for a "treatment of the fall" as the subject of the poem, he is clearly contradicting Milton's own statement of the argument.[8] The "whole Subject," the poet declares, is "Man's disobedience, and the loss thereupon of Paradise."

Part of the difficulty for the twentieth-century scholar lies in the ambiguity of his terms. The words that the Renaissance poet might employ to describe his subject ("argument," "proposition," "theme") also belonged, in a rather different sense, to the technical vocabulary of the logician. Through failing to distinguish between their poetic and logical senses, the modern commentator may all too easily slip into the pitfall of treating a heroic poem as though it were a logical demonstration rather than the probable and "verisimilar" imitation of an action. One cannot emphasize too strongly the fact that the "subject," "matter," "argument" (or "theme" or "proposition") of a Renaissance epic is not a theorem but an action, and that the poet's proper method is not disputation but imitation. Like Andrew Marvell, we may legitimately speak of the "theme" of *Paradise Lost* if we mean thereby the action that constitutes its subject or argument. But we are hardly justified in equating it with a thesis that Milton must somehow "demonstrate."

The fact that such terms as "theme" and "motif" also belong to the vocabulary of music creates a further critical difficulty. Since they play a significant part in the structure of a musical composition we sometimes assume that they must perform a comparable role in the structure and organization of a poem. Though this may be true of much nineteenth- and twentieth-century literature, it scarcely applies to Renaissance epic. When heroic poets of the cinquecento and seicento used the term "theme," they employed it as a synonym for poetic "argument." It pertained to the "matter" or "subject" of the work rather than its structure or form.

When Renaissance theorists spoke of the "theme" of an epic, they were usually referring to its subject. The term "thesis," however, was normally alien to their vocabulary; it belonged less to poetics than to logic and rhetoric. They might speak of the "thesis" of a formal oration (such as a sermon or an academic prolusion) but not, as a rule, of the "thesis" of a poem. The Italian critics who were probably most familiar to Milton usually preferred the terms "argument," "proposition," and "subject"; and they insisted with Aristotle that the poem must be an "imitation of an action."

The search for a "theme" or "moral" in Milton's epic derives in large part from the impact of Le Bossu's poetics on English criticism. According to Dryden, "The first rule which Bossu prescribes to the writer of an heroic poem . . . is to make the moral of the work, that is, to lay down to yourself what that precept of morality shall be, which you would insinuate into the people; as namely Homer's . . . was that union preserves a commonwealth, and discord destroys it.⁹ Bossu's doctrine was destined to play an important role in the evolution of Milton criticism, inasmuch as it directly affected two of the principal neoclassical critics—Dryden and Dr. Johnson—and possibly Addison.¹⁰ It is, however, alien to Aristotle and most of his Italian commentators. For these, the first and most important task for a poet was not the choice of a moral but the selection of a subject or argument. To all appearances, Milton agreed with them. Among his early writings one finds extensive references to the epic or dramatic *subjects* he might subsequently develop—but no list of "themes" or "morals" that he proposed to elaborate poetically!

Much of the heated controversy over the "theme" or "moral" of *Paradise Lost* could have been avoided had the contestants noted the ambiguity of the term "argument" and drawn a sharper distinction between "purpose" and "subject." For the subject and purpose of the poem Milton's own statements provide the clearest evidence, and usually they differentiate distinctly between the two. Milton no more confounded purpose with subject than he confused the poetic and logical senses of "argument." In his eyes *Paradise Lost* was not so much the demonstration of a "thesis" as the "imitation of an action." And that action, surely, was the fall of man.

Fourth, there is the problem of the "crisis" or "climax" of the poem. A few critics have tried to pinpoint it with the mathematical exactness of a cartographer or a geodetic surveying team—fixing its coordinates precisely at book 9, lines 781–82: "So saying, her rash hand in evil hour / Forth reaching to the Fruit, she pluck't, she eat." This (they maintain) is the climax of the plot. Like the earthly paradise itself, it is a sort of continental divide between the rising and the falling action. And here, accordingly, they set up their marker.

In Raleigh's opinion (as Tillyard observes), "there is not an incident, hardly a line of the poem, but leads backwards or forwards" to these lines. For Tillyard himself, on the other hand, the "crisis" in the action could not be pinpointed so precisely. The climax, in his view, appeared to be less a razor's edge than a smoothly rounded knoll: "Instead of a small spot in Book Nine for a watershed you have to take the whole great area of Books Nine and Ten." In the "nodal episode" of the poem, the theme of the fall is inextricably "intertwined" with the theme of regeneration.[11] The crisis includes man's repentance as well as his transgression, and the reconciliation of Adam and Eve in addition to their quarrel. Wilkes, in turn, condemns the entire search for a climax as irrelevant and anachronistic. "May we assume," he asks, "that the structure of an epic depends on such principles as 'crisis' at all?... In Renaissance theorizing about the epic where are such concepts referred to at all? To speak of the 'crisis' of *Paradise Lost*, and fix its situation in this book or that, is to look for effects in the poem not allowed for in its media, not proper to its genre."[12]

Nevertheless he presses his attack too far. Though "crisis" and "climax" are anachronisms, "*peripeteia*" is not—and this is what Raleigh was really talking about. For Renaissance theorists this was a characteristic feature of the complex plot, and they joined with Aristotle in praising Homer's use of it in the *Odyssey*. Though Milton would not have used the terms "crisis" and "climax" in this context, he would certainly have regarded the *peripeteia* as altogether "proper to [the epic] genre."

One should, however, bear in mind the difference between Renaissance and modern interpretations of this term. Unlike Butcher, the majority of Italian commentators did not translate *peripeteia* as "reversal of intention," but preferred to render it as "mutation" or "change of state." In Milton's epic the fundamental "change"— emphasized in the title, prose argument, proposition, and fable alike—is man's lapse from his original state of innocence into a state of sin. This "change of state" occurs in a relatively short space in book 9; moreover, it comprehends Adam's transgression as well as Eve's. Less abrupt than Raleigh believed and less extended than Tillyard maintained, it is clearly a *peripeteia*—though not the only one in the poem.

These "Italian commentaries" are not, of course, an infallible guide. (There is no infallible guide in Milton studies, and no single methodology or combination of methods can guarantee consistently valid results.) The commentators on Aristotle and Horace are themselves often at variance, as were the commentators on Milton's scriptural sources and his classical models. Nevertheless, insofar as they reflect the central critical emphases of the Renaissance, they are of potential, though limited, value; and utilized with discretion and restraint they may illuminate the structure of *Paradise Lost.* The principal outlines of Milton's "vast design" are to be found in the organization of his *mythos,* or plot. Though there are other architectonic patterns in the poem—his cosmic mise-en-scène, his hierarchy of creatures and faculties, his scale of nature and contemplation, his web of interlacing images and themes, his "metaphoric structure" and structure of ideas, the rhetorical patterns of individual speeches or meditations or lyric forms, prosodic and syntactical patterns—these are, on the whole, carefully subordinated to the poem's central narrative design. Studies of these subsidiary structures have often proved invaluable, but they have sometimes diverted attention from the primary structure and can be fully appreciated only within the larger frame of reference of the central design. It is to the plot that we must look for the "form" and "soul" of *Paradise Lost.*

For the matter of his major poetry Milton turned to biblical history, imposing upon it the form or "idea" of the heroic epic or tragedy. For the invention of his argument, he relied on the supreme authority of the divine word; for its disposition and arrangement he depended on the principles of art, on the models left by the ancients (both classical and Hebraic) and by a few of the moderns, on scriptural exegesis, and on his own imaginative fictions. Though the dramatic plans in the Trinity manuscript include national as well as biblical history, they nevertheless show a marked preference for the latter. All of the more detailed sketches and the majority of the briefer entries concern sacred themes. Of the longer poems, only the masque at Ludlow is based on a poetic fiction, and even here the concrete historical realities appear clearly through the transparent veil of allegory. The case of *Comus* is different, not only because it was composed "before the deluge," when it was still possible for Milton to write a courtly entertainment in a fashionable genre for the family of a royal official (all of them future "cavaliers"). The fictional subject, the allegorical mode, the symbolic exploitation of pagan fable and classical pneumatology reflect the conventions and requirements of the masque genre rather than the demands of neo-Aristotelian epic and tragedy. Even the concept of catharsis or purification is conceived largely in Pythagorean or neoplatonic rather than in Aristotelian terms—the lustration rite symbolically effecting the spirit's emancipation from the fetters of the body and the appetites of the flesh.

In all three of Milton's major poems, the *constitutio rerum*—the logical and affective structure of the plot, the probable and verisimilar imitation of the action, the arrangement of incidents, and the interrelationship between character, thought, and deed—is, of course, his own addition. In the fable of *Paradise Lost*, only the crucial events—the temptation and fall, the sentence of judgment (containing the protevangelium), and the expulsion from paradise derive directly from the account in Genesis. The remaining incidents in the plot—all that precedes the actual temptation and all that intervenes between temptation and judgment or between judgment and expulsion—is the poet's own contribution. Though much of this additional material is traditional, it is interspersed with fictional details and episodes of his own invention; and the ordering and arrangement are the product of his own conscious art. The poetic image of the historical action is a deliberate construct—an artificial likeness—no less than a consciously contrived painting or sculpture of the same event. Constructed in time as these are in space, it must conform to the same laws of proportion and *vraisemblance*. In the interests of proportion and structural unity, the rest of the hexameral materials found in Genesis and other biblical matter must be relegated to prospective or retrospective episodes.

In *Paradise Regained*, in turn, where extended passages of prophecy or history would seem prolix and the conventional devices of amplification would have limited scope, only the barest outline— the sequence of baptism, temptation, and angelic ministry—is directly supplied by Scripture. The celestial and infernal councils, the disguises of Satan, the complaints of the disciples, the meditations of the Virgin and of Christ himself, and the details of the temptations are the poet's own addition. The "royalist" or messianic emphasis, which tightens the structure of the fable and links all the biblical materials more closely through the central motif of kingship, similarly exhibits the poet's architectonic skill. The terms of the proposition—"by proof th' undoubted Son of God"—echo the formula for the proclamation of a king. The baptism scene is developed essentially as the formal proclamation of a legitimate heir to the throne, a succession formula. In the temptation sequence the primary emphasis falls on the temptation of the kingdoms of the world and the contrast betwen temporal and spiritual kingship. The angelic ministry serves as a confirmation of supreme kingship, a supernatural acclamation of the "Heir of both worlds." In adding his own fictional inventions to biblical history, the poet has enhanced the structural unity as well as the thematic and logical coherence of his plot.

In the plot of *Samson Agonistes* only the catastrophe is based on biblical history. Samson's meditations and the visits of his friends and foes are Milton's own inventions. Even though some of these dramatis personae are scriptural personages, their intervention in the drama at this particular point is a poetic fiction.

In all three poems the principal action is firmly based on scriptural history, but the structuring of events and the interaction of character, thought, and action to achieve organic unity, probability, and verisimilitude, and "passion or admiration," belong to the poet's architectonic craft, to his command of the principles of disposition or "oeconomy" as well as of problems of invention and elocution.

In all three of his major poems Milton endeavors to arouse "passion or admiration" through the same dual means—external and internal *peripeteias*—that he has proposed long before in his *Reason of Church Government:* "changes of that which is called fortune from without" and "the wily subtleties and refluxes of man's thoughts from within." Nevertheless, the relation between these "turns" of thought and event is sometimes significantly different from the usual relationship between plot and thought (*mythos* and *dianoia*) in Renaissance epic and tragedy. In substituting spiritual for physical combat and moral crisis for the trial of arms, Milton tended to place the temptation ordeal in the central and crucial position in his fable. The major reversal in his plot tends, accordingly, to coincide with the major reversal in thought. The incidents of the fable must be organized in such a way as to lead directly or indirectly to the central and crucial temptation scene (or, in a series of temptations, to the climactic temptation). *Dianoia* (thought) and *ethos* (moral decision) would thus occupy the cardinal position in the *mythos* (plot). The development or complication of the epic fable would be oriented toward the temptation crisis, a passage of debate or soliloquy culminating in a moral decision.

The drama of action—the incidents of both plot and counterplot, events furthering or delaying the fulfillment of the action—would culminate, accordingly, in a drama of the mind, an action of the intellect and will. As the imitation of an action, the epic would depict a pattern of incidents, but the central figure in this pattern would be an image of thought. The movement of the plot would center upon the movements of the soul; the principal *peripeteia* in the plot would depend in large part on the *peripeteias* within the human mind. In *Paradise Lost* the action and counteraction of the infernal and divine polities finally converge on the battlefield of the human soul. The *demonomachia* contracts to a *psychomachia*; the warfare of angelic and diabolical hosts narrows gradually to the moral struggle between good and evil within the individual conscience. Paradise is lost and regained by an action of the will, an act of *proairesis*.

The isolation of the hero in Milton's epics (it seems) is partly attributable to his preference for the spiritual warfare of the temptation ordeal over the trial of strength and the "mean" skill of proficiency in arms. Patience is the exercise of saints; and sanctification itself involves the isolation of the hero as a person "separate" to God. Unlike the fortunes of the battlefield, the outcome of these moral conflicts is largely determined from within. The crucial decision, the crisis of spiritual battle, must take place within the conscience of the individual *agonistes*, in moral solitude; and the poet must accordingly isolate the hero in order to portray his moral struggle. The exemplar of the higher heroism is thus inevitably isolated by the nature and conditions of the kind of heroic virtue he exemplifies, by the kind of combat in which it is exercised, and by the artistic limitations imposed on the poet himself by the theme of moral warfare. By isolating his protagonist, Milton can bring the crisis of the will and the labors of the mind into sharper focus and bolder relief.

The moral crisis within the individual may, accordingly, either coincide with or precipitate the major reversals of fortune in the plot. Nevertheless this is (as a rule) only one facet of Milton's *peripeteias*. His phrase "that which is called fortune" is significant; for in his opinion fortune is more than a chimera. It is a misnomer for the obscure workings of Providence. As he was well aware, Boethius had attributed the belief in chance to ignorance of causes; and chance or fortune could have no place in the Miltonic cosmos, ordained as it was by "some supreme efficient Power ... for a specific end." In *Paradise Regained* Milton's supreme hero censures the Gentile philosophers for accusing the Deity "under usual names / Fortune and Fate, as one regardless quite / Of mortal things." In the *Christian Doctrine* (book 1, chap. 2) Milton denies that "nature or fate is this supreme Power" and declares that "fate can be nothing but a divine decree emanating from some almighty power." The apparent changes of fortune, therefore, are providentially governed; they represent the operations of natural or moral law, the execution of divine decrees, or the results of voluntary actions by free agents.

The reversals and catastrophes in Milton's plots may have a dual significance, therefore, insofar as they result from human or divine decision (or from both), and insofar as the Deity actively participates in, or withdraws from, the action. In *Samson Agonistes* Jehovah intervenes actively at a crucial moment to precipitate the catastrophe. In *Paradise Lost* he permits Adam's temptation and fall, but intervenes actively—directly through the Son and indirectly through his angels—to pass judgment and inflict the evil of punishment. The apparent changes of fortune in Milton's poetry are often acts of divine justice—the *crises* or judgments of the supreme judge—on human sin, as in the punishment of Adam and Samson, the overthrow of the rebel angels and the Philistines, or the destruction of Pharaoh's hosts and the antediluvian giants and the men of Sodom. They may also serve, however, as occasions for testing and exercising heroic virtue, as in the adversity sequence of *Paradise Regained*, the trial of Samson's faith and patience, and the temptation of "patient Job," the biblical exemplar of the better fortitude.

Dramatically and ethically, the changes of fortune are often closely associated with the temptation crisis and with the hero's meditations and moral decisions—the "subtleties and refluxes" of his thought. As divine judgments, the hero's misfortunes are frequently the fruit of his own misdeeds and his own ethical decisions; they are the consequence of moral defeat. The fall of Adam and Satan from their lofty stations and their expulsion from their respective paradises are the external results of their internal fall or spiritual apostasy, the failure of heroic virtue and constancy when subjected to trial. In other cases, however, evil fortune may be the principal occasion or means for testing and manifesting the hero's virtues (especially his obedience and his constancy); they are thus the procatarctic (i.e., external) and also the instrumental causes of temptation. Adversity performs both these functions in *Samson Agonistes*. In both cases (misfortune as the punishment of sin and as the test of heroic fortitude), the turns of thought and the reversal of fortune are closely interrelated—either as cause and effect or vice versa. A poet conscious of the demands of logic and probability, a poet committed to the celebration of God's justice and the delineation of human virtue or vice, would have ample cause and opportunity to portray both. It is not surprising that *dianoia* occupies so central a position in the structure of Milton's epic and tragic fable.

Finally, the "changes of fortune" and the "refluxes of man's thoughts" are further interrelated through the Stoic doctrine of the superiority of virtue to fortune and through the Christian doctrine of the invulnerability of conscience to force and the warfare of the spirit against the world. Patience is "more oft the exercise / of Saints," the chorus in Milton's tragedy exclaims, "Making them each his own Deliverer, / And Victor over all / That tyranny or fortune can inflict." Insofar as adverse fortune is the "trial of . . . fortitude," it serves as the occasion for exercising strength of mind, and (as in the Book of Job) it finds its natural and most appropriate expression in the delineation of the labors of the mind. Here again, the nature of the heroic virtue Milton is imitating requires an "imitation of an action" that is also an imitation of thought and character.

2 The regularity with which Milton frequently conforms to principles of epic structure make his occasional (but nevertheless fundamental) variations on the epic tradition all the more striking by contrast. The most important departures from epic decorum—the rejection of a martial theme, and the choice of an argument that emphasizes the hero's transgression and defeat instead of celebrating his virtues and triumphs—are paradoxically conditioned by a concern for the ethical and religious decorum of the epic genre. On the whole, Milton has retained the formal motifs and devices of the heroic poem but has invested them with Christian matter and meaning. In this sense his epic is (to borrow a geological term) something of a "pseudo-morph"—retaining the form of classical epic but replacing its values and contents with Judeo-Christian correlatives.

Such revaluations are not unusual in the epic tradition; they were in fact inevitable. The values of a heroic society do not, as a rule, meet the standards of a mature civilization; still less can they bear the rigid scrutiny of philosophical or theological critics. Later generations tended, accordingly, to refashion the heroic *ethos* and heroic conventions in conformity with the values of their own societies, subjecting Homer and Vergil to allegorical interpretations—Stoic, Neoplatonic, Christian—or endowing their epic heroes with loftier virtues than those of earlier heroes. In Homer's epics critics have recognized an implicit critique of the values of the heroic age; in Vergil's heroic poem, a critique of the Homeric *ethos*; and in Tasso's epic, a critique of both. In Vergil's Turnus they have perceived a degraded Achilles; and in Milton's Satan, a degraded Turnus. In Lucan's *Pharsalia* they have recognized an implicit (and frequently explicit) denunciation of Caesar's ambitious and victorious enterprise and the horrors of civil war; and in Satan's world conquest—no less ambitious and (temporarily at least) no less victorious—they have detected the lineaments of Lucan's Caesar. In Tasso's Egyptian ambassadors and in Milton's Satan they have recognized a deliberate critique (involving conscious imitation and intentional degradation) of the *ethos* of Homer's Achilles and Odysseus.[1]

Insofar as later poets continued to imitate Homer (or Vergil or Lucan), they tended to adapt the conventions of classical epic to the values of their own national and religious cultures. The history of the European literary epic thus appears to be a series of revaluations, and revaluations of revaluations. It is a sequence of moral revolutions or counterrevolutions. The *ethos* of the poet's heroes is frequently conditioned partly by the heroic exemplars left by earlier poets (including the large body of allegorical and moral commentary that had developed around several of these poems) and partly by the moral and religious values of his own society.

Milton consciously imitates the literary conventions of classical (and, to a certain extent, of Renaissance) epic, but he also transforms them in endowing them with a moral and theological content strongly conditioned by Reformation piety and possibly (as in the case of certain Silver Latin poets) by personal disillusion resulting from the civil war and its political aftermath. He observes the basic principles of the heroic poem but adapts them to his own conception of the nature and limitations of heroic virtue. While exploiting the conventions of Homeric and Vergilian epic and many of Aristotle's conceptions of the epic or tragic plot, he partially transforms them by accommodating them to his biblical subject matter and his theological frame of reference. He follows, but also revalues, the European heroic tradition. Like other poets of his age, Milton adapts the traditional machinery of councils and messengers to the Christian marvelous—the agency of God and devil, and fallen and unfallen angels—and transforms the celestial council into a vehicle for revealing the hitherto secret "counsel" or providence of the biblical God. He retains the traditional changes from felicity to misery or vice versa but adapts them to Christian conceptions of beatitude. He retains the epic marvelous but combines it with Christian doctrines of the miraculous and distinctions between divine miracles and diabolical wonders.[2] He relates the classical hubris to Christian conceptions of pride and combines the *hamartia* of the Aristotelian tragic hero with Christian conceptions of sin (usually signified by the word *hamartia* in the Greek New Testament). He substitutes spiritual conceptions of deliverance, salvation (*salus populi*), conquest, and benefaction for their secular equivalents. He portrays warring polities, but these are spiritual dominions—the City of God and its infernal and worldly imitation and antagonist. He adapts the prospective and retrospective conventions of the epic to the material of world history. The conventional relation between heroic virtue, heroic action, heroic merit, and the reward of honor and glory has been altered. Verisimilitude must be conceived in terms of techniques of accommodation. *Pathos* and *catharsis* are adapted to the motif of disordered passion and tranquility of mind, the corruption and restoration of inward purity.

The mixture of modes within *Paradise Lost*—heroic and tragic, satiric and comic, lyrical and elegiac and pastoral—is now a critical commonplace. To the studies of Arnold Stein, Hallett Smith, Irene Samuel, Rajan, Knott, Kranidas, Toliver, Mueller, Empson, Hartman, and other scholars[3] we owe an increasing awareness of the flexibility and variety of Milton's "fitted" style and the breadth of his concept of epic decorum. An admirer of the *Georgics* once observed that Vergil could even toss dung with dignity; and in the *Aeneid* Renaissance critics praised the poet's ability to accommodate the level of his style to that of his subject matter without violating the demands of the *genus grande* proper to heroic poetry.[4] Perhaps the same tribute can be paid to Milton's verse; one carves a melon, or extracts a fruit juice, differently in an epic and in a pastoral.[5] In the same way the epic ridiculous differs from that of comedy. The pranks whereby Milton's sportive judge dashes the pride of men and angels, subjecting hell and Babylon to merited ridicule, possess significant political and ethical implication, shattering the idols of affected divinity, tyrannical kingship, and false heroism. These divine practical jokes are *epic* comedy and demand a style lower than the prevailing epic style but higher than the style of comedy. Homer and Vergil could also lighten heroic gravity with ridicule—toppling an athletic hero in dung or blood—but there is a world of difference between such heroic slapstick and the slapstick of farce: the pompous magnate slipping on a banana peel. The eschatological afflatus[6] that scatters the vain hopes of men over the backside of the world is highly relevant to Milton's heroic theme, both as a parody of the heroic apotheosis and as an allegorical demonstration of the "vanity of human merits." In occasionally stooping to the techniques of comedy[7] and invective, the heavenly muse usually avoided too abrupt a descent, precipitous plunges that might dizzy the poet or unhorse him like Bellerophon. In this passage, as in the discomfiture of the Philistine champion in *Samson Agonistes*, Milton exploits the ridiculous to discredit the false-heroic; and the mise-en-scène of this low-comedy motif is in fact one of the traditional sites of the classical Elysium reserved for heroes and benefactors. Like Vergil, Milton could stoop with dignity; and, in comparison with those of Boiardo and Pulci (and his partial source, Ariosto) his jests are usually heroic jests—the levity of a divinity who finds sublime amusement in "making the punishment fit the crime"—composed on a grand scale and in the grand manner.

Similarly, domestic scenes require a higher mode of presentation than in comedy. As an epic tragedy, *Paradise Lost* exhibits affinities with both the domestic and the political dramas cited in *Of Education*, with "those tragedies . . . that treat of household matters" (such as *Trachiniae* and *Alcestis*) and "tragedies of stateliest and most regal argument." The fall of Adam and Eve is a domestic tragedy; but it also has political consequences. It results in the loss of that inner government which is the essential form of sovereignty and the precondition of Adam's universal dominion— the "naked majesty" that (like *nuda veritas*) needs no external trappings and exposes the extrinsic magnificence of earthly kings as counterfeit. The pomp of monarchs—the retinues "besmeared with gold," the gorgeous thrones of despots, the quasi-divine honors, the splendor of Pandaemonium and of the Egyptian and Mesopotamian Babylons—is superficial; like the rhetorical and poetic techniques that celebrate the vicious benefits and brutal heroism of the tyrant, it is meretricious ornament and sophistic illusion. The world monarch wears his state without; the true king derives his majesty from within, and "in himself" is "all his state." The loss of inner sovereignty as a consequence of the fall not only destroys man's dominion over the earth and its creatures, it leads to anarchy and lawless violence and ultimately to tyrannical rule. In Milton's domestic tragedy, the "tragic deed . . . is done within the family"[8] —the wife administering the poisoned apple to the husband—but the implications of their act extend far beyond its immediate consequences for themselves. They have doomed their entire posterity to slavery, to the tyranny of the prince of the world and his vicegerents Sin and Death. Satan's successive alliances with the infernal jailers and with Chaos, the hoary anarch of the abyss, will be progressively fulfilled in the microcosm of the human soul, in the universal macrocosm, and in human society. Each will be subject to confusion—to anarchy or tyrannical order—until confusion is once again confounded, and the peace of divine order restored.

Pastoral elements and rural or sylvan scenes are not uncommon in epic and romance; and in certain instances—such as the Medoro-Angelica idyll in Ariosto's *Orlando Furioso*[9]—they may undercut the conventions of chivalric epic and the mannered code of its aristocratic heroes. The adventures of the knight errant may lead him not only to courts and castles and savage wildernesses but to pleasure-gardens, enchanted groves, bowers of bliss, and earthly paradises. The paradox that courtesy may be found not only at court but also (and sometimes in a purer and more essential form) in the country—that (like most other virtues) it depends on the inner nobility of the *cor gentile* rather than on the external circumstances of fortune and place—was a Renaissance commonplace; and both Spenser and Milton exploit it.

Nevertheless these conventions not only were complex, they were frequently ambivalent or contradictory. The imagery of garden and pleasure-grove could be applied to divine or sensual delights, to the paradise of earthly or heavenly love. It could refer to a spiritual peace superior to the endeavors of the active life, or it could symbolize ignoble ease and the temptations of the *vita voluptaria*. It could serve as a type of the world or of heaven, of the church or of the brothel, and of virtue or vice. A grove of trees could serve as a test of fortitude (as in Lucan's *Pharsalia;* Tasso's *Jerusalem Delivered* apparently adapts the motif of the enchanted grove not only from the romance tradition but also from Lucan's epic) or as a test of obedience (as in *Paradise Lost*). The garden might symbolize innocence or corruption.[10]

Given Milton's theme (the fall of man) and its necessary setting (the garden of Eden), sylvan descriptions and garden imagery appear to be inevitable. He could not, obviously, place Adam and Eve in a court or palace; and in fact he poses them against the backdrop of the conventional *scena satyrica*. His first description of the hill of paradise compares it to a "Silvan Scene," a "woody Theatre Of stateliest view." This theatrical allusion suggests the classical distinction—transmitted by Vitruvius[11] to Palladio and Serlio—between the settings of comedy, tragedy, and satyr play (a genre that Renaissance critics and dramatists sometimes associated with pastoral drama or indeed with the masque). It is against the background of a similar *scena satyrica* ("a wild Wood") that the Lady of *Comus* encounters her Bacchic and Circean tempter; and Comus himself retains attributes of the lustful satyrs of Renaissance pastoral drama. In Andreini's *L'Adamo* the mise-en-scène is essentially that of the satyr play; an illustration portrays the conventional woodland scene and indeed heightens decorum by including the traditional horned and hoofed devil—a shape equally appropriate to satyr and to demon. Milton's allusions to Pan and Sylvanus and Faunus, which surprised Bentley and Empson,[12] are consistent with Milton's *scena satyrica* and with the theme of corrupted innocence. The subsequent comparison of Eve to a "Wood-Nymph"—the customary prey of fauns and Pans and satyrs—in the crucial temptation scene is equally appropriate.

Forests and pastures, satyrs and shepherds, nymphs and shepherdesses—the conventions of the satyr play and the pastoral—these are by no means identical, but in Renaissance tradition they often overlap. Since few satyr plays had survived, since Vergil had introduced Silenus himself in an eclogue, and since shepherds often dwelt in close proximity to forests, it was comparatively easy for Renaissance writers to combine satyric and pastoral conventions, both in pastoral drama and in epic-romance. Much of the pastoral element in *Paradise Lost* is, in fact, sylvan or garden imagery rather than the imagery of the pasture or sheepfold; nevertheless the strong intermixture of sylvan imagery in classical and Renaissance pastoral poetry justifies the application of this term to much of the poetry of *Comus* and *Paradise Lost*. We should recognize, however, that the primary considerations underlying Milton's use of such imagery are the demands of epic decorum—the necessarily sylvan character of his mise-en-scène. He had to portray Adam and Eve in a woodland or garden setting; he had to present this setting as the perfect *locus amoenus*, archetype of all the pleasure-gardens in the myths and romances and histories of the fallen world; and he had to employ sylvan or rural imagery to describe it.

In such a setting, it is natural—and consistent with the *decorum loci*—that Eve's lament over her imminent exile should recall the elegiac complaints of banished shepherds in pastoral poetry:

> Must I thus leave thee Paradise? thus leave
> Thee Native Soil, these happy Walks and Shades,
> Fit haunt of Gods? ... O flow'rs,
> That never will in other Climate grow,
> My early visitation, and my last
> At Ev'n ...?
> Thee lastly nuptial Bower, by mee adorn'd
> With what to sight or smell was sweet; from thee
> How shall I part?
>
> [11.269-82]

Though pastoral conventions and the *scena satyrica* are in a sense forced upon the poet by the nature of his argument and the demands of *decorum loci*, they nevertheless perform a more complex office. As Professor Knott has rightly noted, they enable the poet to emphasize the principle of hierarchy. The contrasts between the magnificent state banquets and the rural repast in Eden exemplify the distance between God and man, between the state of the supreme suzerain and that of his lowly vassal. Milton emphasizes the ontological gulf between God and man, heaven and earth, in terms of the antithesis (conventional in sixteenth- and seventeenth-century literature) of court and country. In the language of medieval and Renaissance poetics, God and his Son are *curiales;* the angels, *cives* or citizens of heaven; Adam and Eve, *rurales*.

At the same time the natural beauties of paradise and the magnificence of created nature contrast with the artificial magnificence of Pandaemonium. The latter, in turn, is an idol or imitation of the true magnificence of heaven. The Satanic court, centering on an idol of divine majesty, can display only the superficial trappings of true glory; and its fallacies become more apparent when, upon Satan's first entrance into Eden, he beholds the naked and unadorned glory of uncorrupted innocence. Though inferior in the scale of beings, Adam and Eve need no external attributes of glory, for they possess the glory of the divine image and unfallen virtue. In comparison with their essential glory, the magnificence of the

Satanic court is exposed as merely extrinsic and counterfeit; it is accident, not substance.

"We first see Paradise," Empson observes,[13] "through the eyes of the entering Satan, seated jealously like a cormorant on the Tree of Life"; and we first glimpse Adam and Eve through his eyes. In this scene, heroic and rural conventions are juxtaposed, and the latter undercut the former. The warrior encounters a vision of rural peace. The prince of hell, bearing hell within him, enters the *locus amoenus* and remains undelighted by all delight. His passion for revenge is brought face to face with their tranquillity, his experience of sin with their innocence, his ambition for dominion with their content. Some of these moral antitheses were traditional in Renaissance pastoral—the innocence and content of the country life, its simplicity and peace, and its contrast with the intrigues and ambitions of the court.[14] In exploiting these contrasts, Milton not only undercuts the conventional heroic image of the conqueror and destroyer but also exposes as diabolical the *ragione di stato* ("public reason just") and the transmaritime conquests of Renaissance states. The defenseless natives of paradise are (it seems) comparable to the noble savages of other earthly paradises, dispossessed or enslaved by monarchs intent on "Honor and Empire" if not revenge.

Nevertheless Adam and Eve are epic persons, not protagonists of pastoral. Despite their sylvan dwelling and garden labors, they are lords and sovereigns; and in their original high estate they possess (under God) an essential and intrinsic kingship and a legitimate right to world dominion that would be denied to their posterity. In rank and station they are higher than the kings and tyrants who will descend from them; and in depicting them Milton develops the paradox of *rurales* who are kings, and *curiales* who perform the lowly offices of gardeners. His pastoral imagery serves the ends of heroic poetry. It defines and delineates a native majesty and an inner heroism that are based on the divine image and that discredit the regal and heroic values affected by their adversary (archetype of the kings and captains of the fallen world) as spurious.

Like the comic and satiric elements in *Paradise Lost*, the pastoral element reinforces the heroic, serving to bring into sharper focus the contrasting moral values underlying the action of the poem and the *differentiae* of true and false heroism, genuine and counterfeit virtue, and valid or vain glory. These variations in mode or style reinforce ethical oppositions. They enable the poet to emphasize moral or metaphysical distinctions, to underline diverse political or spiritual values. They permit him to juxtapose contrasting blocks of materials and to integrate them firmly within the unified structure of a coherent and carefully articulated plot. They allow him to achieve material and stylistic variety within formal and thematic unity. By comparison or contrast, they illustrate the majesty of humility, the heroic wisdom of being "lowly wise."

"THOSE   EPIC FABLE
NOTES TO   AND THE
TRAGIC"   TRAGIC
         ILLUSTRIOUS

3 Two of the most prominent objections that neoclassic critics leveled against *Paradise Lost* were that its subject and plot structure were essentially tragic and therefore inappropriate in a heroic poem. In *The Original and Progress of Satire*, Dryden protested that Milton's "subject is not that of an Heroic Poem, properly so called. His design is the losing of our happiness; his event is not prosperous, like that of all other epic works."[1] Similarly, Addison maintained that, though the type of plot in which "the chief Actor in the poem falls from some eminent Pitch of honour and Prosperity, into Misery and Disgrace" and "the Event is unhappy" is "the most perfect in Tragedy," it is "not so proper for an Heroick Poem." The "Hero in *Paradise Lost*" is unsuccessful, and by no means a Match for his Enemies.[2]

On the whole, these observations on the tragic nature of Milton's argument and fable are just. Though both critics regarded this as an irregularity and an "imperfection," the tragic element in *Paradise Lost* is an inescapable fact which Milton himself must have recognized. In the first place, he was well aware that, in terms of Aristotelian critical theory, his "whole Subject, *Mans disobedience, and the loss thereupon of Paradise*"[3] was essentially tragic, inasmuch as it involved a "change in the hero's fortunes . . . from happiness to misery."[4] Moreover, the theme of exile ("loss of *Eden*") had been singled out as an ideal tragic argument; Minturno had cited "l'infelice esilio di Edipo" as one of the themes best suited to arouse pity and fear.[5]

29

In the second place, Milton himself describes his argument as "Tragic," but this designation does not deter him from also describing it, a few lines later, as "Heroic." In contrasting his theme with the conventional epic subject of "Warrs, hitherto the onely Argument Heroic deem'd," he makes no distinction between the proper subject matter of tragedy and that of the heroic poem:

> I now must change
> Those Notes to Tragic; foul distrust, and breach
> Disloyal on the part of Man, revolt,
> And disobedience: . . .
> Sad task, yet argument
> Not less but more Heroic then the wrauth
> Of stern *Achilles*.

[9.4–15]

Third, the very theme which, after "long choosing," Milton had selected as a "Subject for Heroic Song" had previously appealed to him as a subject for tragedy. On the whole, the treatment of the fall of man in *Paradise Lost* is not less tragic than in the drafts for a drama on *Adam Unparadised*. Although Addison believed that Milton had introduced Adam's vision of "his Off-spring triumphing over his great Enemy," in order to overcome the "Imperfection" of a tragic catastrophe in an epic plot, this detail was not peculiar to Milton's epic. In the final act of his projected tragedy, Mercy appears to Adam, "comforts him, promises him the Messiah; then calls in Faith, Hope, Charity; instructs him."[6] As Milton exploits the "paradox of the Fortunate Fall"[7] in his drama and in his heroic poem alike, the "event" of *Adam Unparadised* is not more unfortunate than that of *Paradise Lost*.

To what extent was Milton's apparent reluctance to differentiate strictly between the "epic" and "tragic illustrious" consistent with Renaissance poetic theory? Did his choice of argument violate the laws of the epic genre as defined by the "sublime art[8] of poetics, so highly extolled in his tractate *Of Education?* In this chapter I shall examine the fable of *Paradise Lost* against the background of Renaissance conceptions of these two literary species—their similarities and differences in subject matter, characters, structure, and emotional effects.

For Aristotle, epic and tragedy differed in manner of imitation, but resembled each other in subject matter ("noble actions" of "noble personages," "imitation of serious subjects in a grand kind of verse"), construction, and species. Though the marvelous was requisite to both genres, the epic afforded greater scope for the "improbable, the chief factor in the marvellous, because in it the agents are not visibly before one."[9]

By definition, "incidents arousing pity and fear" were essential to tragedy. Were they likewise essential to heroic poetry? Renaissance commentators were divided on this issue. In Tasso's opinion, purgation through pity and fear was the proper function of tragedy, but the "proprio diletto" and "proprio operazione" of the epic was to arouse wonder ("muover maraviglia"). Differing in their effects, they differed necessarily in subject matter:

Se l'azioni epiche e tragiche fossero de l'istessa natura, pro-
durrebbono gli stessi effetti ... ; ma producendo diverse passioni,
ne séguita che diversa sia la natura. Muovono l'azioni tragiche
l'orrore e la compassione; e dove manchi il miserabile e lo
spaventoso, non sono piú tragiche. Ma gli Epici non sogliono ne
l'istesso modo contristar gli animi; ne questa condizione in loro
si richiede come necessaria.... Non è ancora illustre parimente
l'azione del Tragico e quella de l'Epico; o quello illustre è quasi
diverso di natura e di forma. L'uno consiste ne la inaspettata e
subita mutazione di fortuna, e ne la grandezza de gli avvenimenti
che muovono misericordia e terrore; ma l'illustre de l'eroico è
fondato sovra l'eccelsa virtú militare e sopra il magnanimo
proponimento di morire, sovra la pietá, sovra la religione, e sovra
l'azioni ne le quali risplendono queste virtú, che sono proprie de
l'epopeia, e non convengono tanto ne la tragedia.

The epic poet should avoid "le materie ... infelici, com'è la morte de' Paladini, e la rotta di Roncisvalle; perché fra' Greci ancora, o fra' Latini, niuno è che celebrasse in poema eroico la sconfitta de gli Ateniesi o de gli Spartani, e le vittorie de' Persiani, o pur quelle de' Francesi." Statius had erred in choosing a tragic subject for his *Thebiad*, and Pulci in concluding his *Morgante Maggiore* with a tragic ending:

Men savio consiglio veramente fu quello di Stazio, che celebrò
la calamita de gli Argivi, e la morte o la rotta de l'esercito
condotto da' sette Regi; perché quello è soggetto tragico anzi che
no; e fra i Greci fu trattato da Euripide, il quale, come dice
Aristotele, è *tragikōtatos*.... Pulci ...; cominciando da la feste
di Carlo e de' Paladini, finisce ne la *rotta dolorosa* ne la quale
Carlo Magno perdé la santa gesta.

Thus, for Tasso, epic and tragedy diverged not only in their instruments and mode of imitation, but also in "le cose imitate."[10]

Other Renaissance critics, however, acknowledged little difference between the two genres in subject matter and emotional effect.
Like Aristotle, Minturno maintained that Homer's *Iliad* and
Odyssey had provided the "form" of tragedy, and his own definition of the epic includes purgation through pity and fear ("Imitazione di atti gravi e chiari . . . ; acciocchè e per la pietà, e per
la paura delle cose imitate e descritte l'animo purghi di tali affetti
con mirabil piacere, e profitto di lui").[11] In Castelvetro's opinion,
"l'epopea non ha per fine di necessita il movimento della compassione, & dello spavento, come ha la tragedia," but the epic poet
might legitimately choose a tragic subject capable of arousing these
emotions:

Percioche non mi posso imaginare che egli [Aristotele] havesse
opinione, che l'epopea non havesse, o non potesse havere soggetto
spaventevole & compassionevole, inguisa che simile soggetto si
dovesse domandare proprio della tragedia, & non commune alla
tragedia & all' epopea, salvo se non diciamo, che questo soggetto
si puo dire essere soggetto proprio della tragedia, & non commune
alla tragedia, & all' epopea, o ad altre maniere di poesie, in quanto
secondo lui la tragedia non riceve altro soggetto, che questo cosi
fatto, la dove l'epopea, & l'altre maniere di poesia, avegna che
non rifiutino questo, ricevono non dimeno altri soggetti anchora.

The type of delight proper to the two genres differs, however,
inasmuch as the "diletto oblico . . . proprio della tragedia" proceeds from the pity and fear experienced when "una persona da
bene cade di felicita in miseria," whereas the "diletto diritto" of the
epic is produced by the "avenimento delle due diverse persone
buone, & ree, felice per le buone, & infelice per le ree."[12]
Though Milton's choice of an essentially tragic theme as his
"Subject for Heroic Song" violates Tasso's distinction between the
"illustrious" of epic and tragedy, he could have found limited
support in Aristotle's *Poetics* and ample justification in the commentaries of Castelvetro, Minturno, and Cinthio.[13]

In the actual argument of Milton's epic there is comparatively
little of the "illustre de l'eroico" as Tasso had conceived it. In the
central action of the poem—"Mans First Disobedience"—the protagonist displays neither "eccelsa virtú militare" nor the virtues of
piety and religion. On the contrary, his act of disobedience
involves the very opposite of these virtues; in transgressing the
divine commandment, he violates both "pietá" and "religione."

Though Adam does express a "proponimento di morire" ("for with thee / Certain my resolution is to Die"), this decision is by no means "magnanimo," for he is not "actuated by a regard to [his] own dignity, rightly understood."[14] Instead, the central action of Milton's "epic person" obviously represents the "illustre ... del Tragico," inasmuch as the fall of man entails an "inaspettata e subita mutazione di fortuna" and "avvenimenti che muovono misericordia e terrore."

Adam himself conforms in large part to the pattern which Aristotle and his Renaissance commentators had recommended as the norm for the tragic hero: "an intermediate kind of personage, a man not pre-eminently virtuous and just, whose misfortune, however, is brought upon him not by vice and depravity but by some error of judgement, of the number of those in the enjoyment of ... prosperity." In the "perfect plot" (Aristotle had declared) the "change in the hero's fortunes must be ... from happiness to misery; and the cause of it must lie not in any depravity, but in some great error on his part; the man himself being either such as we have described, or better, not worse, than that."[15] In this passage Tasso had found authority for differentiating between the persons of epic and tragedy. Although in both genres the characters possessed royal or princely status, they differed in moral character, inasmuch as tragedy required "persone né buone, né cattive, ma d'una condizione di mezzo," whereas the epic demanded "il sommo de le virtú; però le persone sono eroiche come e la virtú": "E se alcuna volta il Tragico e l'Epico prendono per soggetto la persona medesima, è da loro considerata diversamente con vari rispetti. Considera l'Epico in Ercole, in Teseo, in Agamennone, in Aiace, in Pirro, il valore e l'eccellenza de l'armi; gli risguarda il Tragico come caduti per qualche errore ne l'infelicitá.[16] Similarly, according to Heinsius's *De Tragoediae Constitutione*, the tragic hero should be neither "probus" nor "improbus," but "inter pro-bum improbumque constitutus"—one who transgresses impru-dently or "inconsulto": "Is autem est, qui cum imprudens peccet, neque viri boni meretur nomen; quia officium illius est transgres-sus: neque contra improbi; quia sine praeelectione, ut in scholis loquuntur, hoc est, inconsulto peccat."[17]

The Adam of *Paradise Lost* appears to differ in two significant respects from the type of tragic hero Aristotle and his commenta-tors had recommended. In the first place, the fact that Milton is describing the loss of man's original innocence makes the norm of the "intermediate kind of personage" between the righteous and unrighteous ("inter probum improbumque constitutus") largely inapplicable to Adam. Unlike the Aristotelian tragic hero, who is "not pre-eminently virtuous and just," Adam embodies the pristine excellence of human nature before its fall. Until his "First Disobedience" he must be regarded as one of the righteous ("probi") and after his transgression he falls into the opposite category of the unrighteous ("improbi"). He cannot be regarded as a "persona mezzana," such as "persone né buone, né cattive."

In the second place, the cause of the "change in [his] fortunes . . . from happiness to misery" lies rather in a deliberate sin than in a mere "error of judgement." Though he does indeed commit an error in judgment in imprudently permitting Eve to leave his side and though Eve herself is deceived by the serpent, Adam's disobedience is neither "sine praeelectione" nor "inconsulto."

Despite these divergences, however, Adam bears a marked resemblence to the tragic hero of the Aristotelian critical tradition. Since Aristotle had recommended that such a figure be "either such as we have described, or better, not worse, than that," Milton was quite justified in making his hero "better" than the usual tragic protagonist, such as Oedipus or Thyestes. Moreover, in at least one respect Adam can be regarded as an "intermediate kind of personage." Even in the state of innocence he falls short of the moral excellence of Christ and the faithful angels, but even after his lapse he likewise falls short of the ethical depravity of Satan and his hosts. Unlike the loyal spirits he fails to withstand temptation; but unlike the rebels he repents and implores pardon for his transgression. Intermediate between the ethical extremes manifested in the good and evil angels, he is, of all the personae of *Paradise Lost*, the "one [most] like ourselves."[18] For he is, in fact, the representative of *Humanum Genus*, an exemplar of universal human nature—unfallen, fallen, and repentant and regenerate.

In the second place, the cause of the "change in the hero's fortunes" lies not in innate "vice or depravity," but in *hamartia*.[19] The latter term could be translated not simply as "error" (as Bywater rendered it), but also as "sin." This was the common translation in the Authorized Version of the New Testament,[20] and Heinsius had rendered Aristotle's *hamartia* in a similar sense as "crime": "neque ob improbitatem subito infelix fiat, sed ob crimen

& flagitium aliquod."[21] It is through *hamartia* (in the sense of "sin" rather than of "error of judgment") that Adam forfeits his "happy State." He falls "non ob improbitatem, sed ob flagitium aliquod insigne."[22]

Another apparent violation of the "rules of Aristotle" could also be justified in terms of Renaissance poetics. Since "pity is occasioned by undeserved misfortune, and fear by that of one like ourselves,"[23] the fall of man might provoke fear, but could not (strictly speaking) arouse pity. Adam's woes are not an "undeserved misfortune," but the just punishment for his sin of disobedience. Milton could scarcely have represented them otherwise without impugning the justice of God and contradicting his avowed intent to "justifie the wayes of God to men." Nevertheless, this difficulty had already been anticipated to some extent by Castelvetro. In raising the issue of divine justice in relation to the misfortunes of the tragic hero, Castelvetro had argued that the sufferings of the "tragic person" could be merited, but capable nonetheless of arousing compassion:

Hora parrebbe, sotillmente considerando la cosa, che, se questo trapassamento della persona mezzana da felicita a miseria non presta cagione alla gente di mormorare contra dio, ne di dolersi di lui, che sia reputato giusto, & appresso, che, se questo trapassamento è reputato giusto, che la persona mezzana ne sia indegna, & ultimamente, se la persona mezzana non n'è indegna, che altri non debba, ne possa havere di lei compassione. . . . Se noi concediamo, che la persona mezzana meriti simile disgratia, & che il popolo porti opinione, che ogni mezzana persona sia degna di cosi fatto avenimento, poi che le mezzane persone sono innumerabili, avegna che questa, a cui è avenuto cio, ne sia degna, e non dimeno indegna di patire sola, & le s'ha compassione, che essa sia scielta a patire sola, & le altre tutte risparmiate, & cosi è indegna di quel male, perche le altre, le quali degnamente ne dovrebbono essere partefici, ve sono senza.

Though the misfortune of a very saintly man ("persona santissima") might cause the audience to impugn God's justice, that of the "intermediate" kind of person ("persona mezzana"), who falls into misery through his own sins ("per gli peccati suoi") need not give occasion to the people to murmur against God:

ma, se la persona mezzana trapassa da felicita a miseria, non da cagione alla gente di mormorare contra dio, ne di dolersi di lui, perchioche, si come ci possiamo imaginare, e assai ragionevole, che avenga questo cosi fatto trapassamento a quella persona per gli peccati suoi, avegna che non sieno de piu horribili del mondo, & sieno mischiati tra alcune buone operationi.[24]

Though Milton's choice of argument—Adam's sin and its merited punishment—could be reconciled with Renaissance interpretations of Aristotle's "rules" for tragedy, such a subject represented a striking departure from the type of argument favored in traditional epic theory and practice. Even this apparent irregularity, however, could find support in Renaissance critical doctrine. In his *De Heroico Poesi Tractatus* Masenius had maintained that, like tragedy, the epic might depict a shameful action with an unfortunate outcome ("actio flagitiosa . . . infelici exitu terminata"): "Actio Herois cum culpa non gravissima conjuncta, infelicem sortita, sine scelere novo patientis, exitum, in Epopoeia, non minùs, quàm Tragoedia locu meretur." Though inferior in dignity to an illustrious action with a fortunate ending, this type of argument was, for several reasons, not inappropriate for heroic poetry. First, Aristotle himself had sometimes confused the action of epic with that of tragedy. Second, such an epic could fulfill the end of this species ("finis Epopoeiae") by purging the affections through admiration and delight ("nimirum ut pravi in animis affectus, cum admiratione & voluptate, salubri metu perpurgentur"). Third, by describing the punishment of sin, the epic poet could reconcile the fear and horror aroused by the crime with the worth of virtue ("Metum vèro salubrem & horrorem scelerum, cum virtutis aestimatione, poena inflicta conciliat"). Finally, even though the hero's action may involve some crime, he may excell in other qualities: "si videlicet per actionem herois, quaelibet ejus actio gravis accipiatur, licèt cum aliquo conjuncta scelere, modò aliis dotibus inter homines excellat." To this type of epic belonged Masenius's own heroic poem on the fall of man: "Nos illius Epopoeiae exemplum aliquod in Adami lapsu a Deo justis poenis castigato proposuimus; cujus tamen poematis corpus, magis ad studiosae juventutis emolumentum, quàm absolutae artis leges compositum."[25]

Although Adam's transgression is far more serious than Masenius's "culpa non gravissima," it meets several of the conditions set forth in the *Tractatus*. Adam's disobedience is punished by the sentence of judgment and banishment from paradise ("poena

inflicta"). The "infelix exitus" of his action—his expulsion from his
"blissful Seat"—takes place without an additional crime ("scelere
novo") on his part, but (on the contrary) with contrition, repentance, and faith. Moreover, despite his transgression, he excels in
"aliis dotibus"; even in the act of disobedience, his willingness to
undergo death and his devotion to his wife are not entirely
illaudable.

Though subordinated to the epic effect of admiration, the tragic
elements of pity and fear assume a far greater prominence in
Paradise Lost than in the conventional heroic fable. Besides select-
ing the type of subject and the kind of plot structure which poetic
theorists had recommended as particularly well adapted to producing these tragic *affetti* in the mind of the audience, Milton also
described the pity and fear which the events of the fable inspired in
the characters of his poem. The fall of man arouses pity in God and
the faithful angels, and almost moves Satan himself to compassion.
Meditating man's imminent "change" from "delights" to "woe," the
devil declares that he "could pittie [the gentle pair] thus forlorne /
Though I unpittied." At the "unwelcome news" of Adam's lapse the
blessed angels feel "sadness . . . mixt with pitie." After judging the
transgressors, the Son "in pity cloaths them both":

> then pittying how they stood
> Before him naked to the aire, that now
> Must suffer change, . . . he clad
> Thir nakedness with Skins of Beasts, or slain.
>
> [10.211–17]

Adam experiences "Commiseration" for Eve's "lowlie plight," and
both express their trust in God's pity:

> his timely care
> Hath unbesaught provided, and his hands
> Cloath'd us unworthie, pitying while he judg'd;
> How much more, if we pray him, will his ear
> Be open, and his heart to pitie incline.
>
> [10.1057–61]

Michael's revelation of the future miseries of mankind stirs Adam
to pity the wretched fate of his offspring. At the sight of the
sufferings of the Lazar-house, "compassion quell'd / His best of
Man, and gave him up to tears" (11.493–94). The seduction of the
"Sons of God" by the daughters of men seems to him "pittie and

shame." The "massacher" perpetrated by the giants leaves him "all in tears," and he is overwhelmed by "tears and sorrow" at the vision of the deluge.

Allusions to fear, horror, or terror in *Paradise Lost* fall roughly into three categories: (1) the horrors of hell and the terrifying aspect of its inhabitants, (2) the war of the angels, and (3) man's disobedience and its consequences. Milton frequently attempts to intensify the affective value of these elements either by describing their emotional impact on his characters or by employing terms ("terrible," "horrible," "dreadful") which suggest their ability to arouse the emotion of fear. Let us consider these briefly in order.

1. Although Milton represents hell and its denizens—Satan and his "horrid crew," the "*Gorgonian* terror" of Medusa, Sin's monstrous deformity, and the "grim and terrible" shape of Death—as terrible in themselves, he enhances the element of terror by describing their own horror at their condition. In their exploration of the underworld, the "adventrous Bands" of devils discover only a "Universe of death," which they behold with "shuddring horror pale, and eyes agast." Deformed "with fear and pain," Sin is perpetually tormented by the "conscious terrours" of remorse—"With terrors and with clamors compasst round / Of mine own brood, that on my bowels feed." Unable to escape from the "Hell within him," Satan is tortured by his own evil conscience:

> horror and doubt distract
> His troubl'd thoughts, and from the bottom stirr
> The Hell within him, for within him Hell
> He brings.
>
> [4.18–21]

The fallen angels are filled with horror by the transformation of their leader and his peers into a "crowd / of ugly Serpents":

> horror on them fell,
> And horrid sympathie; for what they saw,
> They felt themselves now changing.
>
> [10.539–41]

Contrary to Belial's prediction (2.220), the infernal "horrours" Satan had boldly hailed (1.250) are intensified instead of growing milder.

2. In his description of the war in heaven Milton alludes, on the one hand, to incidents capable of arousing fear—such as the angelic conflict itself, the appearance of Messiah on the battlefield, and the punishment he inflicts on the rebel hosts—and, on the other hand,

to the terror the apostates experience on these occasions. In describing the clash of the "adverse Legions" he employs such terms as "the horrid shock," "Horrible discord," "Dreadful combustion," and the like. When Satan and Michael engage in conflict, they brandish their fiery swords in "horrid Circles," and expectation stands "In horror." On the first day of battle, the rebellious angels experience fear for the first time:

> what stood, recoyld
> Orewearied, through the faint Satanic Host
> Defensive scarce, or with pale fear surpris'd
> Then first with fear surpris'd and sense of paine
> Fled ignominious, to such evil brought
> By sinne of disobedience, till that hour
> Not liable to fear or flight or paine.
>
> [6.391–97]

Again, on the following day,

> Amaze,
> ... and terrour seis'd the rebel Host,
> When coming towards them so dread they saw
> The bottom of the Mountains upward turn'd.
>
> [6.646–49]

Finally, on the third day, Milton stresses the terror of "Gods indignation on these Godless pourd," as Messiah enters the combat. The Son alters his countenance "into terrour," too "severe to be beheld / And full of wrauth bent on his Enemies." The four cherubim of his chariot produce a "dreadful shade." The revolted angels are torn between two contrary fears. Pursued "With terrors and with furies" to the bounds of heaven, they are filled with horror at the glimpse of Chaos before them, but with even greater terror at the spectacle of "Eternal wrauth" behind them: "the monstrous sight / Strook them with horror backward, but far worse / Urg'd them behind" (6.862–64). Hell itself is "Affrighted" by their expulsion from heaven, and Raphael himself exhorts Adam by this "terrible Example" to "remember, and fear to transgress."

3. Both the actual violation of the forbidden fruit and its disastrous consequences arouse horror or fear. Even in her dream, Eve is appalled at the serpent's audacity in transgressing the divine injunction:

> with ventrous Arme
> He pluckt, he tasted; mee damp horror chil'd
> At such bold words voucht with a deed so bold.
>
> [5.64–66]

When Eve commits the same "fatal Trespass," Adam's reaction is
likewise one of horror:

> amaz'd,
> Astonied stood and Blank, while horror chill
> Ran through his veins, and all his joynts, relax'd.
>
> [9.889–91]

Milton himself (10.687–88) compares "that tasted Fruit" to the
"*Thyestean* Banquet."
Finally, the fall leaves Adam a prey to the terrors of conscience.
The voice of God now seems "dreadful" to him, and he is tortured
by the "fear of worse" than death. He is tormented by the "Horrid"
thought that he "shall die a living Death":

> that fear
> Comes thundring back with dreadful revolution
> On my defenseless head; both Death and I
> Am found Eternal, and incorporate both . . .
> O Conscience, into what Abyss of fears
> And horrors hast thou driv'n me; out of which
> I find no way, from deep to deeper plung'd'.
>
> [10.813–44]

To his "evil Conscience" the gloom of night represents "All things
with double terror." His vision of the murder of Abel by Cain fills
him with horror:

> But have I now seen Death? . . . O sight
> Of terrour, foul and ugly to behold,
> Horrid to think, how horrible to feel!
>
> [11.462–65]

In several significant respects—argument, protagonist, and emotional "effects"—*Paradise Lost* exhibits the "tragic illustrious" as
Aristotelian poetic theory had conceived it. Like the conventional
subject of tragedy, Milton's epic subject involves "la inaspettata e
subita mutazione di fortuna" and "la grandezza de gli avenimenti
che muovono misericordia e terrore." Like the conventional tragic
hero, Adam falls from happiness into misery through *hamartia*.
Like the conventional tragic *affetti*, pity and fear are prominent in
the fable and episodes of *Paradise Lost*.

"MISERABLE PERIPETEIA OF HAPPY" IN PARADISE LOST

4 How did Milton and his contemporaries interpret the Aristotelian term *peripeteia*, and to what extent did Milton exploit this device in his own poetry? Though recent scholarship[1] has noted instances in both *Samson Agonistes* and *Paradise Regained*, its approach has tended to be anachronistic. Thus Tillyard has credited Milton with anticipating Butcher's conception of Peripeteia as a "Reversal of Intention": "A *peripeteia* happens, not when there is a mere change of fortune, but when an intention or action brings about the opposite of what was meant. Now Milton made *Samson Agonistes* answer so closely to this interpretation of *peripeteia* that I believe it was his own interpretation too." The "use in *Samson* of *peripeteia* or at least of that device as interpreted in a certain way" indicated "how seriously and intelligently Milton had studied" Aristotle's *Poetics*.[2]

Now this interpretation directly contradicts that of Milton's immediate predecessors and contemporaries. Though it is conceivable that his own conception of *peripeteia* was closer to the views of certain nineteenth- and twentieth-century scholars[3] than to Renaissance critical doctrine, it seems unlikely, and we can hardly take such an assumption for granted. In this chapter I shall examine the "Italian commentaries of Castelvetro, Tasso, Mazzoni, and others"—works which Milton himself regarded as authoritative for the "sublime art" of poetics[4]—and apply their conceptions of *peripeteia* (along with the later interpretation of the Dutch scholar Heinsius)[5] to the fable of *Paradise Lost*.

In assessing the divergences between Renaissance and modern interpretations of *peripeteia*, two points are of cardinal importance: (1) the relationship between *peripeteia* and *metabasis* (in Butcher's translation, "change of fortune") and (2) the degree to which the former involves what Butcher termed the "Irony of Destiny"—the extent to which *peripeteia* represents "a change by which a line of action intended to produce a certain effect produces the opposite—an overruling of the intention of one of the agents."[6] For the most part, Milton's predecessors seem to have equated *peripeteia*, rather than *metabasis*, with the actual change of fortune and to have seen in the "irony of events"[7] (the unexpected "reversal of intention") a means of heightening the dramatic effectiveness of this change, but *not* an *essential* characteristic of the *peripeteia*, not an inalienable part of its definition.

The divergence between Renaissance and modern conceptions of *peripeteia* has hinged partly on the translation of *metabasis* and *metabole*. Whereas modern English translations have employed the same word ("change") for both terms, Renaissance translators often preferred to render *metabasis* as "transition" and to reserve the word "change" or "mutation" specifically for *metabole*. As Aristotle had employed the latter term (*metabole*) in his definition of *peripeteia*, Renaissance poetics tended to conceive the *peripeteia* as essentially a change of fortune.

To appreciate more readily the extent and significance of this divergence, let us compare Bywater's translation of these two crucial passages with the versions by Castelvetro and Heinsius:

[Bywater:] The action ... I call simple, when the change [*metabasis*] in the hero's fortunes takes place without Peripety or Discovery; and complex, when it involves one or the other, or both.[8]

[Castelvetro:] Et chiamo simplice attione *quella*, il trapassamento della quale ... si fa *aneu peripeteias* (*cio è senza rivolgimento*) o riconoscenza. Et raviluppata è quella, della quale il trapassamento è con riconoscenza, o con rivolgimento, o con amenduni.[9]

[Heinsius:] Actionem autem simplicem, cujus ... sine agnitione fit transitio. Implexam verò, cujus cum agnitione, aut mutatione in contrarium, aut etiam utraque, fit transitio.[10]

Where Bywater translates *metabasis* as "the change in the hero's fortunes" and Butcher renders it as "change of fortune,"[11] Castelvetro prefers the term *trapassamento* and Heinsius the term *transitio*. Indeed, Castelvetro explicitly denies that *metabasis* means "change" in this passage, since by definition no change occurs in the simple fable: "Non si prende *metabasis* in questo luogo per mutatione, come credono alcuni, ma per lo processo dell' attione dal principio al fine. percioche, come si puo prendere *metabasis* per mutatione in questo luogo, se mutatione non ci ha luogo?"[12]

On the other hand, Renaissance versions of the *Poetics* agree with modern translations in rendering the *metabole* of Aristotle's definition as "change" or "mutation":

[Bywater:] A Peripety is the change [*metabole*] from one state of things within the play to its opposite of the kind described.[13]

[Castelvetro:] Hora rivolgimento è la mutatione in contrario delle cose, che si fanno, secondo che è stato detto.[14]

[Heinsius:] Est autem *peripeteia* quam vocant, sicut dictum est, in contrarium eorum quae aguntur mutatio.[15]

Conceiving Aristotle's *peripeteia* as a "change of things into their contrary," Renaissance theorists explained this *mutatio* in terms of the traditional notion of Fortune's changes—the alteration from happiness to misery, or vice versa. Thus Tasso, defining *peripeteia* as a "mutazione de le cose che si fanno, in contrario," explained that the word *contrary* refers to the reversal of fortune: "in contrario, intendiamo da la prospera ne l'avversa fortuna, o da l'avversa ne la prospera. Questo secondo modo si conviene a l'epopeia, a la commedia, o ad alcune tragedie le quali da' moderni impropriamente son dette tragicommedie. Il primo è proprio de la tragedia."[16] Again, "semplici sono le favole di quelle tragedie che non hanno agnizione, né mutamento di felice fortuna in miseria, o al contrario; doppie quelle ne le quali con l'agnizione sono gran rivolgimenti di fortuna."[17]

Castelvetro and Heinsius likewise regarded the *peripeteia* as a change from happiness to misery, or the opposite. According to the latter, it entailed an alteration from prosperity to adversity, or vice versa ("vel è prosperis adversa, vel secunda ex adversis").[18] In Castelvetro's opinion, "la mutatione . . . delle cose, che si fanno in contrario, è il divenire di felice misero, o di misero felice."[19] This conception of the *peripeteia* as a reversal of fortune from felicity to infelicity or from sorrow to joy occupies a central position in

Castelvetro's interpretation of Aristotle's distinction between simple and complex plots. Whereas the simple fable contains a single matter—either happiness or misery—without any alteration from one state to the other, the complex fable contains two diverse matters—felicity and infelicity—and its action involves a change from one condition to its opposite:

& s'intende per raviluppata quella, che è composta di due diverse, o piu tosto contrarie materie, cio è di felicita & d'infelicita, o d'infelicita, & di felicita, & simplice quella che è composta d'una materia sola, cio è di felicita sola, o d'infelicita sola, continuando un tenore di fortuna dal principio infino al fine.[20]

By simple fables (Castelvetro maintained) Aristotle had meant "quelle favole, che conservano uno tenore di stato o misero, o felice," and by complex plots he had intended "quelle favole, le quali non conservano uno tenore, ma hanno mutatione di stato o di misero in felice, o di felice in misero ... & nomina la mutatione *peripeteian*, cio è rivolgimento di stato misero in felice, o di felice in misero."[21] This change of fortune might occur with or without recognition:

Attione raviluppata è quella, che ha il suo procedere di stato felice in miseria, o di miseria in felice in tre modi, per mutatione senza riconoscenza, per mutatione, & riconoscenza separatamente, non essendo la riconoscenza prossima, ne cagione congiunta con la mutatione, & per mutatione & riconoscenza, facendosi la mutatione insieme con la riconoscenza, & per cagione prossima della riconoscenza.[22]

Similarly, in Castelvetro's opinion, *peripeteia*, or the "mutatione di stato felice in misero, o per lo contrario di misero in felice," also distinguished the "unequal" fable ("la favola disuguale") from the "equal" plot ("la favola uguale").[23]

The conception of *peripeteia* which modern scholarship has applied to Milton's plot has been, on the whole, anachronistic. His predecessors had interpreted this term primarily as a "reversal of fortune" rather than as a "reversal of intention,"[24] and it was probably this idea that he had in mind when he lauded the poet's ability to "paint out" and describe "whatsoever hath passion or admiration in all the changes of that which is called fortune from without."[25] Addison's conception of *peripeteia* as a "Change of Fortune ... from Bad to Good, or from Good to Bad"[26] was far closer to Renaissance poetic doctrine than are the more recent interpretations by Vahlen and Butcher.

In Addison's opinion, the plot of *Paradise Lost* was complex (or "Implex") inasmuch as "the chief Actor of the Poem falls from some eminent Pitch of Honour and Prosperity into Misery and Disgrace. Thus we see *Adam* and *Eve* sinking from a State of Innocence and Happiness, into the most abject Condition of Sin and Sorrow."[27] This conception of the principal *peripeteia* of Milton's epic fable is completely consistent with the interpretations of *peripeteia* by Aristotle's Renaissance commentators—with Castelvetro's "rivolgimento di stato ... felice in misero," Heinsius's "felicitas in infelicitatem," and Nascimbene's "commutatio felicitatis in infelicitatem."[28]

The fable of *Paradise Lost* clearly displays the two contrary matters which Castelvetro attributed to the complex plot—felicity and infelicity—the two states which Milton had defined theologically as man's original "state of rectitude"[29] and his "fallen condition," the state of the fall. The contrast between these two conditions is emphasized throughout the poem, both before and after Adam's "original lapse." The first lines stress the antithesis between the "happy State" of original innocence and the universal misery ("all our woe") which followed man's transgression. At his first sight of Adam and Eve, Satan predicts their "mutatio in contrarium":

> yee little think how nigh
> Your change approaches, when all these delights
> Will vanish and deliver ye to woe,
> More woe, the more your taste is now of joy;
> Happie, but for so happie ill secur'd
> Long to continue.
>
> [4.366-71]

After the fall, Adam himself contrasts the lost state of happiness with his present state of misery:

> we had then
> Remaind still happie, not as now, despoild
> Of all our good, sham'd, naked, miserable.
>
> [9.1137-39]

> O miserable of happie! is this the end
> Of this new glorious World, and mee so late

The Glory of that Glory, who now becom
Accurst of blessed, hide me from the face
Of God, whom to behold was then my highth
Of happiness: yet well if here would end
The miserie . . .;
All that I eate or drink, or shall beget,
Is propagated curse.

[10.720–29]

After lamenting the "fleeting joyes / Of Paradise, deare bought
with lasting woes!" he believes himself "miserable / Beyond all
past example and future" (10.741–840).

Eve laments that her own misery is even greater than her
husband's:

On me exercise not
Thy hatred for this miserie befall'n,
On me already lost, mee, then thy self
More miserable.

[10.927–30]

As in Adam's case, her distress is aggravated by the thought of the
miseries of their posterity:

and miserable it is
To be to others cause of misery,
Our own begotten, and of our Loines to bring
Into this cursed World a woful Race,
That after wretched Life must be at last
Food for so foule a Monster.

[10.981–86]

Finally, Michael's revelation of "Th' effects which thy original
crime hath wrought" evokes from Adam a further complaint of the
wretched state of mankind:

O miserable Mankind, to what fall
Degraded, to what wretched state reserv'd!

[11.497–98]

This change from happiness to misery occurs, moreover, in a
single place and within a short period of time. Castelvetro had
argued that the "mutatione epopoeica" would arouse more admiration if it was effected in "uno, & poco tempo, & in uno, & picciolo
statio di luogo", than if it occurred "in piu, & lunghi tempi, & in
varij, & larghi luoghi."[30] As a matter of fact, the chief *peripeteia* in
Milton's epic fable takes place in the course of a single morning in

paradise. Its suddenness is emphasized both by Adam's initial reaction to Eve's transgression:

> How art thou lost, how on a sudden lost,
> Defac't, deflow'r'd, and now to Death devote? . . .
> And mee with thee hath ruin'd, for with thee
> Certain my resolution is to Die.
>
> [9.900–907]

and by Milton's comment on Nature's response to the two stages of the crime:

> Nature from her seat
> Sighing through all her Works gave signs of woe
> That all was lost.
>
> [9.782–84]

> Earth trembl'd from her entrails, as again
> In pangs, and Nature gave a second groan,
> Skie lowr'd, and muttering Thunder, som sad drops
> Wept at compleating of the mortal Sin
> Original.
>
> [9.1000–1004]

Nevertheless Tillyard has denied that "the Fall itself" is the "real crisis" of *Paradise Lost*; in his opinion the fall of man is merely the "apparent" crisis and the "real" crisis is to be found in "the reconciliation of Adam and Eve":[31]

In the bare story Eve was sinless till the precise moment when she reached out her rash hand and plucked the fruit. Milton may have intended to substantiate the story. . . . But intentions could be of no avail against the terms to which Milton submitted himself by offering to present in ample narrative the transition from a state of innocence to a state of sin. Under the terms of the story these two realms must be separated by a definite but dimensionless frontier: there cannot be a no-man's-land between; in the passage, time must not count. Such a lightning-quick change might be effective in a film; . . . it showed itself to be possible in the simple form of the Miracle Plays; but in a narrative poem it could only be ridiculous, and in his heart Milton knew that well enough.[32]

Actually, this assessment of Milton's narrative problem underestimates the importance which Renaissance poetics attached to *peripeteia* in the epic fable. Just as Aristotle had praised the complex plot of the *Odyssey*, so Harington and Nascimbene had commended Ariosto and Vergil for introducing *peripeteia* into their own epics. In view of Castelvetro's recommendation that the "change of fortune" in the epic plot should occur "in uno, & poco tempo," a "lightning-quick change" would not have been regarded as "ridiculous" in a "narrative poem." On the contrary, theorists believed a sudden change to be all the more effective for arousing passion and admiration. Similarly, according to Renaissance poetics, Milton's attempt "to present in ample narrative the transition from a state of innocence to a state of sin" should ideally have involved either a *peripeteia* or a discovery or both, inasmuch as (1) the complex plot was preferable in epic as in tragedy and (2) in this sort of fable the *transitio* or *metabasis* was, by definition, attended by one or both of these devices.

On the whole, there is little reason to regard the crisis of *Paradise Lost* as distinct from its central *peripeteia*—the protagonists' "mutatio in contrarium" from felicity to infelicity and from innocence to sin. This alteration Milton presented in book 9 as occurring within a very short compass of time and space.

Although Renaissance theorists regarded the *peripeteia* rather as a change of fortune than as a "reversal of intention," they sometimes stipulated that this alteration should be both sudden and unexpected. Though this view was largely based on Aristotle's examples from *Oedipus Rex* and *Lynceus*, it was also founded on his statement that "incidents arousing pity and fear ... have the very greatest effect on the mind when they occur unexpectedly and at the same time in consequence of one another."³³ Thus Minturno's *L'Arte Poetica* conceived the *peripeteia* as an "inopinato, e contrario al creder nostro, avvenimento."³⁴ As instances he cited not only Aristotle's example of the messenger in *Oedipus*, but also that of the suitors in the *Odyssey*:

Intendo per l'avvenimento inopinato quella mutazione di fortuna, la qual si fa, o dolorosa, o lieta, ch'ella si sia; quando altramente, che da noi si sperava e credeva, la faccenda riesce, sicome par necessario, o verisimile. Chiamasi da' Greci *Peripezia*, e propriamente ne' tristi e miserabili accidenti, come avvenne appo Sofocle a quel messo, il qual venendo ad Edipo con opinion di apportargli felice novella, e per liberarlo dalla paura di congiungersi carnalmente con la madre, dimostrandogli, che veramente egli fusse, operò quel, ch'egli non pensava. Ed appo Omero i Proci (mentre nell' altrui casa attendono a magnifici conviti, e si ridono di Ulisse, il quale riputavano mendico e pellegrino, ed a Telemaco insidie pongono, ed inganni) sono da quelli uccisi, quando senza di ciò punto temere essi pensano, che sicura e lieta vita menar possano. Ed il Petrarca dove, e quando gli

parea, che potesse andar sicuro e senza sospetto de' colpi di Amore,
si vide ferito, e preso da lui. E nel Trionfo della Castità, come avea di
tanti Iddii trionfato, così stimando Amore di dovere agevolmente di
Madonna Laura trionfare, contro la opinione sua, e del Petrarca, che
sperava la vittoria, ond' esser suole, si trovò vinto da lei.[35]

In Castelvetro's opinion, the best type of *peripeteia* involved an
event directly opposite to that intended. Such a reversal of intention,
however, was not essential to the definition of *peripeteia*, inasmuch
as the "mutatione in contrario" could also be brought about by
causes directed specifically toward this tragic event or else toward
ends not altogether contrary:

Per due essempi ci dimostra Aristotele, come egli intenda mutatione
in contrario delle cose, che si fanno. Prima per l'essempio di colui,
che venuto da Coranto, credendo di recare lieta novella ad Edipo, &
di sicurarlo della paura, che egli haveva d'avincinarsi a quella che
falsamente credeva essere sua madre, facendogli conoscere, chi egli
era, lo contrista, & fa il contrario di quello, che era sua intentione di
fare. Poi per l'essempio di Linceo, & di Danao, essendo avenuto di
loro il contrario di quello, che doveva avenire, cio è, essendo
avenuto, che Linceo scampasse, & Danao morisse, dovendo per le
cose ordinate a contrario fine avenire dirittamente il contrario. Con
questi essempi adunque mostra Aristotele, che hē *peripeteia*, della
quale in questo luogo parla, & la quale egli appruova per la soprana,
è quella, che ha le cagioni ordinate non a questo, o a diverso fine, ma
a contrario.[36]

Castelvetro preferred such a reversal of ends in both the "internal"
and the "external" fable ("favola interna" and "favola forestiera"):[37]

le cagioni della mutatione, & della riconoscenza deono procedere
dalle cose interne della favola ordinate a contrario fine, o dalle cose
di fuori ordinate a diverso fine.[38]

In both types of plot, however, the sequence of dependent events
could proceed in three distinct ways:

alcune [cose] succedono l'une all'altre con dipendenza. & queste in
tre modi, o perche sono ordinate a diterminato fine, o perche sono
ordinate a diverso fine, o perche sono ordinate a contrario fine.[39]

Examples of such "cose . . . ordinate a contrario fine" in the internal
fable were the death of Laius and the incest of Jocasta in *Oedipus
Rex:*

La morte di Laio, & lo 'ncesto di Giocasta succedono con dipendenza
alla partita d'Edipo da Coranto, che fu ordinata a fine dirittamente
contrario.[40]

An analogous instance in the external fable was the fate of Hormisda in Boccaccio's novella:

Et di quelle, che sono ordinate a fine contrario, si puo vedere l'essempio in Hormisda, che corre all' aiuto di Pasimonda, & non che l'aiuti, ma egli è ucciso nella novella di Cimone appresso il Boccaccio.[41]

Where Castelvetro had regarded the reversal of ends as a desirable, but by no means essential, element in *peripeteia*, Heinsius defined *peripeteia* as a sudden and unexpected change:

Priorem Aristoteles Peripetiam dixit. qua voce cum ut plurimum funesti Tragicique in contrarium eventus designentur, (quo sensu & Nicandrum, opus suum, quod Peripetias dixit, inscripsisse existamus) tamen omnia quae praeter expectationem, vel è prosperis adversa, vel secunda ex adversis evenirent, ita in Tragoedia fuisse dicta patet. autor certe optimus loquendi Aristoteles, quod praeter expectationem evenit, in libris De historia animalium,[42] hac voce nuncupavit. Haec, eorum quae aguntur, sive actionis in contrarium mutatio, à maximo magistro definitur.[43]

Like Aristotle, Heinsius cited the messenger in *Oedipus* and the fate of Lynceus and Danaus in *Lynceus* as examples:

Utranque in Oedipode & Sophoclis & Senecae habemus Oedipus praeter omnem expectationem subito fit miser. haec Peripetia est.[44]

Similarly, the *Lynceus* contained a "manifesta ... in contrarium mutatio":

Quarum in altera felicitas in infelicitatem; in altera, quae duplici mutatione constat, in felicitatem Lyncei felicitas [*sic*], Danai in infelicitatem praeter expectationem mutatur felicitas.[45]

Heinsius had derived the phrase "praeter expectationem" from Aristotle's statement that tragic incidents produce the greatest effect on the mind "when they occur unexpectedly." He had, in fact, employed this expression in his own translation of the *Poetics*:

haec ipsa maxime admirationem movent, sed praecipue cum praeter expectationem alterum alterius est causa.[46]

Nascimbene likewise interpreted *peripeteia* as a sudden change. In his commentary on the *Aeneid*, he observed that the simple fable, unlike the complex plot ("implicita actio"), lacked any great and "sudden" change of fortune:

in qua sine aliquo admirabili casu: id est, absque subita, magnaque

rerum vicissitudine, & absque agnitione fit transitus, ingensque
rerum variatio: hoc est, quae peripetijs, & agnitionibus caret.

Just as Aristotle's commentators had cited examples of both
peripeteia and discovery in the *Odyssey*, Nascimbene found
instances of both in the *Aeneid*. The first six books, he maintained,
involved both of these devices, whereas the last six books contained
peripeteia alone:

Igitur Aeneidis anteriorum sex librorum actio, seu Epopoeia
complicita est. Frequens enim extat tum subita fortunae
commutatio: tum crebrae agnitiones fiunt. . . . Posteriores verò sex
libri actionem habent simplicem, veluti Ilias Homeri, ad cuius
imaginem compositi videntur: nullam enim agnitionem habent,
peripetiam tantùm habent, & multis quidem in locis. Saepè enim
Rutuli victores Troiani victi, rursus Troiani victores, Rutuli victi
demonstrantur. Quod quid aliud est, quàm peripeteia, &
commutatio felicitatis in infelicitatem, & infelicitatis in felicitatem?

Moreover, *peripeteia* and discovery occurred not only in the epic
fable, but also in the episodes:

In episodia incidunt agnitiones, & peripetiae . . . , quae cum
delectationem afferunt, tum etiam poemata mirum in modum
exornant.[47]

Sir John Harington similarly regarded the *peripeteia* as recognition of a "sudden" and "unlooked for" change of fortune, and
believed Ariosto's *Orlando Furioso* to contain many examples of this
device:

Briefly, *Aristotle* and the best censurers of Poesie would have . . . an
heroicall Poem (as well as a Tragedie) to be full of *Peripet[e]ia*, which
I interpret an agnition of some unlooked for change thereof: of this
what store there be the reader shall quickly find.[48]

Milton's account of "Mans First Disobedience" exhibits many of
the characteristics of the *peripeteia* as Renaissance theorists had
conceived it. Eve's lapse occurs "praeter expectationem," and its
immediate causes were ordered toward a contrary end. Having left
Adam's side in "confidence . . . / Either to meet no danger, or to
find / Matter of glorious trial," she straightway encounters danger
and yields ingloriously to temptation. Though she eats the forbidden
fruit in "expectation high / Of knowledge" and of "God-head," the
effect of her action is the obscuration of her understanding and
condemnation to death. The "false Fruit that promis'd clearer sight"

darkens the minds of both its victims. Upon leaving Adam, Eve expects to return for "Noontide repast, or Afternoons repose," but in the interim she forfeits both:

> O much deceav'd, much failing, hapless *Eve*,
> Of thy presum'd return! event perverse!
> Thou never from that houre in Paradise
> Foundst either sweet repast, or sound repose.
>
> [9.404–7]

As Adam is "not deceav'd," but sins "against his better knowledge," the ironic reversal of expectation does not, in his case, hinge on ignorance of the effects of the fruit. He experiences, however, two sudden reversals of his expectations. He had promised "Great joy . . . to his thoughts, and new / Solace in [Eve's] return, so long delay'd," but in actuality her return brings the knowledge of her "fatal Trespass" and converts his joy to horror. Similarly, because he cannot bear to "forgoe" her "sweet Converse and Love so dearly joyn'd," he resolves to share her fate. The effect of his decision, however, is to turn "sweet Converse" to "mutual accusation" and "vain contest," to convert their "Love so dearly join'd" to acrimonious hatred.

Though the fall of man is structurally the most significant of the *peripeteias* in *Paradise Lost*, the fable and episodes contain other reversals. First, as in the *Aeneid*, the tide of battle changes frequently in the course of the angelic war. After the "Satanic Host" has "fled ignominious," it achieves a temporary advantage through leveling its "devilish Enginrie" against "the Victor Host," but this momentary triumph is promptly nullified by the faithful angels, who retaliate by hurling mountains. After these vicissitudes of combat, the rebels are decisively routed by the Son. For the most part, these reversals occur "praeter expectationem." Having affected "Honour, Dominion, Glorie, and renowne," Satan and his legions actually incur "oblivion," "dispraise and ignominie." Having expected realms in heaven, they achieve "Chains in Hell" instead. They are defeated by Messiah, whom they had despised, and their evil "Driv'n back redounded as a flood on those / From whom it sprung" (7.57–58). In the initial onslaught of battle Satan undergoes his first reverse, experiencing pain for the first time and discovering

> himself not matchless, and his pride
> Humbl'd by such rebuke, so farr beneath
> His confidence to equal God in power.
>
> [6.341–43]

Instead of fulfilling his boast to drag *Gabriel* bound at his chariot
wheels, Moloch is himself wounded and "with shatterd Armes /
And uncouth paine fled bellowing." Though the initial success of
their artillery induces the rebels to expect an easy victory,

> highthn'd in thir thoughts beyond
> All doubt of Victorie, eternal might
> To match with thir inventions they presum'd
> So easie, and of his Thunder made a scorn,
> And all his Host derided, while they stood
> A while in trouble.
>
> [6.629–34]

their exultation soon changes to "amaze . . . and terrour." They
perceive "all thir confidence / Under the weight of Mountains
buried deep" and themselves overwhelmed and crushed. At
Messiah's appearance their expectations again revive, "hope conceiving from despair,"

> Weening to prosper, and at length prevaile
> Against God and *Messiah*, or to fall
> In universal ruin last.
>
> [6.795–97]

but their anticipation again proves vain. They are vanquished by the
thunders they had scoffed at.

Second, several of the *peripeteia*s in *Paradise Lost* involve
discoveries. In book 2 the obstacles to Satan's escape from hell are
suddenly removed by the recognition of his parental relationship to
Sin and Death, the guardians of the infernal gates. In book 4 his first
attempt to beguile Eve is frustrated through his discovery by the
angelic guard and his flight upon recognizing the futility of
resistance. In book 12 Adam's recognition of Christ as his future
redeemer seals his justification by faith.

Third, hell itself is the scene of two unexpected changes in Satan's
fortunes. At the beginning of book 1 the vanquished angels were
"confounded," "abject and lost"; at the end of the same book they
have recovered, reorganized their military forces, and reestablished
their polity. Satan sits exalted on "a Throne of Royal State," "from
despair / Thus high uplifted beyond hope." In book 10 his humiliation is even more sudden and "praeter expectationem." Having
"returnd / Successful beyond hope," he finds his triumph converted
to shame by an unexpected metamorphosis:

> a while he stood, expecting
> Thir universal shout and high applause
> To fill his eare, when contrary he hears
> On all sides, from innumerable tongues
> A dismal universal hiss, the sound
> Of public scorn.
>
> [10.504–9]

The same reversal of expectation befalls the remainder of his host, who await him without the hall,

> Sublime with expectation when to see
> In Triumph issuing forth thir glorious Chief;
> They saw, but other sight instead, a crowd
> Of ugly Serpents: horror on them fell,
> And horrid sympathie; for what they saw,
> They felt themselvs now changing. . . .
>   Thus was th' applause they meant,
> Turnd to exploding hiss, triumph to shame
> Cast on themselves from thir own mouths.
>
> [10.536–47]

Fourth, Milton alludes frequently to other reversals in subsequent human history—the destruction of Pharaoh's cavalry in the act of pursuing the Israelites (1.306), the mutilation of Dagon's statue by "the Captive Ark" (1.458), the "violent cross wind" which prevents "Embryos, and Idiots, Eremits and Friers" from reaching "Heav'ns Wicket" and blows them awry into the "Paradise of Fools" (3.487), Samson's betrayal through Dalilah (9.1060), and the *peripeteia* whereby Christ's humiliation shall exalt his "Manhood also to this Throne" of heaven and his submission to death shall defeat death of its spoil:

> Though now to Death I yeild, and am his due
> . . . I shall rise Victorious, and subdue
> My Vanquisher, spoild of his vanted spoile;
> Death his deaths wound shall then receive, & stoop
> Inglorious, of his mortall sting disarm'd.
> I through the ample Air in Triumph high
> Shall lead Hell Captive maugre Hell, and show
> The powers of darkness bound.
>
> [3.245–56]

For the theological basis of his reversals of intention Milton relies largely on the doctrine of permissive evil. According to the *De Doctrina*, God permits the existence of evil "by throwing no impediment in the way of natural causes and free agents (indeed, he may even impell "sinners to the commission of sin" by "blinding their understandings" and "hardening their hearts"), but he converts the evil they intend to a contrary end, the production of good:

the end which a sinner has in view is generally something evil and unjust, from which God uniformly educes a good and just result, thus as it were creating light out of darkness.

God eventually converts every evil deed into an instrument of good, contrary to the expectation of sinners, and overcomes evil with good.[49]

From this concept the Christian poet who had extolled "what religious, what glorious and magnificent use might be made of poetry, both in divine and human things"[50] derived much of the irony underlying his epic and tragic fables. In all three of his major works the sinner's evil is converted "praeter expectationem" to the contrary end intended by Providence; "per le cose ordinate a contrario fine" there results "dirittamente il contrario." In *Samson Agonistes* the Philistines "Unweetingly importun'd / Thir own destruction to come speedy upon them." In *Paradise Regained* Satan rashly assays to subvert the Son of God by "temptation and all guile," "But contrary unweeting he fulfill'd / The purpos'd Counsel pre-ordain'd and fixt / Of the most High" (1.126–28).

The same providential overruling of the sinner's evil purpose appears in the treatment of Satan in *Paradise Lost*. The spiritual war between God and his adversary is conceived essentially as a struggle of contrary wills—one attempting to bring good out of evil, the other to produce evil from good:

> To do aught good never will be our task,
> But ever to do ill our sole delight,
> As being the contrary of his high will
> Whom we resist. If then his Providence
> Out of our evil seek to bring forth good,
> Our labour must be to pervert that end,
> And out of good still to find means of evil;
> Which oft-times may succeed, so as perhaps
> Shall grieve him, if I fail not, and disturb
> His inmost counsels from thir destin'd aim.
>
> [1.161–68]

Theologically, such a strategy is *a priori* doomed to failure, for the creature's foresight cannot possibly overrule the Creator's providence. The final result of his action is, accordingly, the direct opposite of what he had intended:

>   the will
> And high permission of all-ruling Heaven
> Left him at large to his own dark designs,
> That with reiterated crimes he might
> Heap on himself damnation, while he sought
> Evil to others, and enrag'd might see
> How all his malice serv'd but to bring forth
> Infinite goodness, grace and mercy shown
> On Man by him seduc't, but on himself
> Treble confusion, wrath and vengeance pour'd.
>
>   [1.211–20]

Thus the infernal plan "to confound the race / Of mankind in one root, . . . done all to spite / The great Creatour" actually achieves the opposite—the greater glory of God and the greater felicity of man: "But thir spite still serves / His glory to augment" (2.382–86).

This divine exploitation of evil for greater good, converting the effects of sin to a contrary end, is manifested on two occasions in *Paradise Lost*—first in the creation of man to fill the place left vacant by the rebel angels and second in the future redemption and exaltation of mankind through Christ. In book 7 the angelic hierarchies acclaim the Father's decree to create the universe, with praise

>   to him . . . whose wisdom had ordain'd
> Good out of evil to create, in stead
> Of Spirits maligne a better Race to bring
> Into thir vacant room, and thence diffuse
> His good to Worlds and Ages infinite.
>
>   [7.186–91]

Again, upon the execution of this decree, their hymn of praise hails the providential reversal of the evil-doer's intent, for the greater glory of God:

>   easily the proud attempt
> Of Spirits apostat and thir Counsels vaine
> Thou hast repeld, while impiously they thought
> Thee to diminish, and from thee withdraw
> The number of thy worshippers. Who seekes
> To lessen thee, against his purpose serves
> To manifest the more thy might: his evil
> Thou usest, and from thence creat'st more good.
> Witness this new-made World, another Heav'n.
>
>   [7.609–17]

Similarly, the latter books of *Paradise Lost* present the providential reversal of Satan's intentions in regard to man's fall. As in the

case of the angelic rebellion, the act of disobedience is inspired by the
devil, permitted by Providence, punished by divine justice, and
transcended by an act of creation. His first attempt to diminish the
number of Jehovah's worshipers had been foiled by the creation of
man; the second effort is frustrated by the renovation of the elect.
Where Satan had purposed man's destruction, Providence converts
his act toward the contrary end of man's salvation. Adam's sin
becomes an occasion for the exercise of divine grace; his expulsion
from paradise becomes a means to a "Paradise within thee, happier
farr"; and death becomes both a "final remedie" for human misery
and a "Gate of Life." Through "the Providence of God . . . operat-
ing in his restoration," man is to be "delivered from sin and death"
through Christ and "raised to a far more excellent state of grace and
glory than that from which he had fallen."⁵¹ Upon learning of this
future redemption and renovation, Adam hails the "goodness
infinite"

> That all this good of evil shall produce,
> And evil turn to good; more wonderful
> Then that by which creation first brought forth
> Light out of darkness!
>
> [12.469–73]

and rejoices that from his sin

> much more good thereof shall spring,
> To God more glory, more good will to Men
> From God, and over wrauth grace shall abound.
>
> [12.476–78]

The promised restoration of mankind is not only directly opposite
to Satan's intent, but also contrary to the expectation of Adam and
Eve. Reminding his wife of the "mild and gracious temper" God had
shown in pronouncing judgment, Adam declares that

> wee expected
> Immediate dissolution, which we thought
> Was meant by Death that day, when lo, to thee
> Pains only in Child-bearing were foretold
> . . . .
> On mee the Curse aslope
> Glanc'd on the ground, with labour I must earne
> My bread; what harm?
>
> [10.1048–55]

Again, beholding "the end of all [his] Ofspring" in the flood, Adam
wonders "whether here the Race of man will end," but is reassured

by Michael's revelation of Jehovah's covenant with Noah and the promise of a "world restor'd." Finally, the prophecy of his restoration through Christ exceeds his highest expectation, his "utmost hope."

There is, however, a significant difference between *Paradise Lost* and Milton's later poems in the relationship between the principal *peripeteia* and the providential reversal of ends. In both *Samson Agonistes* and *Paradise Regained* the *peripeteia* takes place as a *result* of the divine overruling of the sinner's intent, so that "per le cose ordinate a contrario fine" there occurs "dirittamente il contrario." In *Paradise Lost,* on the other hand, the principal *peripeteia* (man's disobedience and lapse from a state of innocence to a state of sin) *precedes* the principal reversal of ends; indeed it is a precondition of this reversal, for it is not until after man's fall that the process of restoration to a loftier estate can begin.[52]

In the major *peripeteia* of *Paradise Lost* there is no reversal of intention on Satan's part. He brings about the fall of man as (virtually from the very beginning of the epic fable) he had intended to do. Nevertheless from the moment of judgment in book 10, with its veiled promise of restoration in the woman's seed, Milton describes the divine conversion of the devil's action toward an opposite end. As this process will be consummated only with the Last Judgment, Milton is compelled, for the sake of the unities of time and action, to represent its final results in an episode, through the indirect medium of Michael's prophecy, rather than directly in the fable itself. Nevertheless, in addition to this episodic revelation of the final salvation of man, he also depicts at least the initial stages of man's restoration in the fable itself, in the spiritual regeneration of Adam and Eve. The providential reversal of Satan's intent to destroy mankind and subject it to sin and death is manifested in their gradual restoration from a state of sin to a state of grace[53] and the revival of "new hope ... Out of despair." The process of regeneration foretold by the Father in book 3 and initiated by the Son at the moment of pronouncing judgment is exhibited primarily through its effects, repentance and faith.[54] Though this spiritual alteration lacks the suddenness of the most effective sort of *peripeteia,* it nevertheless embodies several other characteristics of the *peripeteia* as conceived by Renaissance critics. First, it involves a "mutatio in contrarium" from a state of sin to a state of grace, from despair to faith and hope.

As early as book 11, Adam finds consolation in the promised
victory of the woman's seed:

> His promise, that thy Seed shall bruise our Foe
> . . . .
> Assures me that the bitterness ot death
> Is past, and we shall live.
>
> [11.155–58]

This reassurance is further intensified by Michael's revelation of
man's future restoration through Christ and culminates in Adam's
confession of faith in his future redeemer. Adam and Eve leave
paradise regenerate in spirit and justified by faith. After their
"mutatione di stato . . . di felice in misero," they have experienced
to some extent a counterchange "di misero in felice." Though
"sad, / With cause for evils past," they are to live "much more
cheer'd / With meditation on the happie end."

Second, this psychological alteration occurs "praeter expectationem." Since neither Satan nor Adam had foreseen the future
restoration of man, the spiritual regeneration effected through
divine grace in the final books of the epic is, on the whole, contrary
to the expectation of both. Third, the climax of this spiritual change
of state—Adam's acknowledgment of Christ as his redeemer—
occurs as the result of a recognition or discovery.

5 In the composition of *Paradise Lost* Milton evidently bestowed special care on the construction of his plot. This, in Aristotle's opinion, was "the first essential, the life and soul"[1] of the poem, and (in Tasso's view) "la forma essenziale del poema."[2] Moreover, his own writings over a period of decades exhibit a profound respect for the Aristotelian "rules" for the disposition of the fable.[3] It is thus hardly surprising that in *Paradise Lost* he exhibited a preference for unity of plot, that he chose the complex or "intricate" type of fable, and that the narrative contains all three "parts of the Plot" recognized in the *Poetics—peripeteia*, discovery, and suffering. In this chapter I shall analyze four of several examples of discovery in the plot of this epic: (1) the recognition scene at Hellgate between Satan and his offspring, Sin and Death; (2) his detection by the guardian angels of paradise in book 4; (3) man's "knowledge of Good lost, and Evil got" by eating the forbidden fruit (11.87); and (4) Adam's recognition of Christ as his redeemer in the concluding book of *Paradise Lost*.

Aristotle had defined discovery or recognition as "a change from ignorance to knowledge, and thus to either love or hate, in the personages marked for good or evil fortune." The "most powerful elements of attraction in Tragedy," he believed, were "the Peripeties and Discoveries." Both in tragedy and in epic, the "complex" plot, which contained "one or the other [of these elements], or

60

both," was preferable to the "simple" fable. The *Odyssey* he regarded as complex, inasmuch as "there is Discovery throughout it."[4]

Like the fable of the *Odyssey*, the plots of both of Milton's epics involve recognition and *peripeteia* and should therefore be classified as "complex." In *Paradise Regained*, for instance, Milton utilizes the device of the discovery on three occasions, and in all three cases it proves of considerable structural importance. First, there is the divine testimony at Christ's baptism, when— "obscure, / Unmarkt, unknown"—the "Son of *Joseph* deem'd" is hailed by John the Baptist as "his worthier" and "in likeness of a Dove / The Spirit descended, while the Father's voice / From Heav'n pronounc'd him his beloved Son" (*PR*, 1.23–32). This incident contributes directly to the development of the plot, for it precipitates Satan's resolve to tempt the Messiah with "well couch't fraud, well woven snares" (*PR*, 1.97). It produces on the Adversary's part "a change from ignorance to knowledge," for he learns thereby that the supposed "Son of *Joseph*" is really the Son of God, "the Womans seed" destined to inflict "that fatal wound . . . Upon my head" (*PR*, 1.53–55, 64). This discovery leads to "hate"; Satan is filled "With wonder, then with envy . . . and rage" (*PR*, 1.38).

A second recognition occurs when Christ penetrates Satan's disguise at the beginning of the first temptation. In the suggestion "Command / That out of these hard stones be made thee bread" (*PR*, 1.342–43) the Messiah recognizes the wiles of the archtempter under the appearance of "the Swain":

> For I discern thee other then thou seem'st
> . . . .
> Why dost thou then suggest to me distrust,
> Knowing who I am, as I know who thou art?
> [*PR*,1.348–56]

Like the earlier discovery, this recognition occurs at a crucial moment in the evolution of the fable—that of the initial encounter between the two antagonists. It dramatizes the first trial of strength in this "great duel, not of arms"—emphasizing, on the one hand, Satan's "hellish wiles" and, on the other, the superior "wisdom" whereby Christ is to "vanquish" them (*PR*, 1.174–75).

Third, in the event which concludes the final temptation, when "Satan smitten with amazement fell . . . whence he stood to see his Victor fall" (*PR*, 4.562–71), recent scholarship has found the "finest form of Discovery"—the recognition "attended by Peripeties, like that which goes with the Discovery in *Oedipus*."[5] Hughes observed that the word *stood* (*PR*, 4.561) "marks the moment of Satan's recognition of Christ's full power and identity, and the catastrophe of his own fall is the consequence."[6]

In these three examples of recognition the following character-istics seem especially significant. First, all three are discoveries of *persons*, rather than of "inanimate things" or of past deeds ("whether some one has done or not done something").[7] Second, all three instances involve the same spiritual antagonists—Christ and Satan. Third, of the three discoveries, two, the first and the last, center around two different aspects of the same problem—Christ's divine sonship. Fourth, all three discoveries are of major import-ance for the complication and denouement of the plot. The first precipitates Satan's proud assay to "tempt the Son of God." The second represents Christ's first clear-cut victory over his adver-sary's wiles, when he penetrates the devil's disguise. The third coincides with the *peripeteia* of this "complex" fable, the reversal in the relative positions of the two "personages marked for good or evil fortune." Fifth, the pattern of discovery in *Paradise Regained* belongs to the type Heinsius designated as *duplex*, or double, rather than *simplex*.[8] According to Aristotle, "The Discovery . . . being of persons, it may be that of one party only to the other, the latter being already known; or both the parties may have to discover themselves. Iphigenia, for instance, was discovered to Orestes by sending the letter; and another Discovery was required to reveal him to Iphigenia."[9] Milton's fable, as we have seen, contains the double type of discovery, for it involves the recognition of "both the parties."

In the imminent combat between Satan and Death in book 2 of *Paradise Lost*, Milton exploits the sort of situation which Aristotle had recommended as particularly suitable for tragedy—one involv-ing some "tragic deed . . . within the family," as "when murder or the like is done or meditated . . . by son on father." Of three alternative methods of treating such a situation, *Aristotle* preferred that in which the "deadly injury" contemplated in "ignorance of . . . relationship" is forestalled by a timely discovery.[10] In Milton's episode, father and son—"in ignorance of [their] relation-ship"—are on the verge of engaging in mortal combat:

>Each at the Head
Level'd his deadly aime; thir fatall hands
No second stroke intend ...: and now great deeds
Had been achiev'd, whereof all Hell had rung,
Had not the Snakie Sorceress.... rush'd between.
>[2.711-26]

Sin's timely revelation of the father-son relationship prevents the
"deed of horror" from taking place:

>O Father, what intends thy hand, she cry'd,
Against thy only Son? What fury, O Son,
Possesses thee to bend that mortal Dart
Against thy Fathers head?
>[2.727-30]

Ironically, Sin's dramatic interposition produces no immediate
recognition on Satan's part. The "Portress of Hell Gate" (2.746) and
her companion are so monstrously deformed that he cannot
recognize them, and his initial response to her revelation is one of
detestation rather than parental *storgē*. There is, as yet, on his
part neither a "change from ignorance to knowledge" nor a change
from hate to "love." Discovery is still incomplete, and he requires
further knowledge of their identity:

>till first I know of thee
What thing thou art, thus double-form'd, and why
In this infernal Vaile first met thou call'st
Me Father, and that Fantasm call'st my Son?
I know thee not, nor ever saw till now
Sight more detestable than him and thee.
>[2.740-45]

It is only after her detailed explanation of her own genesis and
transformation and the birth of her offspring that Satan recognizes
his own progeny and acknowledges Sin as his "Dear Daughter" and
Death as "my fair Son" (2.817-18). This fuller revelation of their
nature and identity completes the process of discovery.

In this episode the recognition is double, rather than simple, for
there is discovery on both sides. On the one hand, Satan learns that
the two "formidable shapes" at Hellgate are his own progeny; on
the other hand, Death realizes that the "Traitor Angel" he was
about to slay is his own father. On Sin's part there is, strictly
speaking, no true discovery, for Milton gives no indication that she
had been ignorant of Satan's identity. The only real "change from

ignorance to knowledge" takes place on the part of the devil and his son.

This discovery produces, at least superficially, a "change . . . to either love or hate, in the personages" concerned and a temporary alteration in Satan's fortunes. The "formidable shapes" (2.649) which had formerly seemed an obstacle to his passage now assist him to escape. Without their aid, he could never have left his infernal prison. Only Sin could have opened the ninefold gates, "Which but herself not all the *Stygian* powers / Could once have mov'd" (2.875–76). Nor could any force on Satan's part have overcome Death: "against all force / Death ready stands to interpose his dart, / Fearless to be o'ermatcht by living might" (2.853–55).

It is specifically the recognition of their family relationship which enlists these formidable jailers in Satan's cause.

In the latter part of book 4 Milton describes the discovery of the archfiend by the angelic guard and his subsequent flight upon the further discovery of his own relative powerlessness. The stages of this recognition are gradual. First, Satan's display of passion on Mount Niphates convinces Uriel that his disguise as a "stripling Cherube" (3.636) is really spurious:

> Thus while he spake, each passion dimm'd his face,
> Thrice chang'd with pale, ire envie and despair,
> Which marrd his borrow'd visage, and betraid
> Him counterfet, if any eye beheld.
>
> [4.114–17]

Uriel's eye *does* behold, and marks his "gestures fierce . . . and mad demeanour" (4.128–29). Suspecting him to be "one of the banisht crew . . . ventur'd from the deep, to raise / New troubles" (4.573–75), the angel of the sun alerts the angelic guard, who find the devil "Squat like a Toad, close at the ear of *Eve*" (4.800). At the touch of Ithuriel's spear he reverts to his "own likeness . . . Discover'd and surpris'd" (4.813–14).

Nevertheless, their discovery is still incomplete. Although they have recognized the invader as one of the fallen angels, they are not yet aware of his personal identity. Even "in his own shape" (4.819) Satan is still unknown to Zephon and Ithuriel. In the infernal monarch they see merely one of "Those rebel Spirits adjudg'd to Hell" (4.823).

As in book 2, Milton exploits the device of the incomplete
recognition with fine irony. This is the first occasion when Satan is
unrecognized in his own shape. Death had immediately identified
him as the leader of the rebel angels, and Chaos had instantly
recognized him as "That mighty leading Angel, who of late / Made
head against Heav'ns King" (2.991–92). He is, accordingly, out-
raged by his captors' failure to perceive in him the head of the rebel
forces and the sovereign of hell:

> Know ye not then said *Satan*, filld with scorn,
> Know ye not me? ye knew me once no mate
> For you, there sitting where ye durst not soare;
> Not to know mee argues your selves unknown,
> The lowest of your throng.
>
> [4.827–31][11]

Again, as in book 2, the failure to achieve complete recognition
serves to emphasize the ravages wrought by sin:

> Think not, revolted Spirit, thy shape the same,
> Or undiminisht brightness, to be known
> As when thou stoodst in Heav'n upright and pure;
> That Glorie then, when thou no more wast good,
> Departed from thee, and thou resembl'st now
> Thy sin and place of doom obscure and foule.
>
> [4.835–40]

The recognition scene of book 2 had stressed the moral deformity
of Satan's daughter, Sin; the recognition scene of book 4 emphasizes the spiritual foulness of Satan himself.

Zephon's words give no clear-cut indication that he recognizes
his prisoner as the archfiend himself, and the first explicit awareness of his identity is voiced by Gabriel:

> And with them comes a third of Regal port,
> But faded splendor wan; who by his gate
> And fierce demeanour seems the Prince of Hell.
>
> [4.869–71]

And it is Gabriel who first addresses the stranger as "Satan."

The scene concludes with a discovery of a different sort—a
recognition not of persons, but of an "inanimate thing,"[12] the
"celestial Sign" whereby the Almighty prevents the outbreak of
battle in paradise. At the moment when Satan and the "Angelic
Squadron" are about to engage in violent combat and "dreadful
deeds / Might have ensu'd,"

> Th' Eternal to prevent such horrid fray
> Hung forth in Heav'n his golden Scales....
>   In these he put two weights
> The sequel each of parting and of fight;
> The latter quick up flew, and kickt the beam.
>
> [4.996–1004]

By this providential revelation of his lot—"how light, how weak / If thou resist"—Satan discovers the futility of relying on his own strength, and this discovery precipitates his flight:

>   The Fiend lookt up and knew
> His mounted scale aloft: nor more; but fled.
>
> [4.1013–15]

The pattern of discovery in this scene conforms to the "simple" type. A series of minor discoveries on the part of the angelic guard culminates in their eventual recognition of the archfiend and his mission as "the Spy" (4.948).

In the complex fable, "the change in the hero's fortunes" involves *peripeteia* or discovery, or both. *Paradise Lost* is no exception to Aristotle's rule. For the central event of his epic Milton has selected a "change from ignorance to knowledge"—man's "knowledge of Good lost, and Evil got" (11.87). By partaking of the tree of knowledge, Adam and Eve forfeit their original innocence (an innocence both Eve and Satan condemn as ignorance) and find their eyes opened to the knowledge of evil. The change in their fortunes coincides with this spiritual alteration.

As with other discoveries in the fable of *Paradise Lost*, Milton utilizes the device of the recognition at a crucial moment in the development of his plot. This is the turning point in the fortunes of Adam and Eve—the event which precipitates their fall from "high estate." It is, moreover, the focal point of Satan's enterprise against mankind, the immediate "objective" of the infernal campaign. On first learning of the divine injunction concerning the tree of knowledge, he had evolved the essence of his strategy—to "excite their minds / With more desire to know" in the mistaken belief that "knowledge might exalt [them] / Equal with Gods" (4.522–26). At the first opportunity he had attempted to execute this plan by reaching "The Organs of [Eve's] Fancie" (4.802), and the content of her dream indicated that he had partly succeeded: "is Knowledge so

despis'd?" (5.60). In book 9 he renews the attack, arguing that "your
Eyes . . . shall perfetly be then / Op'nd and cleerd, and ye shall be
as Gods / Knowing both Good and Evil as they know" (9.706–9).
As in book 4, Satan substitutes the word *ignorance* for *innocence*
("and do they onely stand / By Ignorance, is that thir happie state?"
[4.518–19]) and thereby succeeds in convincing Eve that the state of
innocence is an indignity to be eschewed:

> Why then was this forbid? Why but to awe,
> Why but to keep ye low and ignorant,
> His worshippers.
>
> [9.703–5]

> What fear I then, rather what know to feare
> Under this ignorance of Good and Evil,
> Of God or Death, of Law or Penaltie?
>
> [9.773–75]

The act of recognition in this book is gradual. First Satan persuades "The Mother of Mankinde" (1.36) that the knowledge of
good and evil will bring equality with the gods. After tasting the
forbidden fruit, she is intoxicated by the experience of evil and
erroneously believes that her eyes have been opened to sapience.
The discovery of her fatal trespass precipitates Adam's resolution
to share her death by participating in her crime. Finally, after
sealing their "mutual guilt" with "Loves disport" (9.1042–43), they
awake to a recognition of their actual guilt, to the knowledge of
"Good lost, and Evil got":

> each the other viewing,
> Soon found thir Eyes how op'nd, and thir minds
> How dark'nd; innocence, that as a veile
> Had shadow'd them from knowing ill, was gon,
> Just confidence, and native righteousness,
> And honour from about them, naked left
> To guiltie shame.
>
> [9.1052–58]

This discovery—this "change from ignorance to knowledge"—is,
in the final analysis, a change from innocence to experience of evil,
from righteousness to the consciousness of guilt:

> our Eyes
> Op'nd we find indeed, and find we know
> Both Good and Evil, Good lost, and Evil got,
> Bad Fruit of Knowledge, if this be to know,

Which leaves us naked, thus, of Honour void,
Of Innocence, of Faith of Puritie,
Our wonted Ornaments now soild and staind,
And in our Faces evident the signes
Of foul concupiscence; whence evil store;
Even shame, the last of evils.

[9.1070-79]

Like the Aristotelian *anagnorisis*, this discovery of evil leads directly to "hate, in the personages marked for good or evil fortune": "high Winds worse within / Began to rise, high Passions, Anger, Hate, / Mistrust, Suspicion, Discord" (9.1122-24) and they devote "fruitless hours" to "mutual accusation" (9.1187-88).

The final books of *Paradise Lost* contain a further discovery—a progressive "change from ignorance to knowledge" culminating in Adam's recognition of Christ as his future redeemer. This enlightenment is diametrically opposed to that produced by the "fallacious fruit" of book 9 (l. 1046). The knowledge conferred by the forbidden tree—"guiltiness" and the "loss . . . of innate righteousness"— were degrees of death.[13] Conversely, the "comprehension of spiritual things" which Adam displays before his final departure from the garden is an effect of spiritual regeneration—a function of "newness of life."[14]

Milton accentuates the contrast between these two sorts of recognition by applying to Michael's revelation a phrase originally associated with the fall of man—the serpent's promise that "your eyes shall be opened" (Genesis 3:5) and the statement of its fulfillment ("And the eyes of them both were opened," Genesis 3:7). After removing "from *Adams* eyes the Filme . . . Which that false Fruit that promis'd clearer sight / Had bred" (11.412-14), Michael instructs him to "ope thine eyes, and first behold / Th' effects which thy original crime hath wrought / In some to spring from thee" (11.423-25). Adam himself (11.594) hails the angelic seer as "True opener of mine eyes," and the revelation concerning "Just *Abraham* and his Seed" provokes a similar acknowledgment:

now first I finde
Mine eyes true op'ning, and my heart much eas'd,
Erwhile perplext with thoughts what would become
Of mee and all Mankind; but now I see
His day, in whom all Nations shall be blest

[12.273-77]

Thus Adam himself acknowledges that Michael's prophecy has produced a "change from ignorance to knowledge."

In deliberately contrasting the type of knowledge conferred by the forbidden fruit with that achieved through Michael's revelation, Milton was exploiting the antithesis between the obscuration of man's understanding through spiritual death and its restoration in part "to its primitive clearness" through spiritual regeneration. According to the *De Doctrina*, the "new spiritual life and its increase bear the same relation to the restoration of man, which spiritual death and its progress . . . bear to his fall." The "primary functions of the new life are comprehension of spiritual things, and love of holiness. And as the power of exercising these functions was weakened and in a manner destroyed by the spiritual death, so is the understanding restored in great part to its primitive clearness, and the will to its primitive liberty, by the new spiritual life in Christ."[15]

These theological concepts are expressed poetically by Michael's action immediately before his revelation. The removal of "the Film" produced by the forbidden fruit surely indicates the removal of the "obscuration" of Adam's understanding and its restoration "to its primitive clearness." The three drops "from the Well of Life" (11.416) which the angel instills obviously symbolize the "newness of life" essential to a "comprehension of spiritual things."

The terms in which the *De Doctrina* had defined the "comprehension of spiritual things" made it a highly suitable subject for a recognition scene, inasmuch as it involved a "change from ignorance to knowledge":

The comprehension of spiritual things is a habit or condition of mind produced by God, whereby the natural *ignorance* of those who believe and are ingrafted in Christ is removed, and their *understandings enlightened* for the *perception* of heavenly things, so that, by the teaching of God, they *know* all that is necessary for eternal salvation and the true happiness of life.[16]

Thus "by the teaching of God" as enunciated by Michael, Adam comes to "know all that is necessary for eternal salvation and the true happiness of life." The climax of this process of discovery is his acknowledgment of the future Messiah both as a supreme ethical "example" and as his personal "Redeemer" (12.572–73). By recognizing Christ as his redeemer, he performs the act of faith essential for his justification[17] and, accordingly, for his "eternal salvation."

Similarly, by learning from Christ's example "the sum of wisdom" and the means to "a paradise within . . ., happier far" (12.575–76, 587), he may hope to achieve "the true happiness of life". It is specifically "My Cov'nant in the woman's seed renew'd" (11.116) that the Father bids Michael communicate to Adam, and it is this article of faith which the angel instructs Adam to deliver to Eve: "Chiefly what may concern her Faith to know, / The great deliverance by her Seed to come / (For by the Womans Seed) on all Mankind" (12.599–601).

Thus in the final books of *Paradise Lost* the process of regeneration brings a positive change from ignorance to knowledge; Adam puts on "the new man, which is renewed in knowledge after the image of him that created him." As Milton had attached considerable importance to this text (Colossians 3:10) in his discussion of regeneration in the *De Doctrina*,[18] it does not seem altogether unlikely that Adam's verb *acknowledge* may be a deliberate echo of the noun *agnitionem* of the Beza-Tremellius translations of this passage.[19] Moreover, the propriety of constructing a recognition scene around the concept of the regenerated Adam's renewal in "knowledge" was implicit in the very words of this text. Heinsius had consistently employed the term *agnitio* to denote the Aristotelian *anagnorisis* or discovery.[20] In its context Adam's verb *acknowledge* is doubly appropriate. It serves both to indicate the renewed "knowledge" of the regenerate and to underline the moment of recognition.

Finally, like the Aristotelian recognition, this discovery produces a corresponding emotional "change" in the discoverer. Adam is "Surcharg'd" with "joy," "Replete with joy and wonder," at Michael's "glad tidings" of the future victory of the woman's seed over the serpent (12.372–756, 468). And Eve carries from paradise "This further consolation"—that "By mee the Promis'd Seed shall all restore" (12.620–23).

Of the four discoveries we have examined, only the first can be regarded as double, or *duplex*; the other three belong to the type Heinsius designated as *simplex*. The first three are primarily concerned with the knowledge of evil, the fourth with the knowledge of the future redeemer. In all four cases the recognition is, for the most part, extended or delayed rather than instantaneous. Satan does not immediately recognize Sin and Death. The angelic guard do not immediately recognize Satan's identity. Adam and Eve do not immediately perceive their guiltiness after eating the forbidden fruit. Nor do they immediately recognize their redeemer in the prophecy of the woman's seed. Finally, all four occur at highly significant moments in the structure of Milton's fable. The first two instances contribute to its complication; the third coincides with the turning point of the action, the change in the protagonist's fortunes; the fourth is an essential part of the solution, or denouement. Among the several instances of discovery in *Paradise Lost*, these four are particularly important for their bearing on the development and resolution of the plot.

On the whole, these recognition scenes involve a somewhat broader conception of discovery than that of the *Poetics*. Adam's enlightenment by Michael in the final books is far more gradual than most of the instances of *anagnorisis* cited by Aristotle. Milton's discoveries of "fact" are likewise broader in scope. In the *Poetics* these concern the commission or omission of some particular action in the *past* ("whether some one has done or not done something")[21] On the contrary, Adam's acknowledgement of his eventual salvation through Christ involves recognition of an event in the remote *future*. When Adam and Eve find their eyes opened to the fact of their guiltiness and loss of innocence, this recognition does not concern the actual commission of their crime—the question whether they have eaten or refrained from eating the forbidden fruit—but rather the nature and consequences of their act. Similarly, in book 4, Satan is compelled to recognize not so much the *fact* of his rebellion as the moral ugliness and the spiritual consequences of his deed. Finally, Renaissance critics differed in their interpretations of Aristotle's reference to recognition of "inanimate things." Whereas Castelvetro maintained that these "cose inanimate" were properly the *subjects* of a discovery,[22] Tasso regarded them as the *objects* of recognition: "L'agnizione è de le cose inanimate, o del fatto, o de le persone: de le cose inanimate, come quella d'Edippo, il qual riconosce il bosco sacro a le Furie, e di M. Torello che riconosce la chiesa dov'egli fu portato per arte magica."[23] *Paradise Lost* contains, in fact, examples of both types. Though the "mounted scale" (4.1014) wherein Satan reads his lot fits Tasso's definition of a discovery of an inanimate thing, earth's reaction to man's trespass against the forbidden fruit (9.782, 1000) is closer to Castelvetro's conception of recognition *by* a "cosa inanimata." In several of Milton's recognition scenes the primary cause of the delay in achieving full *anagnorisis* lies not in the discoverer but in the person discovered. Because of the altered aspect of an old acquaintance, he fails to identify the familiar figure in its unfamiliar form. Thus, in *Paradise Lost*, Sin seems a stranger to Satan, and Satan himself appears unfamiliar to Ithuriel and Zephon. Though the *Poetics* does not raise the problem, Castelvetro's commentary discusses in detail the failure in recognition due to an alteration in form or to "accidental change":

Anchora pareva, che ciascuna riconoscenza di persona, o di fatto sconosciuto potesse, & dovesse ricevere una distintione atterzata, secondo che sono tre le ignorance delle persone, o del fatto molto separate, & distinte l'una dall' altra nel modo del nasconderne la riconoscenza, la quale nasce dalla ignoranza, ne senza essa andante avanti puo essere riconoscenza. Conciosia cosa che la persona, o il fatto s'ignorino, non apparendo esse sotto forma niuna ne sua, ne d'altra cosa, o s'ignorino apparendo essi sotto forma d'altra cosa, o s'ignorino apparendo sotto la sua forma per mutatione accidentale.[24]

Again, a familiar person may be unrecognized as a result of his miraculous transformation or because of the hardships he has suffered:

La ignoranza nasce dalla persona ignorata per mutatione miracolosa, come, Cephalo è ignorato da Procri per trasformatione miracolosa, & Mercurio non è riconosciuto da Batto per trasformatione miracolosa. Nasce anchora l'ignoranza per affanni sofferti, o malatia patita dalla persona ignorata.[25]

Satan's failure to recognize Sin after her metamorphosis provides a clear-cut instance of "ignoranza ... dalla persona ignorata per mutatione miracolosa"; in her half-bestial shape his daughter no longer wears the form which had seemed "so fair in Heav'n." On several occasions the devil is likewise subject to a "mutatione miracolosa" and appears "sotto forma d'altra cosa." Disguised as a "stripling Cherube," he temporarily escapes recognition by Uriel, and he is able to enter Pandaemonium "unmarkt" by appearing "in shew plebeian Angel militant / Of lowest order" (10.441–43). His altered shape and luster prevent his identification by Zephon and Ithuriel.

Similarly, in *Paradise Regained*, a "mutatione miracolosa" lies at the root of Satan's initial inability to perceive Jesus' identity with God's "first-begot" whose "fierce thunder drove us to the deep" (*PR*, 1.89–90). In the state of his humiliation Christ has laid by the "form of God" and assumed the "form of a servant"; it is his altered form which delays full recognition.[26]

To what extent did Milton consciously exploit the Aristotelian *anagnorisis* for the development of his epic fable? On the whole, the alternative view—that in a poem as long as *Paradise Lost* he could hardly avoid including several episodes involving some sort of recognition and that his use of discovery was really unintentional and fortuitous—seems improbable. His avowed respect for the *Poetics* and its Italian commentaries, together with the structural importance of *anagnorisis* in both of his epics, would appear to justify our regarding these recognition scenes as a deliberate exploitation of the discovery as described by Aristotle and elaborated by his commentators.

6 That the same poem should
appeal simultaneously to reason and emotion, impressing its
twentieth-century readers both as "logical epic" and as "passionate
epic," is indirect testimony to Milton's fidelity to the principles of
Renaissance conceptions of eloquence. Like the orator, the poet
endeavored to teach, delight, and move. He attempted to convince
and persuade by probabilities or apparent probabilities, by appeals
to real or apparent goods and evils, by concrete sensuous images of
abstract and universal ideas. Like the orator, he sought to stimulate
or moderate the emotions, to bestow praise or blame, to exhort or
"dehort," to accuse or defend. Both followed the principles of
invention, disposition, and verbal expression or adornment. Both
recognized the same levels of style. Both conceived the mastery of
eloquence as a combination of art, imitation, and exercise—the
formal discipline of rules, the study and exploitation of classical
models, and painstaking practice and application. Both endeavored
to add reason to imagination in order to move the will. Neo-
Aristotelian poetic and rhetorical theory—together with Ramistic
revisions of logic and rhetoric—tended to reinforce the association
of cognitive and affective values and the combined appeal to
reason, sense, and passion.[1]

For Aristotle the affective power of tragedy and its ability to
purge or moderate the emotions depended in large part on the
principles of correct imitation, on the organic unity of the plot, and

on the causal connection between the thought and character of the dramatis personae and the events of the plot. A probable, verisimilar, and coherent imitation of the events leading up to the tragic *metabolē* (or change of fortune) enhanced the drama's ability to arouse pity and fear. It was on these grounds that Aristotle objected to overemphasis on spectacle at the expense of plot structure, and to the exploitation of devices like the deus ex machina. Since the emotional effects of tragedy could be achieved through the probable structure of incidents without the assistance of dramatic spectacle, actual performance was unnecessary.[2] Milton's *Samson Agonistes*, significantly, was not intended for the stage.

As a component of the plot, *pathos* presents more formidable difficulties than *peripeteia* and *anagnorisis*, the two other parts of the tragic fable.[3] In the first place, the term itself is ambiguous. Like its equivalents, *passio* and *perturbatio*, it may refer both to the emotions and to their external causes, to the tragic event and to its emotional effects.[4] Second, not only did Renaissance critics differ in their interpretations of Aristotle, but twentieth-century scholars still disagree as to his precise intent. Aristotelian theory, accordingly, can provide only limited guidance to Milton's conception of *pathos*; and in attempting to analyze his epic and tragic plot in the light of Aristotle's remarks on the "third part" of the tragic fable, the student must recognize the dubious validity of his criteria. The most reliable evidence appears to be the poet's own practice, rather than twentieth-century (or even sixteenth- and seventeenth-century) interpretations of the eleventh chapter of the *Poetics*.

The third part of the tragic fable, according to Aristotle, is *pathos*. This he defines as an action (*praxis*) "of a destructive or painful nature, such as murders on the stage, tortures, woundings, and the like."[5] Bywater translates *pathos* as "Suffering," Butcher as "Scene of Suffering, Tasso as "la passione, o la perturbazione," and Heinsius as "perturbatio." Like *pathos*, the latter terms are ambiguous; in common usage they may denote either external or internal events—the actions that inflict suffering (and that may, accordingly, arouse emotion not only in the victim but also in the spectators) or the emotions themselves. Though Aristotle employs this term in the former sense in this passage, he frequently utilizes it elsewhere in the latter sense. Renaissance critics did not consistently interpret this passage exclusively in terms of actions; and in considering the *pathos* of Milton's fable we must bear in mind the ambiguity of this term, the possibility of internal as well as external reference. He had written earlier of the "passion and admiration" to be found not only in the external changes of fortune but also in the refluxes of man's thoughts from within. His substitution of the spiritual drama of the temptation ordeal as heroic argument instead of the external conflict of arms would likewise tend to encourage a corresponding emphasis on spiritual agony in preference to physical torment. Samson's mental torture is far more intense than his physical suffering and calls forth keener and more vehement outbursts of anguish. In the theme of Christus Patiens, Milton perceived the opportunity for fine expressions of his hero's agony; but the scene is Gethsemane, not Golgotha.

In discussing *pathos* as a part of the tragic plot, Milton's near contemporaries associated it with one or more of a variety of referents: the tragic incidents themselves; the pity and fear aroused in the audience by these incidents; or the expression of emotion by persons within the dramatic or epic poem. Like Vettori, Riccoboni, and several other cinquecento commentators, Tasso interpreted Aristotle's definition as including lamentations as well as wounds and "deaths shown in public." As an example he cites the section of the *Iliad* where Priam, Hecuba, Andromache, and Helen mourn over the body of Hector.[6] By this definition, the laments of Adam and Eve in *Paradise Lost* after their fall, the choral laments in Milton's dramatic sketches for a tragedy on the loss of paradise, and the choral songs following the hero's death in *Samson Agonistes* would belong to *pathos*. The *pathos* would include not only the "masque of all the evils of this life and world" in "Adam Unparadised" and the analogous scenes of vision and prophecy in *Paradise Lost*, but also Adam's own expressions of grief, remorse, or temporary despair. In *Samson Agonistes* it would include (as Mueller correctly observes) the messenger's account of the violent death of the Hebrew champion and his Philistine victims, in addition to the expressions of passion by the messenger himself and by Manoa and the chorus of Danites. If one accepts Tasso's definition, *pathos* as a part of the fable may comprise not only the tragic actions imitated but also the tragic emotions imitated; for both may arouse the emotions of the reader or spectator.

Besides the intrinsic ambiguity of *pathos* and the brevity of

Aristotle's remarks on this subject, the passage contained additional uncertainties. The phrase *kai hosa toiauta* ("and the like") offered a loophole for critics who wished to apply the term *pathos* to spiritual as well as physical anguish—an interpretation that could be neither proved nor disproved. Again, it was not clear whether Aristotle was referring exclusively to violent actions on stage (rare in surviving Greek tragedies) or whether his *pathos* might include offstage actions that were of "a destructive or painful" nature and were reported by a messenger. Though Bywater and Butcher translated the phrase *en tōi phanerōi* as "on the stage," Else rejected this interpretation. In his opinion, *pathos* referred to the tragic action itself, or even to the imminent but unfulfilled threat of tragic disaster.[7]

Rebarbative as these discussions may seem, they nevertheless involve issues of crucial importance for the critical analysis of *Paradise Lost* and *Samson Agonistes*. If Aristotle is referring specifically to painful actions presented directly *onstage*—and implicitly excluding the indirect descriptions of such incidents through the narratives of messengers—then we must revise our opinions concerning the *pathos* of *Samson Agonistes*, inasmuch as the violent death of the hero and his enemies occurs offstage. (The fact that Milton's drama was not intended for the stage would, moreover, introduce an additional difficulty.) In *Paradise Lost*, similarly, the inevitable limitations of narrative (as opposed to dramatic) presentation would tend to rule out the element of *pathos* in the strictest sense, just as they would preclude the *pathos* that Tasso recognized in the *Iliad*. Clearly, Tasso did not limit *pathos* to the visual representation of painful actions on the stage. Such an interpretation would have made *pathos* a part of the dramatic spectacle and hence irrelevant (in the strictest sense) to the narrative mode of the *Iliad* and other epics. It would also (as Else has perceived) banish the element of *pathos* from a large number (if not the greater part) of the Greek tragedies still extant. In many of these the scenes of violent destruction occur offstage and are reported indirectly through messengers.

On the other hand, if one extends the concept of *pathos* to include lamentations (as does Tasso) and spiritual anguish (as does Bywater), then the distinction between *pathos* as a part of the fable and *pathos* as an element in character, thought, and diction may become blurred. The *pathos* of *Paradise Lost* could include the laments of the fallen Satan as well as those of fallen man, the pain experienced by the rebel angels during the battle in heaven and in hell as well as the spiritual suffering of Adam and Eve and the physical suffering of their posterity. By such an extended definition, moreover, one could regard not only the messenger's speech in *Samson* and the grief of Manoa and the chorus as *pathos*, but also the sufferings of the hero (together with the lamentations and complaints of his father and friends) throughout the drama. The element of *pathos* would thus tend to become diffused throughout both works. To avoid this difficulty, the critic might introduce an arbitrary distinction between the *pathos* specifically associated with the principal "change of state" (or *metabolē*) and the element of *pathos* elsewhere in the plot, or between *pathos* in the plot and in the episodes. Such a distinction, however, would represent a distortion of Aristotle's text and of the views of Renaissance critics. Since the latter sometimes called attention to multiple reversals and recognitions in epic and romance, the possibility of more than one *pathos* or scene of suffering would not seem implausible. Moreover, in the opinion of several commentators *pathos* was not restricted to one section of the plot but should be dispersed throughout the entire fable.

What Aristotle actually meant, however, is less important for the student of Milton than the multiple possibilities that his text offered to the Renaissance interpreter. For several critics, the problem of *pathos* was closely interrelated with Aristotle's classification of the various kinds or species of epic and tragedy. Aristotle had distinguished "four distinct species of Tragedy" in accordance with "constituents" he had previously analyzed: "first, the complex Tragedy, which is all Peripety and Discovery; second, the Tragedy of suffering, e.g. the *Ajaxes* and *Ixions*; third, the Tragedy of character, e.g. The *Phthiotides* and *Peleus*"; and finally the tragedy of "'Spectacle', exemplified in *The Phorcides*, in *Prometheus*, and in all plays with the scene laid in the nether world."[8] He had previously distinguished between two types of plot: simple ("when the change in the hero's fortunes takes place without Peripety or Discovery") and complex ("When it involves one or the other, or both").[9] He had argued that "for the finest form of Tragedy, the Plot must be not simple but complex; and further, that it must imitate actions arousing pity and fear, since that is the distinctive function of this kind of imitation."[10] Subsequently, he had divided the epic into "the same species as Tragedy," declaring that it "must be either simple or complex, a story of character or one of suffering." Homer's *Iliad* was "simple and a story of suffering," whereas the *Odyssey* was "complex (there is Discovery throughout it) and a story of character."[11]

The apparent discrepancy between the classifications of epic and tragedy may be due primarily to textual corruption. Bywater and Butcher differ in their interpretations of the passage concerning the fourth species of tragedy. Though the former regards it as a reference to "Spectacle,"[12] the latter inserts the words *hē haplē* ("the Simple"), for the sake of consistency. In Butcher's translation, accordingly, the disputed passage should read: "The fourth kind is the Simple. We here exclude the purely spectacular element, exemplified by the Phorcides, the Prometheus, and scenes laid in Hell."[13]

Renaissance commentators often diverged widely in their interpretation of this particular crux. Moreover, they frequently encountered other difficulties in attempting to ascertain the relationships between these species. Some of the forms of epic or tragedy—such as simple and complex—were clearly mutually exclusive. Others involved different degrees of emphasis on passion or character; as Aristotle himself had recognized, they could coexist with one of the other forms.

Pazzi's translation had rendered *pathos* as *perturbatio*, and the ambiguous phrase *en tōi phanerōi* as *palàm* ("openly" or "publicly"): "Perturbatio verò actio est laetifera, seu dolore plena: veluti cùm neces, cruciatus, vulnera, caeteraque generis huius palàm fiunt." In commenting on this passage, Maggi argued that the tragic fable is rendered pathetic through its passions ("à perturbationibus pathetica") just as it is made complex through *peripeteia* and recognition. Aristotle's examples of the things that openly produce perturbation (such as "mortes vulnera, cruciatus, quae in aperto fiunt") do not imply that murders ought necessarily to be enacted on the stage. Aristotle has described perturbation by giving examples of the kinds of things which arouse it; "nam in spectatorum animis perturbationes ab eiusmodi eventis fiunt."[14]

The four kinds of tragedy, according to Pazzi's translation, are the complex, the pathetic, the moral, and the kind represented by *Phorcides* and *Prometheus* ("Quartum, veluti, Phorcidas, &

Prometheum: quaecunque insuper, quae apud inferos sunt"). In his
commentary, Maggi argued that the Greek text should be emended
to include a reference to the "simple" plot, in accordance with
Aristotle's distinction between simple and complex fables and his
classification of the four species of epic.[15]

As Vettori interpreted Aristotle, *pathos* (like *peripeteia* and
anagnorisis) is essentially a means for securing the tragic effect. The
finest plot ("pulcherrima fabula") ought to contain those things
which will move the greatest admiration or marvel in the spectators, strike terror into their minds, and excite pity. Three things
accomplish this marvelously ("mirifice"): *peripeteia, agnitio,* and
passio. Pathos or *passio* is an action which leads to death or has the
power of destroying man. Even if it does not bring death, it breeds
the keenest physical sufferings ("acerrimos saltem corporis dolores
gignit"). To illustrate this point, Aristotle mentions slaughters
performed before spectators, or the sharpest torments of body, and
wounds inflicted. All of these actions are called *pathos.*

In Vettori's opinion, *pathos* signifies physical suffering; it does
not, in this passage, refer to perturbation of mind ("perturbationem
& quasi morbum animi"). As he points out, Athanasius had
employed this word in the same sense as Aristotle; in his oration on
the violent death (*nece*) and unmerited execution of Christ, he had
spoken of the "Passion or sufferings of the Lord" (*peri pathous
kuriou*). Vettori similarly interpreted Aristotle's term *perioduniai*
as physical torment; it is a habit of the body ("corporis habitum")
and denotes the sufferings of one who is afflicted with the greatest
anguish ("maximis doloribus"). Pathetic tragedies (or tragedies of
suffering) derive their name from *pathos,* "propter rerum, quae illic
continentur atrocitatem."[16]

Arguing that *pathos* ("perturbatio, & luctus") was proper to
tragedy, since it contained "res . . . tristiae, maerorisque ac doloris
plenas," Robortello observed that many ancient tragedies had
lacked recognition and reversal but had nevertheless possessed
pathos. Interpreting this term as a reference to the actions that
stimulate the tragic emotions rather than as an allusion to the
emotions themselves, he suggested that Aristotle's "definition" was
actually an explication based on the sort of things that arouse
perturbation. Utilizing the definition of pity in Aristotle's *Rhetoric* to elucidate the ambiguous section in the *Poetics,* Robortello stressed the reference to *apparent* or manifest evils in both

passages. In his opinion, the qualifying phrases in the *Rhetoric* (*epi tōi phainomenōi*) and in the *Poetics* (*en tōi phanerōi*) expressed the same meaning. Even the greatest evils will not move the mind sufficiently if they are not known.

In Robortello's opinion, Aristotle's phrase *en tōi phanerōi* (openly or manifestly) did not mean that horrible things ("atrocia") should be presented on the stage. This would have been repugnant to the art of the ancients as well as to nature. Admittedly certain evils could be openly seen, such as wounds, ulcers, and disease. Nevertheless the essential meaning of this passage is that these evils ought not to remain hidden and unknown, but that (as they occur and the complaints of those who suffer these ills are heard) they should be made manifest, so that they would have the power to move. Citing the definition of fear in the *Rhetoric* (pain arising from the imagination or fantasy of impending evil), Robortello declared that when we perceive the evils that have befallen other men, we necessarily consider what these evils are, to whom they have occurred, and for what cause. If these evils are such that they may befall us also, then perturbation arises, and we experience a certain dread in the imagination. This Aristotle clearly intended to signify, not so much in the *Poetics* as in the *Rhetoric*. Moreover, this third part of the fable, which we call *pathos*, ought to be diffused throughout the entire tragedy. It should be represented not only in things (actions), but also in thoughts and in words. As examples of *pathos* in Greek tragedy, Robortello cited the deaths of Ajax, Jocasta, and Haemon; the torments in Sophocles' *Antigone* and Euripides' *Hecuba*; the wounds in Sophocles' *Oedipus*; and the ulcers in *Trachiniae* and *Philoctetes*.

Out of the three parts of the tragic fable (Robortello continues)— recognition, reversal, and perturbation—Aristotle has fashioned two distinct species of tragedy. *Peripeteia* and *anagnorisis* make one genus of tragedy (the complex); *pathos* or perturbation constitutes another genus per se. Several of the tragedies of the ancients contain perturbation but lack recognition and peripeteia.[17]

Piccolomini translated *pathos* as passion in the sense of suffering ("patimento"). In his translation of the text, it is a "corruptive and destructive action, or an action that brings intolerable pains." Such, for example, are the slayings, the deaths, the grievous torments ("dolorosi tormenti"), and similar things that are of a

bloody ("sanguinolente") nature and that are openly and manifestly made known ("in aperto, & manifestamente fatte conoscere"). In his annotations on this passage he sensibly avoided the
question whether the tragic poet could imitate bloody actions and
atrocious and horrible deeds openly on the stage. In this paragraph
Aristotle says nothing on this subject either pro or con, and the
passage itself does not warrant the controversy that has arisen
among expositors over whether these horrible events can occur
"palesemente in scena." Having just discussed two parts of the
fable—recognition and reversal—Aristotle is simply taking up the
third and remaining part of the plot, the *pathos.*

In Piccolomini's opinion, *pathos* does not signify emotion
(*affetto*) in this passage, but suffering ("passione, ò più tosto
patimento"). At this point Aristotle did not intend to raise the
question whether such events were to be openly enacted on the
stage; consequently, here he neither grants nor prohibits it. Though
the practice of the best poets in the most perfect tragedies, as well as
Horace's remarks concerning the representation of horrors onstage
and Aristotle's own statements elsewhere in the *Poetics*, suggests
that the open representation of such events onstage ("fargli
apparari apertamente in scena") would be an artistic defect, the
particular passage in question neither sanctions nor forbids such
presentation. It simply declares that passion or suffering in the
fable is a destructive and lethal action or at least an action full of
the keenest and intensest grief or pain ("dolor"). By *dolor* (grief or
pain), moreover, Aristotle does not mean affliction and grief of
mind, but sensitive pain experienced in the body itself. Such
sufferings ("patimenti") are violent deaths, slaughters, tortures,
wounds, sores, and the like. Accordingly, a plot filled with
imitations of atrocious and painful actions—actions full of deaths,
bloodshed, complaints, laments, outcries, and similar things, which
cause and make manifest the immeasureable gravity of sensitive
and bodily anguish ("sensitivi corporei dolori")—such a plot
contains the part of the fable that we term suffering or *patimento.*

Pathos is a qualitative part of the fable. It is not confined to a
single place in the drama but is dispersed throughout the plot, in
each of its quantitative parts. Hence the fable is called "pathetic"
(i.e., passionate and full of *patimento*). There are many examples
of such pathetic plots in the dramas of good poets, such as the
tragedies of Ajax, Hecuba, Medea, Thyestes, and the like. On the

other hand, there are other tragedies which cannot be called "pathetic," such as the dramas on Iphigenia and Oedipus; these tragedies lack so great a horror ("tanta atrocità") and such bloody actions as occur in "pathetic" tragedies. A tragic plot may contain recognition and reversal without the presence of pathos.

By the words *in aperto, & manifestamente,* Aristotle did not intend to say anything concerning the "palesare, or non palesare cosi fatti patimenti in scena." Instead, he meant that the fable contains (*pathos* or *patimento*) when it is composed in such a way that it obviously appears to be full of such sufferings: "quando ella è composta tale, che ripiena manifestamente si mostra di tai patimenti." This "manifestation" can be made through the reports of messengers, through tearful dialogues, through laments and lamentable complaints. It can also be made through offstage outcries, howls, and laments of the tragic victims who are being slain or wounded, struck or tormented or who are suffering tortures and other painful accidents. Moreover, tragic poets sometimes display onstage the dead bodies of the slain. Such is the suffering (*patimento*) that is a part of the plot; and such are "pathetic" tragedies. The "pathetic" or passionate tragedy ("passionevole") is full of passions and sufferings ("passioni, & . . . patimenti") and of death, torments, and bloodshed.

Piccolomini is understandably puzzled by Aristotle's fourth species of tragedy—understandably, for the text itself appears to be corrupt—but he is franker than most of his contemporaries in admitting his perplexity: "Et quanto all' ultime parole delle tragedie fatte sopra quelle persone che son nell' Inferno, io non mi vergogno di confessare, ch'io non habbia potuto sodisfarmi in comprender, che cosa egli per questo si voglia intendere." He does not see why Aristotle had not classified such dramas among pathetic rather than simple tragedies, since they concern the punishments and torments of hell. Nevertheless, on the analogy with the fourth species of epic, he believes that Aristotle is referring specifically to the "simple" tragedy, which contains the same continuous state of fortune without any mutation or change of state.[18]

Castelvetro's discussion of *pathos* is marked by considerable hair-splitting; it was not for nothing that he bore the nickname "Il Grammaticuccio" (the Grammarian). Scrupulous in his endeavor to preserve the methodical and systematic order of Aristotle's treatise and its logical coherence, he takes pains to avoid confusion between the parts necessary for a well-constructed plot and the parts requisite for producing the tragic effect of pity and fear. Reversal and recognition (*rivolgimento* and *riconoscenza*) are two parts which produce these emotions. Nevertheless *pathos* (*passione*) is also required for their production; this is the third part in generating compassion and terror, but the eighth part in rendering the fable beautiful. In Castelvetro's view, the *pathos* refers to past or future events. Aristotle's definition would have been fuller if he had defined passion as a destructive or painful action ("corruttiva, or dolorosa") that had already occurred or that would occur in the future. The tragic person feels grief and indignation ("dolore, & sdegno") for a horrible deed committed by himself or by others. Alternatively, he may experience these passions for a horrible deed that he has not yet committed but is about to commit, or else for a deed that he has actually performed but that is not truly horrible.

In the first case, there are two alternatives. Feeling grief and indignation for his horrible deed, the tragic person may commit another horrible action. Thus, overcome with grief and indignation over their incestuous marriage (the "prima horribilita"), Oedipus blinds himself and Giocasta hangs herself. On the other hand, the tragic person may not commit a new horror, but may merely remain in his present condition. For instance, having recovered his sanity after slaying his wife and sons in his fury, Hercules feels grief and indignation but does not proceed to a "nuova horribilita."

Noting the obscurity and ambiguity of Aristotle's phrase *en tōi phanerōi thanatoi*, Castelvetro observed that previous commentators had interpreted it in one of three ways: as a reference to deaths enacted onstage, to the exhibition of the bodies of persons who have perished offstage, or to the voices of persons dying offstage (as in the case of Clytemnestra). Nevertheless he is reluctant to limit this definition so narrowly; in his opinion, it may also include the reports of deaths brought by messengers or the full representation of such events onstage, even though the latter is not commonly approved. Other expositors maintain that Aristotle is referring to the deaths described by messengers and other persons in words so vivid and so immediately present to the minds of the people that the latter seem to view these events with the eyes of the mind. This explanation, however, seems very far from Aristotle's intent; for it belongs rather to speech than to plot ("ufficio più tosto della favella, che della favola"). Conceivably Aristotle's phrase may signify deaths that are known through fame and history—"morti famose, & non communi, ne vulgari," such as those of Ajax, Hercules, and Clytemnestra—but Castelvetro himself is doubtful about the validity of this interpretation. Finally, he proposes a further explanation, that the phrase refers to imminent and apparent deaths—"le morti, che non sieno lontane, ma vicine, & apparenti, le quali inducono più dolore, che non fanno quelle, che non veggiamo, o crediamo essere da lunge"—in accordance with Aristotle's discussion of fear in the *Rhetoric*.[19]

Riccoboni interpreted *pathos* as signifying suffering (*passio* or *perpessio*). It is the third of the things that engender fear and pity ("metum, & misericordiam"). While granting that *pathos* often means the perturbation felt by the auditors, he argues that in this passage it bears a different sense. He criticizes Robortello's view that this perturbation belongs entirely to the spectators, who are perturbed by thoughts of the evils that have befallen others. Though *pathos* frequently carries this meaning, Aristotle's definition refers not to the perturbation felt for another's ills, but to the very evil under which the dramatis personae are suffering ("sed ipsum malum, quod illi, qui a poetis inducuntur, perpessi sint"). This is the third element in the fable that moves pity and fear. The *pathos* does not regard the spectators, for the plot does not extend so widely that it should embrace the spectators also. On the contrary, the *pathos* pertains to the persons who are involved in the plot, the same persons to whom the reversal and recognition pertain.

Riccoboni translated Aristotle's term *periōduniai* ("bodily agony") as lamentations or wailings (*eiulationes*). In his version, accordingly, Aristotle's examples of *passio* or *perpessio* are deaths, lamentations, wounds, and the like which are made manifest (*in aperto* or *in manifesto*). Examining the various explanations that had been advanced by earlier critics—Maggi, Castelvetro, and others—for the phrase *in manifesto mortes*, he interprets it judiciously as a reference to deaths made manifest in any way whatever other than through direct representation on the stage: "Nos in tanta explicationum multitudine intelligimus per mortes in manifesto, mortes quomodolibet manifestas, dummodo in scena manifestae non fiant."[20]

In including "laments" as an instance of *pathos*, Tasso was following an interpretation that had already been approved by several expositors and that appeared to rest on the authority of Aristotle himself. In Vettori's edition, the Latin translation of the *Poetics* refers to "mortes, & eiulatus, & vulnerationes," even though Vettori's commentary interprets *periōduniai* specifically in terms of bodily affliction. Riccoboni's Latin translation similarly refers to "mortes, & eiulationes, & vulnerationes." In attempting to adapt Aristotle's theory of tragedy to heroic epic, Tasso endeavored to illustrate the definition of *pathos* with an example from epic poetry. He found such an example in the lamentations over Hector's body in the *Iliad*—a highly appropriate analogue on several grounds. Not only did it recall the "lamentations" of Aristotle's text (as more than one translator had rendered it), but it was drawn from a work that Aristotle had associated with tragedy and had classified specifically as a "pathetic" epic.

In accordance with Aristotle's classification of the epic fable, Tasso found the *Iliad* "semplice e compassionevole" and the *Odyssey* "morata e doppia." Nevertheless he recognized the possibility of other combinations: "il semplice e 'l costumato," and "il doppio e 'l perturbato." Indeed, since the complex or "double" plot involved a reversal, and the reversal was the cause of perturbation, the combination of the complex and pathetic species would seem highly appropriate for both epic and tragedy:[21] "Anzi, se la peripezia o 'l rivolgimento è cagione di perturbazione, non veggio come questa coppia potesse meglio congiungersi insieme; e, s'ella si congiunge ne la tragedia, non so perché non si possa congiungere ed accoppiare ne l'epopeia."

In Heinsius's opinion, Aristotle's *pathos* or *perturbatio* belonged specifically to the complex fable. "Since the main aim of the tragic plot is to stir passions, . . . not through some extrinsic, or histrionic, effort, but through the structure of the incidents and actions, Aristotle made emotion the third part of the complex fable."[22] Tragedy "moves either horror or pity or both through a probable and correct imitation of actions," and the imitation of these perturbations begets the kind of pleasure proper to this genre. Since "in tragedy the fable primarily does the imitating, this kind of pleasure necessarily inheres in this very part. And therefore passions cunningly fashioned have to be worked into it—that is, into the very arrangement of the actions rather than elsewhere, although they are not on this account excluded from thought and

diction, parts which have no relevance to this one."[23] Following
Aristotle in his discussion of "the persons from which tragic
passions spring" and in his insistence that the tragic emotions
should result from the structure and incidents of the play,[24]
Heinsius maintains that "the passions proper to tragedy usually
arise *per se* from a turn in the fortune of such people."[25]

Heinsius reorganizes Aristotle's four species of tragedy by classi-
fying three of them—the pathetic, the ethical, and the legendary
(Bywater's "Spectacle")—under the "simple" plot, as distinct from
the complex. The first is "full of emotions," such as the "raging and
madness" of the heroes of Seneca's *Hercules Furens* and Sophocles'
Ajax. The second portrays the character or ethos of "persons good
or ill," such as "the dutifulness of Aeneas." Though there are no
surviving examples of the legendary fable, this would treat themes
like the first Nekyia in the *Odyssey* or Aeneas's descent to the
underworld.[26]

In interpreting Aristotle's ambiguous remarks on *pathos*, Renaissance critics were painfully aware of the wide range of alternative
explanations advanced by their immediate predecessors. Commentators of the late cinquecento were compelled to compare and
revalue the interpretations advanced by Maggi and Robortello, by
Vettori and Castelvetro, Scaliger and other Italian critics, or (much
earlier) by Averroes in his Arabic paraphrase. Moreover, many of
them read the *Poetics* in the light of Aristotle's discussion of pity
and fear in the *Rhetoric*, Horace's remarks concerning onstage
actions and announcements of offstage events, or the evidence
available in surviving Greek tragedies.[27]

Aristotle's approach to the problems of tragic structure (in the
view of many Renaissance commentators) had been essentially psychological, moral, and political. Tragedy served the state and the
welfare of the individual by purging and moderating the passions;
the essential role of the tragic poet was to arouse the tragic
emotions. He could achieve this end most effectively by eschewing
the most obvious appeals to the emotions—the resources of
spectacle—and concentrating instead on the logical (or probable)
development of the plot. In a well-constructed drama the tragic
effect—the delight peculiar to tragedy—would result naturally and
inevitably from the complication and unraveling of the fable. The
structure of events[28] could convince the judicious reader even

without the aid of spectacle, provided the "change of state"—the tragic *metabolē*—seemed to occur probably or necessarily. The primary concern of the *Poetics* appeared to be the kind of plot, the kind of matter, the kind of tragic *persona* and tragic incident, that could most effectively arouse pity and fear in a critical and discriminating audience. Tragic effect was dependent, in large part, upon the apparent probability of the tragic fable.

In their interpretations of *pathos*—the most important element in the tragic fable, according to Heinsius—Renaissance commentators differed widely. Some of them (as we have seen) identified it specifically with those painful and destructive events which were actually represented onstage; others extended the term to laments and to reports of offstage actions of a painful and destructive nature. Some restricted it to physical torment; others emphasized mental suffering. Some interpreted it as a trope, signifying incidents capable of arousing the tragic emotions in the spectator; others restricted its application to the dramatis personae. Some associated it with the complex plot, some with the pathetic tragedy, some with all species of tragedy. Some limited it to one point or section of the drama; others regarded it as an element recurring throughout the dramatic action.

If Milton had read even superficially in the criticism of the period (and it seems implausible that he did not read carefully and widely) he must have been aware of the diversity of critical opinion on this subject. On the whole, no single critic can serve as an authoritative guide to his own interpretation; and (as I suggested earlier) the most reliable evidence seems to be his actual practice.

Insofar as Milton conceived the role of the tragic or epic poet in neo-Aristotelian terms ("conservative" and anachronistic though they may seem today), he would have regarded passion as contingent (in large part) upon logic, or the appearance of logic. If developed logically and plausibly, the tragic incident would per se possess the power to arouse admiration and passion, whether the source of tragic effect resided in the external events of the fable or in the internal reflections of the protagonists—in *mythos* or in *dianoia* and *ethos*.

"SCENE OF SUFFERING"
PASSION IN PARADISE LOST AND SAMSON AGONISTES

7 "Whatsoever hath passion or admiration in all the changes of that which is called fortune from without, or the wily subtleties and refluxes of man's thoughts from within. . . ." When Milton wrote this passage he was apparently still undecided as to his poetic plans for the immediate future—still examining the potentialities and weighing the merits of lyric, drama, and heroic poem.

In neo-Aristotelian and neo-Horatian dramatic theory, as in the passing remarks on tragedy by Terentian commentators, tragic structure and tragic effect are closely interrelated; and Milton's own remarks on the subject, both in the *Reason of Church Government* and in his dramatic sketches—and much later in the preface to *Samson*—emphasize both of these factors. In the early 1640s he was looking for a subject that could arouse (and allay) the tragic emotions and that could receive the form or "idea" of the tragic fable. Like many cinquecento or early seicento critics, he believed that the delight peculiar to tragedy sprang from the imitation of actions arousing pity and fear. As Robortello had observed in his commentary on the *Poetics*, "peculiaris tragoediae voluptas . . . est, quae paratur per commiserationem, & terrorem, adhibita imitatione . . . sed per imitationem cum exprimantur incommoda, calamitatesque quamlibet maximae, luctum pariunt cum voluptate, omnis enim imitatio, quamvis truculentarum, miserabiliumque rerum sit, iucunda. & sanè in luctu por oc etiam

89

voluptas est, declarat Aristoteles libro Rheto. I." In the oratory of
Demosthenes, "Tota verò ratio movendae commiserationis est
ducta ab ipsis rebus quae commiserabiles sunt"; and for the same
reason "etiam poêtae tragici à rebus ipsis, ad eas verba commiserabilia adaptantes, ducere commiserationem non ab apparatu; aut
scena, quae horribilem aliquam praeseferat speciem." As Robortello comments, Aristotle had condemned the attempt to arouse
pity and fear ("duas has animi perturbationes movere") through the
theatrical spectacle ("ex theatri scenaeque apparatu") at the expense
of plot-structure ("neglecta rerum constitutione ac fabula ipsa").[1]

Tragic effect belonged to oratory as well as to poetry, as
Robortello's references to Hermogenes' discussion of Demosthenes
and Homer, and Aristotle's discussion of the emotions of pity and
fear in his *Rhetoric* and *Poetics*, seemed to indicate. Orator and
poet alike attempted to arouse passion and admiration. In view of
the interconnection of poetic and rhetorical theory, the conception
of poetry as an imitation of passion and character and thought as
well as an imitation of action, and the widespread interpretation of
pathos in terms of spiritual as well as physical suffering, Milton's
emphasis on the "refluxes" of thought as well as the changes of
fortune as a potential source of passion and admiration is not
surprising.

His emphasis on admiration or marvel reflects the common
opinion of earlier critics. Though Aristotle maintained that the epic
offered greater scope for the marvelous (*admirabile*), he had
nevertheless emphasized its role in tragedy: "Ac oportet quidem in
Tragoedijs efficere id, quod admirabile est."[2] When tragic incidents
"occur unexpectedly and at the same time in consequence of one
another" they produce the "very greatest effect on the mind" and
seem more marvelous "than if they had happened of themselves or
by mere chance."[3] In his commentary on the *Poetics* Riccoboni
devoted an entire chapter to the element of the marvelous in the
tragic fable ("Fabulam admirabilem esse oportere"), reducing Aristotle's argument to syllogistic form: "Probat fabulae Tragicae
admirationem in hunc modum; Imitatio terribilium, & miserabilium est admirabilis. Atqui fabula Tragica est imitatio terribilium, & miserabilium. Ergo admirabilis."[4]

In addition to Italian (and possibly Dutch) commentaries on the
Poetics, Milton would have read rhetorical discussions of the tragic
emotions and the tragic style. As we have noted, Robortello cites

Hermogenes' *Ideas*. Tasso borrows liberally from Demetrius's treatise *On Style*. Vettori illustrates the term *periōduniai* with a reference to Cicero. Several poetic theorists refer occasionally to Longinus or to Dionysius of Halicarnassus. In *Of Education* Milton proposed to teach the principles of "a graceful and ornate rhetoric ... out of the rule of Plato, Aristotle, Phalereus [i.e., Pseudo-Demetrius], Cicero, Hermogenes, Longinus";[5] and it is safe to assume that he was familiar, in varying degrees, with most of these writers. In his *Art of Logic* he elaborates Ramus's teachings with technical terms and concepts derived from Aristotle, Cicero, and other authorities on rhetoric or dialectic.

Like many cinquecento expositors, he would (almost certainly) have interpreted the theory of tragic effect set forth in the *Poetics* in the light of Aristotle's *Rhetoric*. This provided a more detailed and more comprehensive account of the nature and causes of pity and fear; and Renaissance critics borrowed liberally from it in their commentaries on the *Poetics*.

In the *Rhetoric*, Aristotle had defined fear as "A sort of pain or agitation arising out of an idea (*phantasia*) that an evil, capable either of destroying or giving pain, is impending on us." People fear "all those evils whose effect is either a considerable degree of pain, or destruction, and these, provided they be not far removed, but give one the idea of being close at hand." Hence "all those things are to be feared which appear to possess great power either of destroying, or of hurting, in points whose tendency is toward considerable pain." Even the "symptoms of such things are alarming, for the evil appears to be at hand; since this in fact is danger, viz. 'the approach of what excites fear.'" Injustice combined with power, "insulted virtue, invested with power," the fear of our enemies, "the hatred and the anger of those who have it in their power to do us any harm" are objects of fear. Also to be dreaded are dissemblers, rivals, and those "who have been wronged, or who conceive themselves to have been wronged."[6]

Aristotle defines pity as "a sort of pain occasioned by an evil capable of hurting or destroying, appearing to befall one who does not deserve it, which one may himself expect to endure, or that some one connected with him will; and this when it appears near." The circumstances which excite pity are those which "have a tendency to destroy" and those evils "which involve the quality of greatness, and of which chance is the cause." The former evils include "death, assaults, personal injuries, and age, and sickness, and want of food." Among the latter are "absolute want, or fewness of friends, . . . ugliness, infirmity, deformity, and the circumstance that evil befalls one from a source whence it were becoming for some good to have arisen." Men "feel pity while the evil is yet approaching. And they feel it towards their equals," for "the evil is seen with greater clearness as possible to befall also one's self." Since "the disasters which excite pity always appear to be close at hand," it follows that "those characters which are got up with the aid of gesture, and voice, and dress, and of acting, generally have the greater effect in producing pity. For thus, by setting the evil before our eyes, as either being on the eve of taking place, or as having happened, men make it appear to be close at hand." These circumstances "produce pity in a higher degree from its appearing *near*; also the fact of the person's being *unworthy*, and his disaster appearing in view before our eyes."[7]

According to Aristotle, then, as several Renaissance commentators interpreted his *Poetics* and *Rhetoric*, the *pathos* of a drama would appear to be the cause or occasion of pity and fear, for an evil capable of destroying or giving pain underlies all three definitions.

To arouse and maintain fear and pity, the poet must make a future evil appear immediate and imminent. Throughout the opening books of his epic Milton emphasizes the imminence of the doom that awaits the protagonists. Foreshadowings of the fall, comparisons drawn from the fallen world, the strength and multitude of man's infernal enemies, the horrors of hell (man's future habitation), apostrophes ("O for that warning voice"), Satan's threats and menaces ("yee little think how nigh / Your change approaches") all lend immediacy to the impending catastrophe. Even the visit of the sociable archangel contains tragic implications, with its exemplum of the "terrible reward of disobedience" and the destructive force of divine wrath and justice. The epic motif of the hero as destroyer (a pattern based partly on the "destroying wrath" of Homer's Achilles and adapted to Milton's paradigms of infernal and divine wrath) gives additional emphasis to the imminent destruction of mankind, heightening the sense of danger, "the approach of what excites fear." In an age of witch-trials and homiletic hellfire, an age of spiritual monomachias with the prince of this world or daemonomachias against legions of darkness,

Milton did not need to instill fear of the devil. Nevertheless, even if fortuitously, he has invested his adversary, the accuser and destroyer of mankind, with many of the characteristic objects of fear outlined in the *Rhetoric*. Satan is man's rival. He believes himself wronged, and suffers from a sense of "insulted virtue" and injured merit. He is moved by hatred and anger, and possesses the determination and power (albeit limited by man's moral freedom) to harm. As the archetypal tyrant, he combines injustice with power. He fears his divine and angelic enemies and is compelled to dissemble.

One function of the "masque of all the evils of this life and world" in Milton's draft for the tragedy of *Adam Unparadised* and of the visions and prophecies of world history in the final books of the epic is to make the future miseries of mankind seem imminent and near at hand and thus to increase their affective force, for the poet's audience as well as for his protagonist. Both of Adam's angelic instructors—the divine historian and the blessed seer—present tragic events of the past and future through means that are simultaneously "simple, sensuous, and passionate" and that bear a recognizable resemblance to established literary genres. If Michael has presented a tragic masque, Raphael has recited a brief epic, a tragic "Angeleida" followed by a brief "Mondo Creato." Aristotle had stressed the greater effectiveness of dramatic representation in producing pity by literally "setting the evil before our eyes" and thus making it "appear to be close at hand." Michael's tragic masque—depicting the corruption and destruction of the world, the general miseries of mankind, the persecution of the just by the unjust, and the execution of divine vengeance on the latter—literally sets the evil world history before Adam's eyes (and our own), making these events seem "close at hand" and hence more efficacious in arousing pity or fear. Finally, this vision of future evils includes many of the evils that Aristotle had specifically identified as causes of pity: "death, assaults, personal injuries," age and sickness and famine.

In the *Christian Doctrine* Milton argued that the passions attributed to God are real rather than figurative; they do not have to be rationalized or explained away as a rhetorical figure, a form of *anthropopathia*. In *Paradise Lost* the passions he ascribes to both Father and Son can enhance the tragic effect: divine wrath can be an object of fear; and divine pity (*misericordia*) for man, both before and after his fall, can intensify the pity felt by the reader, yet also mitigate the effect of terror. If divine justice, like Satanic injustice, can arouse fear, divine mercy (*misericordia*) may temper and allay grief for the fall and fear of divine wrath.

In certain respects, Milton's epic protagonists differ from the kind of tragic hero preferred by Aristotle and many of his Renaissance commentators. Though they fall from high estate and bring death and misery upon themselves and their posterity through their own action, they do not fall undeservedly. Though Eve is deceived, Adam sins with open eyes; he knows what he is doing, and he is aware of the consequences. Both fall through *hamartia*; but this is *hamartia* in the New Testament sense (the error of sin) rather than in a strictly Aristotelian sense. Writing in a different theological tradition from that of the Greek dramatists and poetic theorists, Milton found it expedient to alter and adapt their artistic conventions to meet the requirements of his own theodicy.

This detail would not, however, diminish sympathy for his protagonists or the possibilities of tragic effect. Milton's contemporary audience had, for the most part, been reared in an ecclesiastical tradition that had stressed their inherent frailty and propensity to sin, their liability to fall, and their need for utter dependence on divine grace rather than their own merits. As "public persons" (*publicae personae*) Adam and Eve had determined the fate of their posterity; they were representatives and archetypes of universal humanity, the *Humanum Genus* or Mankind of the morality plays. All men had fallen through Adam's fall; all shared the guilt and consequences of his sin; and all had been born in the image of the "old Adam"—an image that they must "put off" for the image and likeness of the new Adam, the "one greater Man." The fate that had befallen Adam and Eve might easily "befall also one's self," and the evil that they had experienced the reader might "himself expect to endure."

The mode of Adam's transgression, like that of Samson's, would tend, moreover, to strengthen rather than weaken the reader's sympathy. Both had fallen through sensual weakness, through uxoriousness. This the *homme moyen sensuel* could understand, even if he did not approve. Adam's transgression may break the great chain of being and the cosmic "bond of Nature"; but in relation to Eve and in his own opinion it is the "bond of Nature" that draws him to his destruction. It was the violation of the bond of nature (as one sixteenth-century commentator argued),[8] by persons closely related through natural ties, that intensified the tragic emotions. In violating the order of nature, Adam appeals paradoxically to the "bond of Nature" itself; and even though the reader is aware of the paradox he must feel that Adam has acted naturally, if injudiciously. In the case of Samson's transgression, where the hero violates his covenant with Jehovah by entrusting God's secret to his wife, pity for the hero may coexist with horror at Dalila's betrayal. He has sinned in apparent obedience to the bond of nature; she has broken the same bond. Samson is additionally pitiable (by Aristotelian standards) since he has encountered "wedlock-treachery endangering life" where he should (by the laws of nature) have received fidelity and love.

Paradise Lost is both a domestic tragedy (like *Trachiniae* and *Alcestis*) and a domestic epic (like the *Odyssey*). The domestic scenes in the central books of the poem serve to heighten the reader's sympathy and sense of identification with the protagonists; at the same time they make the motivation of Adam's fall seem more understandable, and the fall itself more probable and more logical. They also intensify the emotional impact of the fall (the change of state or *metabolē*); the picture of unique earthly felicity must serve as a foil for the miseries resulting from the fall. The poet must emphasize the bliss of the "happy Garden" in ʾer to heighten the tragic implications of its loss.

In *Paradise Lost*, as in *Samson*, passion is specifically associated with the effects of sin; and the *pathos* or *passio* is both internal and external. It is found both in the changes of fortune "from without" and the "refluxes" of thought "from within." The moderation (and/ or catharsis) of the passions is also achieved through internal and external agency. Like many of Milton's early funeral elegies,[9] his epic and tragedy conclude with a *consolatio*. Traditionally, the consolation belonged to deliberative rhetoric; it was intended to allay grief and similar passions, and in Boethius's *Consolation of Philosophy* it was associated with medicinal imagery. In *Samson* the emphasis falls on the inadequacy of formal "Consolatories writ / With studied argument, and much persuasion sought / Lenient of grief and anxious thought" in comparison with the comfort and cure administered by the divine spirit·

But with th' afflicted in his pangs thir sound
Little prevails, or rather seems a tune,
Harsh, and of dissonant mood from his complaint,
Unless he feel within
Some source of consolation from above;
Secret refreshings that repair his strength,
And fainting spirits uphold.

[*Samson Agonistes*, lines 660-66]

Eventually (as recent critics have recognized) Samson is in fact purified by his ordeal of suffering, gradually regaining control over his passions and subjecting them to the command of his own reason and the dictates of the spirit. Before his successive (and successful) encounters with the Philistines, the torments of his own conscience and the sense of heaven's desertion are his greatest misery; near the end of his ordeal, he is conscious of "Favor renew'd" and can speak in the same breath of conscience and "internal peace." A partial catharsis, a partial moderation of the passions, is achieved through the hero's own struggle with his passions, just as it is subsequently achieved by Manoa and the chorus—the audience *within* the drama, who likewise depart in "peace and consolation," and in "calm of mind, all passion spent."

As Mueller and Gossman have recognized,[10] Milton not only attempts to arouse and allay the passions of his readers (the audience *without* the drama); he also imitates the passions of his dramatis personae, their subjection to passion, their struggle with passion, their victory over passion. *Pathos* (passion), as we have noted earlier, frequently becomes *ethos* (character); the passions serve as the matter for virtue. The inner psychological drama, like the external action, moves to contraries; from fear to faith or confidence, from fainting spirits to fortitude of mind and magnanimity, from impatience toward patience, from despair (or near-despair) to hope. We have encountered a similar progression from distrust and impatience to patient faith in the complaint of the disciples in *Paradise Regained*. The process of consolation and the process of moderating and tempering the passions belong primarily to the "refluxes" of man's thoughts. They may be depicted in soliloquy and meditation, or in dialogue and dialectical encounter; but (as Milton portrays them) they are essentially labors of the mind and/or operations of the spirit.

In *Paradise Lost* the moderation of the passions, turbulent and

stormy after the fall, is accomplished both through inner regeneration and through external revelation. Instructed to "dismiss them
not disconsolate," Michael "promises the Messiah" (as in Milton's
sketch for a drama on the fall); remorse for sin and the bitterness
of exile are alike mitigated and tempered by joy and admiration—
wonder at the paradox of the *felix culpa* and the production of
good out of evil, and rejoicing in the expectation of future
restoration. Catharsis is effected within the epic not only through
regeneration but also through the revelation of providential design.
Fear and pity for the future miseries of mankind and sorrow for their
own change and banishment are allayed, for Adam and Eve, by
confidence in the promise of the woman's seed. The tragedy of
forbidden knowledge concludes with a consolatory revelation of the
ways of divine providence and with an act of faith.

Milton's conception of the epic or tragic fable cannot be reduced
to a single formula or model. There are too many differences—
some of fundamental importance—in his various plans for tragedy,
and in the epics and tragedy he actually composed. There was even
greater diversity, of course, in the epic and tragic traditions he had
inherited. Nor, for that matter, could Aristotle's conception of the
plot be reduced to a single pattern. Despite his concern to outline
the prerequisites for a perfect plot, he distinguished four different
species of epic and tragedy. The simple and complex kinds were
mutually exclusive; and the pathetic and ethical species differed in
emphasis.

These distinctions are not irrelevant to Milton's poetry. If (as
various scholars have argued)[11] *Samson Agonistes* is partly modeled
on certain "pathetic" tragedies—dramas of suffering like *Ajax* and
Philoctetes, *Trachiniae* and *Heracles*, *Oedipus at Colonus* or
even *Prometheus Bound*—one would not expect the same kind of
plot or the same kind of dramatic situation as in *Oedipus Rex*, or
the same kind of emphasis as in an essentially "ethical" tragedy.
Conversely, if *Paradise Regained* is essentially an "ethical" poem,
an epic of character, one should not look for the pathetic or
passionate element in the same degree as in a tragedy of suffering
(such as Milton's projected tragedy on the agony in Gethsemane).

In a limited degree, these classifications may be useful in
analyzing some of the principal differences in the plot structure or
in the pathetic or ethical emphasis of Milton's major poems; but

they may serve only as tentative (and potentially unreliable) means to this end rather than as categorical distinctions. Since heroic patience is exercised and perfected in adversity, *pathos* may serve to illustrate *ethos*, and pathetic tragedy merge into ethical tragedy. Though *Samson* is a "passionate" tragedy, adversity tests and refines the hero's moral fortitude; he learns through suffering, and his tragedy of suffering is also a tragedy of character. Conversely, though *Paradise Regained* is a "moral" epic, it is also (and primarily) an exercise in suffering, and apprenticeship for the hero's ministry of redemption and the supreme *pathos* of the Passion. In both cases *pathos* and *ethos* complement each other; and they cannot be strictly differentiated.

In *Paradise Lost*, both of these elements are prominent; more "pathetic" but less "ethical" than *Paradise Regained*, more "ethical" but less "pathetic" than *Samson Agonistes*, it is (in the strictest sense) neither a tragedy of suffering nor a tragedy of character, but exhibits aspects of both. It is not purely a "passionate" epic,[12] nor altogether a "moral" epic. In the case of Adam and Eve, as in that of Satan, the element of *pathos* is the direct result of an ethical decision, an act of choice that exposes them to divine retribution. In Samson's case this is partly true, though in a different sense; though his death results in part from moral choices made within the drama, the pains of captivity and blindness and remorse result from an act of moral folly committed before the events of the plot. In all three poems, the core of the dramatic action is an act of *proairesis*, an act of moral decision.[13]

Finally, Milton's remarks on *epitasis* in his dramatic plans and his direct allusion to the *summa epitasis* of *Samson* suggest that he conceived the development of plot in terms of increasing tension and perturbation (a term frequently associated with the *epitasis*—the complication or middle section—of the tragic or comic fable). The element of *pathos* or perturbation, accordingly, would not (as a rule) be confined to one section of the fable but would (as several neo-Aristotelian critics also maintained) be dispersed throughout the plot. With this in mind, let us consider the relationship between *pathos* and *mythos*, passion and plot, in Milton's major poetry.

In *Samson*, as Mueller has correctly observed, the final pathos—the suffering and passion associated with the catastrophe of the drama—occurs offstage and is reported by the messenger. It is physical suffering, in the traditional sense. Nevertheless the element of *pathos* is not restricted to this passage alone. It occurs throughout the drama (for Samson is a "pathetic" tragedy, a tragedy of suffering); and it includes not only the physical suffering of the protagonist through blindness and hard labor but (in a far greater degree) his spiritual anguish, the torture of the mind and the agony of remorse. The hero's fiercest tormentors are his own thoughts, armed with deadly stings. Physical blindness is not the worst of his ills (as he had once believed); and the sting of that "manifest serpent," his wife, proves to be less painful than that of his own conscience. Samson's suffering extends throughout the tragedy—in solitude, in converse with friends and father, and in the successive confrontations with his wife, the Philistine champion, and the public officer. These are (as the chorus correctly recognizes) labors and ordeals of the mind.

In *Paradise Regained* (an epic of character), on the other hand, the tragic passions are subdued. The hero himself is a god as well as man; though he is once exposed to mortal danger, in the episode of the temple tower, he promptly discountenances his adversary. Though he experiences hunger, he is not subjected to physical or spiritual torment; his tragic agony and passion lie in the future. The stronger emotions of grief, the ordeals of fear and doubt, belong to minor characters in the epic—to his disciples and his mother—and these are soon allayed by faith or confidence, the contrary of fear.

The plot of *Paradise Lost* is complex inasmuch as the "change in the hero's fortunes" involves a *peripeteia*—a "change from one state of things . . . to its opposite . . . in the probable or necessary sequence of events."[14] Eve's aspiration to divinity produces "the opposite state of things,"[15] in the forfeiture of immortality and the obscuration of the divine image. The pursuit of elevation leads to the fall, and the ambition for a higher dignity results paradoxically in the loss of original excellence. Whether the change of fortune (*metabolē*) also involves a discovery or recognition is less certain; it depends on whether the knowledge of good and evil—the experience of evil and the illusions wrought by the delusive fruit—can be regarded as a genuine *anagnorisis*. More conventional recognitions occur frequently elsewhere in Milton's fable, and after waking from their drunken sleep Adam and Eve recognize their fallen condition. This is a delayed reaction, however; and the actual fruition of forbidden knowledge is a "discovery" of a different sort, attended with delusion rather than disillusion.

In *Paradise Lost*, the *pathos* of Adam and Eve is, for the most part, spiritual rather than physical—the pain of remorse and the milder grief of exile. Their *pathos* follows (or, in Adam's case) attends their fall. Nonetheless the element of *pathos* is not confined to the first man and first woman alone; it pertains to the fallen angels as well as to fallen man, and in this respect it extends throughout the greater part of the epic—the initial scenes in hell, Satan's monologues on Mount Niphates and in paradise, the civil war in heaven, and the vision of Adam's posterity.

Milton's shift to "tragic" notes in the final books of his epic is mirrored not only in events but also in the emotions of his principal characters. The violent passions that afflict the protagonists after their fall stand in striking contrast to their former tranquillity, when the affections were ruled and moderated by reason. The antithesis between postlapsarian and prelapsarian psychology is roughly analogous to Quintilian's distinction between the emotions associated with *pathos* and *ethos*: "in the one case the passions are violent, in the other subdued, the former command and disturb, the latter persuade and induce a feeling of goodwill. . . . For *pathos* is almost entirely concerned with anger, dislike, fear, hatred, and pity."[16]

Though all three of Milton's major poems contain reversals and thus belong to the complex species of epic or tragedy, they differ significantly in other respects. Though all three involve *pathos* as well as *ethos*, the former is more pronounced in *Samson*, and the latter in *Paradise Regained*. Though both present suffering as an heroic ideal, transforming *pathos* into *ethos* and vice versa, *Samson* is essentially a "pathetic tragedy," a "tragedy of suffering," and *Paradise Regained* a "moral epic," an "epic of character." The difference is significant for Milton's treatment of the passions, but it should not be exaggerated. Samson's virtue is perfected in adversity; the moral education of the hero of *Paradise Regained* involves the *paideia* of suffering and obedience, as preparation for his redemptive mission as suffering servant. Nevertheless Christ's supreme *agon*, the true *pathos* of the Passion, lies beyond the scope of the fable; in the plot of *Paradise Regained* there are recognitions and reversals contrary to expectation, but no major "change of

state" from felicity to misery and no tragic *pathos* (except for the
brief complaints of the disciples and the Virgin after the unex-
plained disappearance of the Messiah). The brief adversity sequence in the poem leaves the hero "no worse than wet." His
choice, as we know, will lead to the crucifixion—but not in the
immediate future. On the other hand, Samson's tragic fall—his
metabolē or "change of state"—has occurred *before* the events of
the fable; and the entire drama is one of *pathos*. The action consists
in his moral recovery, his return to his role as Jehovah's champion,
and the final *agon* that leads simultaneously to his greatest victory
and his own death. The drama thus moves between two tragic
events—the defeat and triumph of the hero, human weakness and
heroic fortitude—and between two *metabolē*s or "changes of
state": from deliverer to slave, and from slave to deliverer; from
God's elect to apparent derelict, and vice versa.

In *Paradise Lost* the elements of *pathos* and *ethos* are more
equalized. In the case of fallen angel and fallen man alike, misery is
(on the whole) the just penalty of moral guilt, and *pathos* the result
of ethical decision. Suffering or passion possesses ethical significance as both cause and effect of sin, as a symptom of the internal
and external disorder introduced into microcosm and macrocosm
as a result of man's disobedience. Since *Paradise Lost* is an
etiological epic, presenting the origin and causes of "Death and all
our Woe," *pathos* is closely associated with the *metabolē* (or
"change of state") of the human protagonists in the fable itself (and
in the prophetic vision of Adam's posterity) as well as with the
metabolē of the rebel angels. In the case of man and angel, it
accompanies and follows his fall.

The fact that *Samson* is both a complex tragedy and a tragedy of
suffering is significant both for the *pathos* of the drama and for its
catharsis. For the greater part of the tragedy Samson is suffering the
effects of the *metabolē* that had occurred before the events of the
drama. It was this fall, prompted alike by hubris (insolence) and by
sensual folly, that had blinded and enslaved him, plunging him (in
the words of the chorus) from the highest glory to the lowest pitch
of abject fortune. It was this "change of state" that would make him
an "example" for the ages—from medieval sermons and Renaissance frontispieces to Hollywood films—and it is the *pathos*
directly resulting from this fall that prompts his own lamentations

and the laments of his friends and his father in the first scenes of the drama. The tragic scene described by the messenger at the end of the play involves a second, and different, *pathos*.

Tasso was not alone in including "laments" in the *pathos* or scene of suffering of a tragedy. This detail occurs in the actual text of several Renaissance translations of the *Poetics*. Accordingly, there are probable (though not definitive) grounds for interpreting the laments in *Paradise Lost* and in *Samson* as part of the *pathos* or *perturbatio*. The hero's most intense expression of grief occurs comparatively early in the drama, in his lament with the chorus shortly before Dalila's arrival; and it stands in striking opposition to the tone of the final *commos*. The contrast between the near-despair of this *threnos* and the fierce jubilation of the final *commos* accentuates the further contrast between the failure of human consolation and the final consolation bestowed by the Deity. In *pathos* and in *ethos* the two passages present a violent contrast; and their opposition is enhanced by their generic resemblance. Each is a *threnos*, but the first is a chant of defeat, the second a victory song. Milton has counterpointed the two *threnoi*, playing them against each other, just as he has counterpointed the two *pathoi* or scenes of suffering, and the two *metabolēs* or "changes of state." Both are tragic, but one is an exemplum of human weakness, the other of heroic fortitude and magnitude of mind.[17]

In Milton's tragic epic (as Mueller has justly termed it) passion and character are so closely interrelated that it would be unwise to emphasize either of these qualities at the expense of the other. Both *pathos* and *ethos* were theoretically necessary for a perfect tragedy, even though Aristotle himself spoke of tragedies that contained plots but lacked character and though some of his Renaissance commentators spoke of tragedies without *pathos*. Though it is a complex epic, like the *Odyssey*, it cannot be neatly pigeonholed under labels like "pathetic" and "ethical"; both of these categories are almost equally applicable.

In *Paradise Lost* the elements of pathos—the painful and destructive or "corruptive" action—are scattered throughout the fable and episodes; from the horrors of hell to future miseries of mankind, from the ruin of the revolting angels and the ruin of man to the successive destructions of the world, from the *me miserum* of the fallen Satan to that of the fallen Adam. In *Samson* the catastrophe

is sufficiently sanguinary and destructive to fulfill the conditions of
pathos as Piccolomini and his contemporaries conceived them; and
Milton emphasizes the pathetic element through reiterated allusions
to horror, bloodshed, destruction, and death ranging from the
"hideous noise" and "universal groan" that arouse the fears or
hopes of Manoa and the chorus ("Blood, death, and deathful deeds
are in that noise, / Ruin, destruction at the utmost point") to the
messenger's report, the choral celebration of death and destruction,
and Manoa's final allusion to the hero's body "Soak't in his
enemies' blood" and "clotted gore" (lines 1508–1728). This is an
Aristotelian *pathos* par excellence, and Mueller has correctly identified it as such.

Nevertheless Samson's earlier lamentations—his initial complaint
of blindness among enemies (lines 63–109) and his subsequent
complaint over the torments of the mind, concluding with the
petition for "speedy death" as the "close" and "balm" of misery
(lines 606–51)—also constitute *pathos*, as Renaissance commentators conceived it. The pathological and medical imagery (noted by
Svendsen and other commentators on this passage)[18] derives much
of its relevance from the medical associations of *pathos* (in the
technical sense of "disease" or "malady") and of terms like *catharsis*
and *consolatio*. Like many of the Renaissance commentators on the
Poetics and *Rhetoric*, Milton extends the meaning of *pathos* to
include inner as well as external suffering; in this context, his
pathological imagery reinforces and heightens his imitation of
spiritual *pathos*, the "anguish of the mind." Samson's "torment" is
a literal translation of *pathos* and of *periōduniai*. His allusions to
"maladies innumerable" and to "ling'ring disease" evoke the medical and pathological sense of *pathos*. His allusions to the "body's
wounds and sores" and his metaphorical exploitation of terms like
"mangle," "exulcerate," and "inflammation" find their point of
departure in the wounds and ulcers that Renaissance exegetes had
discussed as examples of Aristotle's "destructive or painful" incidents. His reference to "deadly stings" recalls neo-Aristotelian
discussion of *pathos* as "acerbissimus dolor." His allusion to
"corporal sense" parallels Renaissance analyses of *pathos*; implicit
in his complaint is the argument that the torments of the mind are
more painful than physical torments inasmuch as they afflict the
"apprehensive tenderest parts," more sensitive than "corporal
sense." Both the element of *pathos* and the concept of consolation

receive clearer and more passionate definition through the use of medical imagery.

For Samson, as for Adam and Satan, the keenest *pathos* is the torment of remorse.

8 In Tasso's *Gerusalemme Libera-ta*, as in the heroic poems of Homer and Vergil, Milton perceived a "diffuse . . . model" of the "epic form." In the commentaries of the same author, as in the writings of other Italian or classical theorists, he recognized a guide to poetics, the "sublime art" which taught the "laws" of the literary genres and the principle of decorum, which might show "what religious, what glorious and magnificent use might be made of poetry, both in divine and human things." In Tasso's *Discorsi del Poema Eroico* he would have found a clear statement of the end and characteristic affect of heroic poetry—the evocation of wonder as a means of delighting and profiting the reader. The utility of the epic resulted from its power to persuade—to move the minds of an audience—with admiration. Though modeling his definition of the epic on Aristotle's description of tragedy, Tasso significantly substitutes "marvel" for "pity and fear." The heroic poem, he declares, is an "imitazione d'azione illustre, grande e perfetta, fatta, narrando con altissimo verso, *a fine di muover gli animi con la maraviglia, e di giovare in questa guisa.*" Whereas other genres "muovono maraviglia per muover riso, o compassione o altro affetto," the epic poet has no other end than admiration, "ed a l'incontro muove compassione per muover maraviglia; però la muove molto maggiore e più spesso." Whereas "l'operazione de la tragedia è di purgar gli animi col terrore e con la compassione," the "proprio diletto" and "propria operazione" of

the epic consist in "il muover maraviglia." To achieve this characteristic epic effect, the heroic poet must choose the loftiest subjects
and employ the noblest style: "Elegga, fra le cose belle, le bellis-
sime; fra le grandi, le grandissime; *fra le maravigliose, le maravigliosissime; ed alle maravigliosissime ancora cerchi d'accrescere novità
e grandezza.*"[1] The epic fable, character, thought, and diction were
oriented toward the goal of admiration.

Though most Renaissance theorists avoided so sharp a distinction between the effects of epic and tragedy, they acknowledged the
greater scope for the marvelous afforded by the narrative mode of
imitation, as set forth in Aristotle's remarks on *to thaumaston:*[2]
"The marvellous is certainly required in Tragedy. The Epic,
however, affords more opening for the improbable, the chief factor
in the marvellous, because in it the agents are not visibly before
one. The scene of the pursuit of Hector would be ridiculous on the
stage—the Greeks halting instead of pursuing him, and Achilles
shaking his head to stop them; but in the poem the absurdity is
overlooked. The marvellous, however, is a cause of pleasure, as is
shown by the fact that we all tell a story with additions, in the
belief that we are doing our hearers a pleasure." In Mazzoni's[3]
opinion, admiration was the proper effect of the heroic poem.
Minturno[4] follows Aristotle in asserting that "benchè ad ogni
Poeta sia richiesto il destar meraviglia negli animi degli Uditori, pur
niuno il fa meglio, nè più, che l'Eroico; nella cui Poesia molte cose
maravigliose ci si mostrano, le quali nella Tragedia, ... dove a
vedere si dessero, rider più tosto ci farieno, che meravigliare."
Among the distinguishing characteristics of the epic genre, Castelvetro[5] lists the "maggiore maraviglia, che può havere, & dee
l'epopea, laquale non può havere la tragedia." The "Italian
commentaries" Milton extolled so highly as teaching the "rules" of
the epic species[6] were virtually unanimous in emphasizing the epic
effect of wonder. Underlying his extensive exploitation of the
marvelous in *Paradise Lost* was a solid foundation of Aristotelian
critical doctrine.

To what extent did Milton consciously attempt to arouse wonder
—the "propria operatione" of the heroic poem? What particular
elements of the marvelous did he employ in order to produce this
effect? This chapter will consider two aspects of the question:
(1) Milton's own references to the wonder aroused by divine or
diabolical agency in the course of the poem, and (2) the traditional

theological distinction between God's "miracles" and Satan's "wonders."

Tasso had advised the epic poet to reconcile "il maraviglioso e 'l verisimile" by introducing the Christian supernatural: "Attribuisca il poeta alcune operazioni che di gran lunga eccedono il potere de gli uomini a Dio, a gli angioli suoi, a' demoni, o a coloro a' quali da Dio o da' demoni è conceduto questa potestà."[7] Milton similarly seeks the marvelous in divine or infernal *mirabilia*. In *Paradise Lost* the marvel aroused by diabolical wonders in associated principally with shape-shifting, monuments, and Satan's enterprise against man. The rebel angels are described as "admiring" the work of Mulciber (1.730–31), which (Milton suggests) is far more marvelous than the greatest monuments of men:

> And here let those
> Who boast in mortal things, and wond'ring tell
> Of *Babel*, and the works of *Memphian* Kings,
> Learn how thir greatest Monuments of Fame,
> And Strength and Art are easily outdone
> By Spirits reprobate, and in an hour
> What in an age they with incessant toil
> And hands innumerable scarce perform.
>
> [1.692–99]

This achievement is followed by a further demonic "wonder" when the giant angels become "less than smallest Dwarfs" (1.777–79). The "Bridge of wondrous length" (2.1028) which Sin and Death build over Chaos "by wondrous Art Pontifical" (10.312–13) wins admiration from Satan himself:

> near the foot
> Of this new wondrous Pontifice, . . . at sight
> Of that stupendious Bridge his joy increas'd.
> Long hee admiring stood.
>
> [10.347–52]

When he enters Pandaemonium in disguise and resumes his own "shape Star-bright," his peers are "amaz'd" by the "sudden blaze" (10.450–53). After this dramatic epiphany he attempts to enhance the effect of admiration by contrasting the magnitude of his achievement with the insignificance of the instrument and the cost. He has purchased a "World . . . with a bruise" and overcome its erstwhile ruler by a trifle: "and the more to increase / Your wonder, with an Apple" (10.486–87).

These infernal wonders stir admiration in fallen angels, so it is scarcely surprising that Satan succeeds in astonishing Eve. It is through an apparent miracle that he persuades her to disobey, and the appeal to the marvelous figures prominently both in the dream of book 5 and in the temptation scene of book 9. In the preliminary temptation, the "Tree of interdicted Knowledge" seems so "much fairer to ... Fancy than by day" that Eve looks "wond'ring" (5.51–54). Like the sight of the tree, the effects of its fruit inspire admiration, leaving her "wond'ring at my flight and change / To this high exaltation" (5.89–90). In the actual temptation, Satan skillfully manipulates her initial wonder at the articulate serpent to induce belief in the miraculous virtues of the forbidden tree. In fact, he himself introduces the theme of wonder, and the first lines of his speech provide an ironic counterpoint to her admiration. Knowing that she must perforce marvel at the prodigy of a beast endowed with discourse, he begins by entreating her *not* to marvel (a statement calculated to produce precisely the opposite effect) and protesting that, instead, it is she who is the proper subject for admiration: "Wonder not, sovran Mistress, if perhaps / Thou canst, who art sole Wonder" (9.532–33). This address leaves Eve, naturally, "much marvelling" and "not unamaz'd" at the "miracle" and "wonder" of an animal "reasoning to admiration"—at "Language of Man pronounc't / By Tongue of Brute, and human sense exprest" (9.551–66, 872). His next speech leaves her "yet more amaz'd" (9.614), and she allows herself to be convinced, gradually, of the miraculous virtues of the fruit—"Wondrous indeed, if cause of such effects" (9.650) and "worthy to be admir'd" (9.746). This apparent miracle belongs to a type of the marvelous already discussed by Castelvetro—a rational act in a brute beast: "La maraviglia negli animali senza ragione, & nelle cose insensate fanno, o paiono fare le loro operationi secondo ragione, & secondo che sogliono operare gli huomini consigliatamente.... Anzi ... genera maraviglia, perche fa quello fuori di sua natura, che fa l'huomo per ammaestramento d'intelletto."[8]

Primarily, however, Milton reserves the epic effect of wonder for the works of God rather than for the operations of the devil. His chief sources of the marvelous are the *magnalia Christi*—the defeat of the rebel angels, the creation of the world, and the redemption of man. Raphael's account of the war in heaven fills his human audience

> With admiration, and deep Muse to hear
> Of things so high and strange, things to thir thought
> So unimaginable as hate in Heav'n,
> And War so near the Peace of God.
>
> [7.52–55]

These are matters "above Earthly thought" and "human knowledge," and Adam hails them as "Great things, and full of wonder" (7.70–82). Messiah's appearance on the celestial battlefield is attended by "Signs" and "Wonders," as the "uprooted Hills" return to their places "at his command" (6.781–90). When he turns his wrath against his enemies, "they astonisht all resistance lost" (6.838). When Satan recoils under Abdiel's "noble stroke," "Amazement seiz'd / The Rebel Thrones . . . to see / Thus foil'd thir mightiest" (6.189–200).

A further source of the marvelous is the creation of the world—an action nobler than the angelic battle, for "to create / Is greater than created to destroy" and Messiah is "greater" in his return from "Creation and the Six days' acts . . . Than from the Giant Angels" (7.601–7). Angel, devil, and man marvel at the initial act of creation and its result, the completed universe—"a Fabric wonderful" (10.482). Satan's first reaction to "the sudden view of all this World at once" is "wonder . . . though after Heaven seen" (3.542–53). Allured by the splendor of the sun, he observes how "wondrously was set his Station bright" (3.587). To Uriel he explains that the desire to behold God's "works so wondrous" had brought him to visit "this new Creation" (3.661–65), and it is with "new wonder" that he beholds paradise and its human inhabitants (4.205, 263). Uriel likewise avows that "wonderful indeed are all his works" (3.702). Wonder at the beauty of creation leads Adam and Eve to marvel at its Creator: "thine this universal Frame, / Thus wondrous fair; thyself how wondrous then" (5.153–55). Adam listens "with wonder, but delight" to the divine historian's narrative of creation (8.11), and Raphael himself explains that heaven is "as the Book of God . . . Wherein to read his wond'rous Works" (8.66–68). Adam's first reaction to the world is (like Satan's) one of wonder (8.257–58).

A still higher source of the epic marvelous is "the marvel of God's salvation" (Wisdom v. 2), Arranging the *opera Dei* in order of

climax, Milton describes the creation as "greater" than the destruction of the rebel angels, but declares that the redemption of man is
even "more wonderful" than the creation. Adam receives Michael's
prophecy of future salvation "with joy and wonder":

> O goodness infinite, goodness immense!
> That all this good of evil shall produce,
> And evil turn to good; more wonderful
> Than that which by creation first brought forth
> Light out of darkness!
>
> [12.468–73]

When the Son offers himself as a sacrifice for man and "attends the
will" of the Father, the angels listen with marvel: "Admiration
seiz'd / All Heav'n, what this might mean, and whither tend /
Wond'ring" (3.269–73). The Father prophesies Christ's "wondrous
birth"—"Made flesh, when time shall be, of Virgin seed" (3.282–
85). Similarly, in the *De Doctrina*[9] Milton describes Messiah's
advent as a "miraculous conception" and observes that theologians
regard the Incarnation "as, next to the Trinity in Unity, the greatest
mystery of our religion." In the final books of the poem Noah's ark,
the Exodus, the acts of the apostles are presented as marvels. The
completion of the "wondrous Ark" is succeeded by another "wonder strange": "Of every Beast, and Bird, and Insect small / Came
sevens, and pairs, and enter'd in, as taught / Thir order" (11.733–
36, 819). God endows Moses with "wondrous power" to hold back
the waters of the Red Sea (12.200). The Holy Spirit confers on the
apostles "wondrous gifts ... To speak all Tongues, and do all
Miracles, / As did thir Lord before them" (12.500–502).

These explicit allusions to "wonder" and the "wonderful" indicate Milton's concern to achieve the characteristic epic effect of
admiration, but they represent only a part of the element of the
marvelous in his poem. Let us note briefly a few of the more
significant points of similarity between Milton's treatment of the
marvelous and Renaissance poetic theory.

1. In describing the single-handed rout of the rebel forces by
Messiah, after commanding his own army to refrain from further
combat, Milton may have been influenced by the classic instance of
the epic marvelous in Aristotelian critical tradition—the pursuit of
Hector by Achilles. Tasso cites "Aristotele ed Omero istesso ne la
fuga d'Ettore" as authorities for his opinion that "a niuna altra

specie di poesia tanto conviene il muover maraviglia, quanto a la epopeia" and adds that "quella maraviglia che ci rende quasi attoniti di veder che un uomo solo con le minacce e co' cenni sbigottisca tutto l'esercito ... rende mirabile il poema eroico."[10] Minturno declares that the reader of the *Iliad* derives "maraviglia grandissima" from this passage, seeing "Achille girne dietro ad Ettor volto in fuga, e col ciglio vietare, che niuno il ferisca, temendo per avventura, che alcun non gli prevenga a quella gloria conseguire."[11] Castelvetro agrees that the flight of Hector involves the marvelous, but denies that it should seem ridiculous, even on the stage, for the Greek army to refrain from combat "per ubidire ad un suo maggiore":

Hora, se la caccia, che diede Achille ad Hettore raccontata nel libro X dell'Iliada fosse avenuta veramente tale, senza dubbio l'essercito de Greci havrebbe circondata Achille cacciante, & Hettore cacciato, & si sarebbe stato otioso, & scioperato, & si come si suole dire con le mani a cintola senza far nulla & solamente veditore per non disubidire ad Achille, che col capo accennava loro, che non fedissono Hettore, accioche egli solo havesse la gloria d'haverlo ucciso, & d'haver vendicato Patroclo con le sue proprie mani, & lo stare dell'essercito senza perseguitare, & senza fedire Hettore non havrebbe mosso punto a riso, chi l'havesse allhora veduto.

What *would* have seemed ridiculous on the stage would have been the unnecessary "diminuimento della maravigla" resulting from the presence of the Greek hosts supporting Achilles against a solitary enemy:

Hora, perche Aristotele ha fermata questa conclusione, che l'epopea poteva fare la maraviglia molto maggiore, che non poteva la tragedia ... si doveva dire, che la caccia data da Achille ad Hettore sarebbe piu maravigliosa, se si fosse mostrato, che Achille solo senza havere il caldo dell'essercito de Greci, o che l'aiutasse, o che fosse presente a fargli animo, havesse cacciato Hettore, poi che Hettore era solo senza l'essercito de Troiani, che l'aiutasse, o che fosse presente a fargli animo. & percio Homero nascose ne suoi versi la presentia dell'essercito de Greci, ne narrò come fosse pronto, & presto per fedire Hettore in tanto, che nol facesse, accioche la caccia datagli da Achille fosse piu maravigliosa, & fosse congiunta con maggiore sua lode.

In a tragedy such a scene would make the poet himself appear ridiculous for wantonly sacrificing the marvelous; "altri si beffera del poeta, che voglia fare rappresentare la fuga d'Hettore maravigliooa & lodevule per Achille, se con Achille accompagnera l'essercito favoreggiantelo, & fara Hettore solo." The *Aeneid* utilizes a similar pursuit as a source of the marvelous, but, unlike the *Iliad*, it attributes an army to both parties:

Laonde Virgilio, havendo in pensiero di fare una caccia simile, che desse Enea a Turno maravigliosa & lodevole per Enea, non fa, che Enea habbia l'essercito che lo favoreggi, & Turno non l'habbia, ma fa, che ciascuno di loro habbia il suo essercito.[12]

Moreover, an exploit is all the more marvelous if it is performed by a single man rather than by several persons; "piu maraviglia prendiamo dell'operatione d'un solo, quando l'operatione è degna di maraviglia, che non facciamo d'una operatione degna d'ugual maraviglia per se, quando è operata da piu persone."[13]

Like Achilles, the Messiah commands his own side to refrain from combat, so that he may defeat the enemy single-handed. His opponent, however, is not a lone warrior, but an entire army—the third part of heaven's host. As in the *Iliad*, "un uomo solo . . . sbigottisca tutto l'esercito"; but in Messiah's case the army so discountenanced is the hostile force, not his own side. In Milton's epic, as in Homer's, the glory of winning a single-handed victory is a significant factor in the hero's refusal to allow his own army to participate. Both Minturno and Castelvetro attributed this motive to Achilles, and in *Paradise Lost* the Father specifically declares that he has reserved for Messiah "the Glory . . . Of ending this great War, since none but Thou / Can end it." Ethically, however, he stands in striking contrast to Homer's hero, for his primary motive is filial obedience and he seeks not his own glory, but to "glorify" the Father (6.725).

Thus Milton enhances the element of the marvelous by pitting the Son alone against an entire army. Achilles had routed Hector—but in the presence of the whole Greek host. Aeneas had defeated Turnus, while the Trojan and Rutulian armies stood by. Messiah routs the entire rebel force while his own armies remain disengaged. In exploiting the single-handed victory of one against many as a source of the marvelous, he had a notable precedent in Odysseus's massacre of the suitors,[14] and he was to make use of the same device subsequently in *Samson Agonistes*.

Elsewhere in *Paradise Lost* Milton achieves "piu maraviglia" through presenting the marvelous as "operatione d'un solo." The creation of the world and the redemption of man are exploits the Son performs alone, in obedience to the Father, as in the earlier expulsion of the rebel angels. Abdiel fights "the better fight" alone, maintaining "single" against "revolted multitudes the Cause / Of Truth, in word mightier than they in Arms" (6.30–32). Enoch is "the only righteous in a World perverse," hated "for daring single to be just" (11.701–3). Noah is "the only Son of light / In a dark Age," the "one just Man alive" (11.808, 819). Satan's desire for "high repute" leads him, like Achilles, to forbid his companions to share his "enterprise" (2.465–72), and he performs his great exploits—the voyage through the abyss, the defeat of man, the conquest of the world, and the deliverance of his followers from hell—alone.

"To mee shall be the glory *sole* among / The infernal Powers, in one day to have marr'd / What he *Almighty* styl'd, six Nights and Days / Continu'd making" (9.135–38).

2. In the devils' metamorphosis into serpents, as in Sin's similar transformation into a viper, Milton exploits a "mutatione miraculosa"[15] as a source of the marvelous. Upon hearing the "sound / Of public scorn" instead of the "high applause" he had anticipated, Satan "wonder'd, but not long / Had leisure, wond'ring at himself now more" (10.504–10). Tasso's *Discorsi* had, significantly, cited the analogous transformations in Ovid and Dante as examples of "maraviglie" highly effective in the epic but unsuited to the theater:

Non sarebbe ancora convenevole ne la scena la trasmutazione di Cadmo in serpente, la quale convenevolmente fu narrata da Ovidio; . . . non quella di Proteo in tante sembianze descritta nella Georgica, e prima nell'Odissea; non quella nel cerchio de' ladroni, de la quale Dante si vanta con queste parole:
    Taccia di Cadmo e d'Aretusa Ovidio;
    Ché se quello in serpente, e quella in fonte
    Converte poetando, i' non l'invidio;
non quella . . . del mago in tante forme appresso il Boiardo . . . ; non tante altre che si leggono con maraviglia in tanti altri poeti moderni e antichi; non tante maraviglie le quali nel teatro sarebbono peraventura sconvenevoli, e ne l'epopeia sono lette volentieri, sí perché sono sue proprie, sí perché il lettore consente a molte cose, a le quali nega il consentimento colui che risguarda.[16]

Milton's extensive use of metamorphoses as a source of the marvelous is in keeping with Tasso's recommendations. Besides the analogy between the serpentine metamorphosis of book 10 and the similar transformations of Ovid's Cadmus and Dante's robbers, Satan's numerous disguises—as stripling cherub, as cormorant, as toad, as lion and tiger—resemble the metamorphoses of Proteus "in tante sembianze" and those of Boiardo's magician "in tante forme."

Tasso also includes machines among the "maraviglie" especially suitable in the heroic poem. Though tragedy can make little use of this device, "ne l'epopeia spesso scendono da cielo gl'Iddii e gli Angeli, e s'interpongono ne l'operazioni de gli uomini, dando consiglio ed aiuto ... *Laonde tutti questi poemi paiono quasi fatti e condotti a fine da la provvidenza.*"[17] Milton's dual exploitation of supernatural machinery both as a source of the marvelous and as the agents of divine providence is especially appropriate in an epic dedicated to the assertion of "Eternal Providence." Both divine and infernal machinery operate to fulfill the divine intent. The extended revelations of divine and human events by Raphael and Michael are introduced into the narrative as "consiglio ed aiuto." Conversely, Satan's "dark designs" are ultimately subservient to "the will / And high permission of all-ruling Heaven"; they bring greater damnation on himself, but "Infinite goodness, grace and mercy shown / On Man by him seduc't" (1.211–20).

3. Events which "occur unexpectedly and at the same time in consequence of one another"[18] also contribute to the element of the marvelous in *Paradise Lost.* The discovery of Satan by Zephon and Ithuriel, the transformation of the devils into serpents, the promise of redemption Michael extends to Adam—these events occur "praeter expectationem"[19] and evoke surprise, but their causes are rooted in previous events or in the divine will, or in both. Here, as in *Samson Agonistes,* "divine disposal" is a highly important factor in the marvelous, for the unexpected event which arouses marvel stems from divine providence. Minturno makes this very point in his *L'Arte Poetica,* in developing Aristotle's observation that even matters of chance seem "most marvellous if there is an appearance of design ... in them"[20]: "Meraviglianci di quelle cose, che oltre alla nostra opinione accadano, massimamente dove elle si attamente sien congiunte, che l'una paja dopo l'altra ragionevolmente seguire." In matters of chance, "quelle specialmente ci fanno meravigliare, che o per divino consiglio, o di lor proprio movimento crediamo avvenire." Thus the statue of Mitys, which killed "the author of Mitys' death by falling down on him" seemed to act "per divina disposizione, o studiosamente per punire il nimico."[21]

4. Mazzoni regarded recognition as the basic of the marvelous in the poetic fable,[22] and *Paradise Lost* contains several examples of this principle. When Zephon and Ithuriel discover Satan in book 4, they recoil "half amaz'd / So sudden to behold the grisly King"

(4.820–21). The discovery of Eve's trespass leaves Adam "amaz'd" and "Astonied . . . and Blank, while horror chill / Ran through his veins" (9.889–91). The "wonder" he experiences at Michael's revelation of his future redemption likewise depends on *anagnorisis*. 5. Wonder and "delight" are conjoined not only in Adam's response to Raphael's narrative of creation (8.11), but also in neo-Aristotelian poetic theory. According to the *Poetics*, the "marvellous . . . is a cause of pleasure," and this opinion was reiterated by Renaissance commentators.[23]

To reconcile the demands of verisimilitude with the element of the marvelous, Renaissance critics appealed to a theological commonplace—God's indisputable power to suspend the laws of nature and perform whatever miracles he chose. Mazzoni's *Discorso* employs this argument to defend Dante's *Commedia* against the charge of violating verisimilitude. As the Christian faith acknowledges two powers in God—an ordinary power which operates according to natural laws and an absolute power which accomplishes supernatural and miraculous works—no Christian can doubt that God is able, by his absolute power, to send a living man to heaven, hell, and purgatory. In this way Dante achieves the marvelous without forfeiting verisimilitude. His hell is "una somma maraviglia":

Perciò che io son ben sicuro che, se costoro havranno a mente come l'inferno di Dante dovea essere descritto, in maniera che verisimile paresse caminare vi possa un huomo vivo, e che le pene deveano essere appropriate a' delitti di modo, che nel senso si potessero intendere bene, et allegoricamente convenissero a' delitti; tosto mutaranno parere, e vedranno ch' in alcun modo, con queste conditioni, non potea descriver l'inferno e le sue pene con cose degne di maggior maraviglia de quelle ch' egli elesse.[24]

For Tasso, likewise, the basis of verisimilitude in representations of the marvelous consisted in regard for the "virtue and power" of the forces who accomplish these "miracles":

Queste opere, se per se stesse saranno considerate, maravigliose parranno; anzi miracoli sono chiamati nel comune uso di parlare. Queste medesime, *se si avra riguardo a la virtú ed a la potenza di chi l'ha operate*, verisimile saranno giudicate. . . . Può esser dunque una medesima azione e maravigliosa e verisimile: maravigliosa, riguardandola in se stessa e circonscritta dentro ai termini naturali;

verisimile, considerandola divisa da questi termini *ne la sua cagione, la quale e una virtú sopranaturale, possente, ed usata a far simile maraviglie.*[25]

Though Milton's treatment of the Christian supernatural conforms in large part to the principles enunciated by Mazzoni and Tasso, his representation of divine and infernal *mirabilia* carries the principle of verisimilitude considerably beyond either of these critics. In Tasso's *Discorsi* the term "miracoli" embraces not only the works of God and his angels, but those of the demons and their agents as well ("a Dio, a gli angioli suoi, a' demoni, o a coloro a' quali da Dio o da' demoni è conceduta questa potestá, quali sono i santi, i magi e le fate"). Milton, on the other hand, appears to preserve the theological distinction between God's "miracles" and Satan's "lying wonders" and thus shows greater "riguardo a la virtú ed a la potenza di chi l'ha operate"—a more consistent fidelity to decorum, "the grand masterpiece to observe."[26]

In the *De Doctrina* this distinction is implicit, though never expressly stated, in Milton's definition of *miraculum* as "providentia Dei extraordinaria": "The extraordinary providence of God is that whereby God produces some effect out of the usual order of nature, or gives the power of producing the same effect to whomsoever he may appoint. This is what we call a miracle. Hence God alone is the primary author of miracles, as he only is able to invert that order of things which he has himself appointed." As proof texts Milton quotes Psalm 62:18 ("qui facit *mirabilia solus*"), John 10:21 ("*num daemonium potest caecorum oculos aperire?*), and 2 Thessalonians 2:9 ("cuius adventus est ex illa vi efficaci *Satanae, cum omni potentia, et signis ac prodigiis mendacibus*").[27] These three texts supplement each other in distinguishing the different character of the divine and infernal marvelous. The first insists that God alone can work miracles. The second denies this power to the devils. The third describes Antichrist's operations as "after the power of Satan, with . . . signs and lying wonders."

Though the *De Doctrina* does not explicitly formulate this distinction, it is a commonplace in Scholastic and Reformed theology. According to Keckermann, "Etiam Diabolus opera edere potest mira; sed tamen proprie loquendo non edit miracula; quia semper utitur causis secundis, nec etiam scopum habet miraculis proprium."[28] Similarly Wolleb observes that "Mali Angeli mira faciunt, sed miracula facere nequent. Miracula enim sunt opera,

omnem creaturarum potentiam superantia."²⁹ Zanchius lists three
"discrimina, quae sunt inter *mirabilia*, quae possunt Daemones, &
quae Deus edere solet *miracula*"—in nature, authenticity, and
ends. First, divine and infernal wonders differ "à natura ipsorum
factorum," for although the devils can perform many things
"praeter ordinem naturae consuetum," God alone can perform such
miracles as bringing the dead to life, dividing the Red Sea, and
preserving the youths in the fiery furnace. Second, they differ "à
veritate & falsitate factorum," for the devil's miracles are not what
they seem: "Omnia Dei miracula, sunt revera id quod apparent:
proinde vera sunt miracula. At quae Diabolus edit, non omnia sunt
talia, qualia esse videntur. . . . Miracula igitur diabolica non sunt
vera miracula: quando neque ipsa facta sunt semper id, quod
videntur esse: sed imposturae sunt & praestigiae." Third, they
differ "à finibus"; whereas God's miracles are performed for man's
salvation and his own glory, "diaboli signa contra salutem hominum & contra gloriam Dei facta sunt. . . . Mirabilia tamen edunt,
& portenta magna; sed quae indigna sunt nomine miraculorum."
Zanchius further observes that many things seem miraculous to
man simply because he does not know their real causes. An
ignorant rustic would regard a solar eclipse as a miracle, but an
astronomer, aware of its true cause, would recognize it as a purely
natural phenomenon:

Non enim miraculum est quodvis admirabile factum, cuius
caussam ignoremus. Multa enim fiunt, quorum caussae nos latent:
ac proinde, quae admiramur & miracula nobis esse videntur, quae
tamen alij non admirantur, illi nimirum, qui illorum caussas
tenent.³⁰

In his commentary on Thessalonians, Saint Thomas Aquinas
gives three similar explanations for the reference to the "lying
wonders" of Antichrist and Satan (2 Thessalonians 2:9): "Miraculum mendax dicitur, vel quia deficit a vera ratione facti, vel a
vera ratione miraculi, vel a debito fine miraculi." In the first place,
the devil's wonders are not what they seem: "Primum fit in
praestigiis, quando per daemones illuduntur aspectus, ut aliud
videatur, quam est." Second, the marvel they arouse is due to
ignorance of their causes: "Secundo modo illa dicuntur miracula
improprie, quae plena sunt admiratione, quando effectus videtur et
ignoratur causa. Quae ergo habent causam occultam alicui et non

simpliciter, dicuntur mira, et non miracula simpliciter.... Ali-
quando vero fiunt aliqua mira, sed non praeter ordinem naturae,
sed occultas causas habent: et haec multo magis faciunt daemones,
qui virtutes naturae sciunt. et qui habent determinatas efficacias ad
speciales effectus ...; sed non quae habent veram rationem
miraculi; quia non possunt in illa quae sunt supra naturam." Third,
as miracles are "ordinata ad attestandum veritati fidei, ad reducendum fideles in Deum, ... aliquis praedicans falsam doctrinam
non potest facere miracula."[31] Again, in the *Summa Theologiae*,
Saint Thomas declares that, though demons cannot perform true
miracles, they can achieve actions which exceed "humanam facul-
tatem et considerationem" and therefore seem miraculous. "Sic
igitur cum daemones aliquid faciunt sua virtute naturali, miracula
dicuntur on simpliciter, sed quoad nos."[32]

Satan's numerous *mirabilia* in *Paradise Lost* are, therefore,
merely "lying wonders" rather than true miracles. He effects his
various metamorphoses "sua virtute naturali" by exercising the
natural power of spirits to appear "in what shape they choose"
(1.428). His shape-shifting would seem miraculous only to someone
ignorant of its cause. The sudden transformation of the devils from
gigantic stature to dwarfish size is indeed "a wonder" (1.777), but
not a miracle.

To accentuate the contrast between true miracles and "lying
wonders" Milton brings Satan's marvels into dramatic juxtaposition with those of God at several points in the narrative. Unlike
Satan's voluntary shape-shifting, the metamorphosis of the fallen
angels into serpents in book 10 is an authentic miracle; "a greater
power" overrules the natural ability of the devils to assume
whatever shape they choose. The same principle is involved in the
effect of Ithuriel's spear, which compels Satan to revert to his "own
likeness" as "no falsehood can endure Touch of Celestial temper"
(4.811–13), but on this occasion God accomplishes the miracle
through second causes.

Satan's temptation of Eve involves most of the characteristics of
the *miraculum mendax* noted by theologians. In the biblical
account, the woman does not marvel at the serpent's gift of rational
speech, but in *Paradise Lost* her belief in "this miracle" (9.562) is a
principal factor in her seduction.[33] In the first place, this "lying
wonder" involves imposture and illusion, for the miracle is not
what it seems to be. Contrary to appearances, the serpent has

neither tasted the forbidden fruit nor acquired the power to reason and speak. It is simply a passive instrument under the influence of a demonic power. Second, it seems miraculous only because Eve is ignorant of the cause. She does not suspect that the phenomenon stems from diabolical possession, whereby Satan has inspired "his brutal sense.... With act intelligential" (9.188–90). Third, as his own soliloquy amply attests (9.135–78), Satan performs the apparent miracle "contra salutem hominum & contra gloriam Dei." Similarly, in arguing that "ye shall not Die" (9.685), he exploits his *miraculum mendax* in the cause of "false doctrine" rather than "ad attestandum veritati fidei" and "reducendum fideles in Deum."

According to the *De Doctrina*, miracles are designed not only "to manifest the divine power, and confirm our faith," but also "to increase the condemnation of unbelievers, by taking away all excuse for unbelief."[34] When Messiah appears on the celestial battlefield, the miraculous manifestations of "Power Divine" (6.780 ff.) which accompany him are sure signs of his divine authority, but Satan and his cohorts remain unconvinced by them, "hard'n'd more by what might most reclaim." The introduction of the true miraculous at this point intensifies the guilt of the rebel angels and underlines the justice of their punishment.

EPILOGUE   EPIC DESIGN
PLOT AS   AND DIVINE
PARADIGM   IDEA

Although problems of genre and
ideal form no longer possess the fascination they held for neoclassical critics, they were operative in the compositon of seventeenth-
century epic, and hence indispensable for the study of seventeenth-
century literature. For Milton and his contemporaries, considerations of plot not only conditioned the choice of subject matter, they
altered and reshaped the material in the interests of a generic or
universal idea of form. It was through the plot, the formal
disposition of incidents, that the poet succeeded in realizing the
norms of a literary species, the paradigm of an epic or comedy or
tragedy. Design conferred generic identity—and indeed metaphysical status—entitling the poem to an intelligible (though sometimes
debatable) position in the scale of being: the order of natural,
artificial, and ideal forms.

Combining the Aristotelian conception of plot as idea and the
Platonic conception of art as the imposition of ideal form on
matter, Renaissance critics—theorists of the visual as well as the
verbal arts—usually regarded the primary task of the poet or
painter as the realization of a design. This was the key not only to
the unity and integrity of the work and to its generic identity, but
also to its beauty and its power to delight, its moral value and its
power to teach, its logical inevitability and its power to persuade,
its emotional force and its power to move the passions. "Beauty is a
matter of size and order," wrote Aristotle, and it was through "the

imitation of an action . . . complete in itself, as a whole of some magnitude," that the beauty of a well-constructed epic or tragedy resembled that of a living creature. To "be beautiful, a living creature, and every whole made up of parts, must not only present a certain order in its arrangement of parts, but also be of a certain definite magnitude." Just as "a beautiful whole made up of parts, or a beautiful living creature, must be of some size, a size to be taken in by the eye, so a story or Plot must be of some length, but a length to be taken in by the memory."[1]

In the case of Milton's poetic argument, the process of composition was one of eliciting as well as imposing design. The matter he selected for his heroic poem was not altogether formless. It possessed implicit structures—most obviously the temporal and causal sequence of temptation, disobedience, judgment, expulsion —and in accommodating these to the idea of epic design, he also incorporated elements of other patterns or systems: a cosmological and theological system, a pattern of universal history, an image of the role of divine providence in the creation and government of the world. Although none of these designs—providential, cosmic, or (for that matter) microcosmic—determines the formal design of his work, they nevertheless bear an intelligible relationship to its theme and structure.

Structurally, *Paradise Lost* represents the accommodation of a temptation ordeal to an ideal of epic form abstracted from classical heroic poetry and systematized through Renaissance speculation on Aristotle's advice concerning the disposition of the epic and tragic fable. The pattern of incidents is governed not only by patterns implicit in the biblical argument (the fall of man) and by the larger and more comprehensive pattern of spiritual warfare (as developed in both biblical and postbiblical temptation crises), but also by notions of the ideal or paradigmatic epic structure, concepts of the perfect tragic plot and its relevance for heroic poetry.

Though all of these narrative patterns influence the formal structure of the poem, they also involve other and more comprehensive patterns, both intrinsic and extrinsic to the plot itself. Logical and ethical patterns not only condition the structure of events within the fable, but also help to integrate the episodes— both causally and thematically—within the design of the main plot. Finally, in both matter and theme, Milton's fable and episodes involve a design even more comprehensive in scope: the decrees of divine providence, partially revealed not only in Scripture but in the order of nature itself—in the pattern of the world (human microcosm as well as universal macrocosm) and in the structure of world history.

These patterns do not always coincide; they sometimes conflict with one another, as well as with literary and philosophical tradition. Though they frequently occur elsewhere in isolation from one another, in *Paradise Lost* they are closely involved with problems of narrative design. Each of them, to a degree, has influenced the disposition of Milton's plot.

Except for a few critical asides on epic conventions, Milton himself said little about the formal structure of his epic. It was on the basis of subject matter rather than narrative design—on the choice of a higher argument rather than a more perfect realization of epic form—that he aspired to outsoar the heroic poets of antiquity. Like other dedicated artists of his period, he apparently took technical and formal perfection for granted; to master the rules was an artistic imperative, even for a writer who dared to transcend them. For his earliest critics—even those who most extolled his choice of subject matter or those who questioned its propriety as an epic argument—the design of *Paradise Lost* was the principal object of concern, and its regularity or irregularity a primary criterion for praise or blame.

Dryden objected that Milton's design was "the losing of our happiness."[2] Samuel Wesley protested that the action was not uniform.[3] Dennis acclaimed *Paradise Lost* as the loftiest but "most irregular Poem" ever written.[4] Voltaire praised its happy combination of uniformity and variety: "All its Episodes being necessary Lines which aim at the Centre of a perfect Circle." Addison, methodically examining the poem by the "rules of epic poetry," emphasized its superiority to the works of the ancients in the unity, entirety, and greatness of its action: it possessed "all the greatness of plan, regularity of design, and masterly beauties which we discover in Homer and Virgil."[5] In Samuel Johnson's opinion, *Paradise Lost* could claim the first place "among the productions of the human mind" with "respect to design." There was "perhaps" no poem of the same length from which so little could be "taken without apparent mutilation."[6]

On the whole, neoclassical critics showed cautious respect

toward Milton's design—in sharp contrast to their frequent condemnation of Spenser's epic as barbarous and formally corrupt. To
many of them *The Faerie Queene* seemed to violate the fundamental principles of unity of action and uniformity of design: Spenser
"wanted a true Idea." In structuring his narrative, he had followed
unreliable guides—the will-o'-the-wisp of the romancers—instead
of imitating the ancients.[7] In the case of *Paradise Lost*, on the other
hand, the majority praised its formal design—its economy of
incident and its structural unity and coherence—even though some
of them doubted that this design was suitable for heroic poetry.
Addison commended the poet's regard for the unities of time,
place, and action and his ability to achieve variety in unity.
Paradise Lost contained "no other episodes than such as naturally
arise from the subject, and yet is filled with . . . a multitude of
astonishing incidents." Since the account of the fall of the angels
runs parallel to the main action of the poem, it does not break "the
unity so much as another episode would have done, that had not so
great an affinity with the principal subject." As in the *Spanish
Friar*, "the two different plots look like counterparts and copies of
one another."[8]

Similarly in Johnson's opinion, Milton had equaled all other
poets in the disposition of his fable (i.e., "a narration artfully
constructed, so as to excite curiosity, and surprise expectation").
Nothing could be objected to the "compleatness or *integrity* of the
design"; it possessed "distinctly and clearly what Aristotle requires,
a beginning, a middle, and an end." In his account of Adam's fall
Milton had involved prior and subsequent events, interweaving
"the whole system of theology with such propriety, that every part
appears to be necessary." In the entire poem there were only
two episodes, and both were "closely connected with the great
action; one was necessary to Adam as a warning, the other as a
consolation."[9]

Though the preoccupations of neoclassical critics with ideal form
—the principles of the genres, the "rules of Aristotle, the unities,
the structure of the plot—may seem obsessive, they are not, on the
whole, irrelevant; for they are an outgrowth of Renaissance critical
attitudes that influenced the composition of *Paradise Lost*. Despite
their diversity and their occasional tendency toward polemical
distortion, these commentators still offer suggestive insights into
the technical problems that confronted the poet in structuring his

fable. They become misleading when they insist too emphatically and too narrowly (like Addison and Dennis) on the poem's regularity or irregularity, its conformity with or violation of the rules. Though the principles of Renaissance and neoclassical poetics no longer possess intrinsic authority, the degree to which the poet observed, neglected, or even inverted them may help to elucidate his intent and to clarify the formal structure he imposed on his materials.

In adapting the argument of his intended tragedy to a narrative instead of a dramatic mode, Milton elaborated his plot through such conventional epic devices as divine and infernal councils, voyages from heaven or hell, and retrospective or prospective episodes; but he did not radically alter the basic design of his tragic plot. The epic concludes, like the abortive drama, with Adam's expulsion from paradise after a *consolatio* that mingles sorrow with joy, mitigating temporary defeat with the prospect of ultimate restoration and victory. The paradox of the fortunate fall, the *topos* of the *felix culpa*, is as integral to the tragic drama as to the tragic epic. In comparison with the epic fables of Homer, Vergil, and Tasso, *Paradise Lost* concludes "unfortunately" for the protagonist; and the reactions of neoclassical critics to this point reflect both the strength and the weakness of their methodology. In Dryden's opinion, the tragic ending compromised Milton's achievements as a heroic poet.[10] For Voltaire, it demonstrated the fallibility of the "pretended Rules"; Milton had proved, in defiance of critical precepts, that "a very good Poem" might end unfortunately for its hero.[11] Addison regarded the conclusion of *Paradise Lost* as an "imperfection" in Milton's plot, inasmuch as it conformed to a tragic rather than a heroic model. The pattern that Milton had followed—the kind of "implex fable" in which "the chief actor . . . falls from some eminent pitch of honour and prosperity, into misery and disgrace"—was "the most perfect" model for tragedy, but it was "not so proper for an heroic poem."[12]

In developing the tragic pattern inherent in his biblical argument, Milton brought the epic fable demonstrably closer to Aristotle's conception of the perfect tragic plot. But *Paradise Lost* also approaches the norms of tragedy in other respects: its strict regard for the unity of action, its close integration of episodes into the action of the fable, its exploitation of dramatic structure[13] and dramatic dialogue, and (so far as the central and crucial scenes are concerned) its economy of personages and incidents and its respect for the unities of place and time. Milton's technical mastery over both his form and his materials is nowhere more evident than in his reduction of events of universal significance to a comprehensive but nevertheless severely restricted design: the imitation of a single action, accomplished for the most part within comparatively narrow temporal and spatial boundaries. Within little more than a week, Satan has accomplished his enterprise and, within a period considerably shorter, drastically altered the destinies of mankind. The world has been lost within the boundaries of an enclosed pleasance.

These limitations were partly imposed on the poet by his subject matter—and Dryden was not alone in regarding them as blemishes. Formally, however, these potential obstacles to variety might encourage a stricter observation of the unities. Structurally, the fable of *Paradise Lost* seems to meet at least one of Aristotle's objections to the epic as inferior to tragedy: "In saying that there is less unity in an epic, I mean an epic made up of a plurality of actions, in the same way as the *Iliad* and the *Odyssey* have many such parts, each one of them in itself of some magnitude; yet the structure of the two Homeric poems is as perfect as can be, and the action in them is as nearly as possible one action."[14] In its treatment of time, place, and action—and in its cast of principal characters— *Paradise Lost* achieves a radical unity and a concentration that are more characteristic of the qualities Aristotle found in the best Greek tragedies than typical of epic poetry. In his opinion, the epic had "no fixed limit of time"—in sharp contrast to tragedy, which endeavored "as far as possible" to keep "within a single circuit of the sun, or something near that."[15]

Nevertheless, however closely the structure of Milton's fable seems to approximate that of tragedy, he does not confuse the genres; he adapts the tragic paradigm of epic structure. He seeks the characteristic "affects" of heroic poetry as well as those of tragedy; and he portrays man's seduction as an archetypal epic enterprise. Accommodating the venerable *topos* of spiritual combat to the formal structures of heroic poetry, he both maintains and subverts the traditional epic decorum. In his heroic poem, as in his projected drama on the fall, the tempter's role is essentially that of the *Malus Angelus* of the morality tradition; and in the context of an epic conflict, the principal agents in the conventional temptation ordeal acquire heightened stature as spiritual warriors. Intensifying the military imagery of his poem, Milton converts hell into an armed camp and invests the tempter himself with attributes of an epic hero, a prototype of all world conquerors and world destroyers. By thus dramatizing the spiritual conflict between divine and infernal agents in terms of the strategies and counterstrategies of warring kingdoms, Milton places the psychological combat in the garden firmly in the context of cosmic warfare, the continuing battle between God and Satan for world dominion and for sovereignty over the human soul. He frames his central action (the temptation of man) between the apocalyptic battle in heaven and the spiritual struggle between divine grace and Satan's vicegerents Sin and Death in the future history of the world.

The temptation of Eve (and of Adam through Eve) is the prototype of man's spiritual combats against the powers of darkness; and it concludes, significantly, with a decisive, albeit temporary, victory for the tempter. The conventional *Bonus Angelus* is significantly absent from the moral battlefield; Raphael has already delivered his admonition and made his exit on a sunbeam; Michael has yet to offer mingled warnings and consolations. Sufficient to stand or fall, the ancestors of mankind are to be tested in isolation, exercising their divinely given prerogative of voluntary decision. From their example their fallen posterity are to learn the vanity of human merits and the necessity for relying utterly on God: the meaning of Milton's biblical motto, "My strength is made perfect in weakness." In contrast to the ideal pattern of spiritual warfare, where the Christian warrior foils the devil and his wiles, Adam and Eve meet overwhelming defeat. The pattern Milton follows is closer to the ordeal of Faustus (a pattern that ends in damnation) than to that of the triumphant saint—yet this pattern too is altered through the regeneration of Adam and Eve and the humiliation of their victorious adversary. The reversals in Milton's epic fable, as in his dramatic plans, comprehend the sinner's repentance and pardon as well as his fall. The psychomachia at the center of the poem is deliberately placed in the larger context of a theomachia, a contest between rival divinities. The devil's victory over the first Adam is significantly framed by complementary episodes protraying Satan's defeat by the Son of God.

In the context of epic warfare, Satan's degradation after his return to Pandaemonium does not compromise the structural coherence, or indeed the probability, of the plot; it belongs clearly to the counteraction that one anticipates from the divine strategist, and it is directly linked with the sentence of judgment passed on the serpent in paradise. Up to this point, however, Satan has consistently maintained the stance of a traditional epic hero, conceiving and executing a program of world conquest, consigning viceregal authority to his satraps and returning in triumph to receive the expected applause. In a conventional temptation drama the initiative would normally belong to the tempter, regardless of his ultimate victory or defeat. In this epic, carefully centered on a temptation ordeal, the tempter assumes a role commonly associated with an epic hero; and, even though his heroism is specious, he carries, up to book 10, the greater burden of the plot. The central event in the poem follows, logically and all but inevitably, from the devil's own character and thought—his *ethos* and *dianoia*. His own moral decisions, his rhetorical arguments, his actions lead directly to the principal reversal in the fable, the fall and condemnation of man.

As a successful but vicious hero, Satan has justly been compared to the protagonist of Lucan's *Pharsalia*; driven by ambition, Caesar rebels against the authority of the Senate and precipitates the entire Roman state—virtually a cosmos in itself—into a disastrous civil war. In adapting his argument to an epic framework Milton represents Adam's lapse as a rebellion: "foul distrust, and breach / Disloyal on the part of Man, revolt, / And disobedience" (9.6–8); in instigating man's rebellion, the archrebel of the angelic revolt is still challenging divine sovereignty, still prosecuting (albeit more indirectly) the civil conflict begun in heaven. Like Caesar—and unlike Turnus, who likewise plunges Italy into internecine war— Satan is, in this instance, victorious; his enterprise terminates fortunately.[16]

Satan's role as tempter is (to be true) a licensed office—though here he is far less aware of the fact than in his temptation of Job. The threads of the action are placed safely in the hand of God; the fallen archangel, enslaved by his own desires, is in fact a puppet— albeit a very lively one. The divine strategy controls the actions of infernal and angelic powers alike, ruling the events of the plot by the iron scepter as well as by the golden. Milton successfully asserts eternal providence; and his narrative action appears (as Tasso had advised) to be providentially governed from beginning to end. In the fable of *Paradise Lost* the devil proposes; man chooses; deity disposes.

Structurally, however, there are significant differences between Milton's epic and those of his major predecessors in representing the execution of a divine decree in the epic action and in portraying the rivalry of "machining persons" favorable or hostile to the hero. In the epics of Homer, Vergil, and Tasso the supreme deity himself decrees the epic action. Zeus concedes the Trojans a temporary victory, in spite of strong opposition by Hera and Athene, in order to fulfill his oath to honor Achilles by discrediting the Greeks; subsequently he permits the hero (this time with Athene's aid) to win further glory by slaying the principal defender of Troy. At Athene's intercession Zeus decrees the *nostos* of Odysseus, whose homecoming has been delayed by Poseidon's anger. By Jove's decree and Venus's aid, Aeneas achieves a permanent settlement in Italy in spite of the continued hostility of Juno. In Tasso's *Gerusalemme Liberata*, God himself hastens the liberation of Jerusalem against the opposition of the powers of hell. In the majority of these poems, the burden of the delaying actions—the countermovements which prolong the execution of the providential design—belongs to gods or demons inimical to the hero.

In *Paradise Lost* the conventional pattern was untenable on theological grounds and by the nature of Milton's argument. The epic action—Adam's disobedience and loss of paradise—springs from infernal rather than divine providence. It is the result of man's volition at the devil's instigation, not the effect of a divine decree. Even though the event is foreseen and permitted by Providence, Adam and Eve transgress of their own free will; "they themselves decree'd / Thir own revolt, not I." The design, however, originates with Satan; and in the structure of Milton's fable the actions and counsels that help or hasten the crucial event in the poem belong to the devil himself, adversary of man and God. The delaying actions fall to the part of heaven, and heaven itself foresees that they will be unavailing.

Milton's plot is nonetheless an image of a providential design; for the divine government of the world comprehends both good and evil temptations and the actions of both good and evil instruments. Through a skillful organization of *kairoi* (occasions) man and angel and devil alike are offered a series of opportunities for rebellion or fealty. In comparison with the certainty of divine foresight, the infernal strategy appears myopic; for all its ingenuity, it remains tentative and groping, a sequence of brilliant improvisations. The method of Providence, though devious or seemingly contradictory, is clearly conceived from the start. The divine delays themselves emphasize the contrast between long-range and short-sighted vision, reinforcing theological *topoi* concerning the delay in the divine justice, the contrast between divine and human measures of time, the imperative of "waiting upon God."

In *Paradise Lost*, as in *Samson Agonistes* and *Comus*, plot may also serve as proof or testimony of providential guidance, a confirmation of faith through experience of the "event." Evoking doubts as well as hopes, expectations and counterexpectations, the fable moves darkly but inevitably toward its "close"—the moment of truth where all is seen as "best." Controlled by an uncontrollable intent, the events of the plot demonstrate the justice of the divine plan by which the universe is governed—a providential design that comprehends the activities of both good and evil agents and reconciles the logical and moral oppositions within the plot under a higher unity. The architecture of *Paradise Lost*, like the walls of Cusanus's paradise, is built of contraries.[17]

Logical structures are assimilated to the narrative design not only through the element of *dianoia* (the valid or specious reasoning of the dramatis personae themselves) but also, and primarily, through the poet's concern for probability in the construction of the plot—his emphasis on the causal relationships between character, thought, and action. Milton's assertion of eternal providence and his justification of God's ways to men depend, in large part, on an analysis of causality; and in delineating the pattern of cause and effect underlying Adam's fall and regeneration he relies heavily on distinctions between principal and auxiliary causes, contingency and necessity, to rationalize the verdicts passed on apostate men and angels:

> They trespass, Authors to themselves in all
> Both what they judge and what they choose; for so
> I form'd them free, and free they must remain,
> Till they enthrall themselves.
>
> [3.122–25]

The first sort by thir own suggestion fell,
Self-tempted, self-deprav'd: Man falls deceiv'd
By th' other first: Man therefore shall find grace,
The other none.

[3.129–32]

In the strictest sense, these passages pertain to *dianoia* and *ethos* (the "character" and "thought" of Aristotle's *Poetics*), but they subsequently become operative in the plot itself. Milton's fable is not only logically organized, it also serves the ends of logical demonstration and rhetorical persuasion. The poetic argument becomes, in effect, the vehicle of a logical argument.[18]

Despite the technical distinction between them, logical or rhetorical arguments normally reinforce the poetic argument, and vice versa. Allegories like the parentage and vicegerency of Sin and Death, or Satan's alliance with the powers of the abyss, may illustrate an argument drawn from systematic theology or moral philosophy. Raphael's account of the revolt of the angels functions as a dehortatory argument; like Satan's exhortations to Eve it belongs to deliberative rhetoric. Insofar as it involves praise or blame, it exploits the characteristic *topoi* of demonstrative rhetoric. Milton's endeavor to justify the ways of God inevitably entails arguments drawn from forensic rhetoric; though they occur primarily in the Father's own speeches, they recur in the reflections of Adam, Eve, and Satan himself on the justice or injustice of God.

In an epic centered on an act of moral decision, disjunctive structures—the alternatives of *either/or*—acquire major importance in the thought, and ultimately in the action, of the principal characters. Adam and Eve may stand *or* fall, obey *or* disobey, believe God *or* Satan. Fallen mankind may accept *or* reject grace, rely on their own strength and wisdom *or* on the strength and wisdom of God; they may either degenerate through their fallen nature *or* be regenerated by divine grace, bearing the image of either the old *or* the new Adam. The principle of conditional necessity, in turn, entails hypothetical reasoning. *If* Adam and Eve continue in obedience, they will continue to live, and they may in the course of time ascend to a higher, more spiritual state; *if* they disobey, they must die and return to dust. *If* they accept grace and repent, they will be saved; *if* they reject grace and remain obdurate, they are inevitably damned.

In Milton's fable, moreover, logical processes are operative in the very structure of the plot as well as in the reflections and speeches of the principal characters. The pattern of heroic conflict dramatizes the dialectical conflict between contrary ideas: love and hate, creation and destruction, regeneration and degeneration, liberty and servitude, true kingship and tyranny, good and evil. Adapting the logical principle—that the meaning of an idea appears more clearly through juxtaposition with its contrary—to the conventions of epic conflict, Milton imitates the concept in action, in dynamic relationship with other ideas. The fable depicts a conflict between universals as well as a personal struggle, a clash of archetypes as well as characters.

The events of the plot similarly emphasize distinctions between complementary rather than contradictory concepts (such as mercy and justice) or between the different meanings of a term (internal and external happiness or misery, internal and external bondage or freedom, secular and spiritual heroism). Or, again, the internal logic of the fable itself proposes and resolves traditional moral or theological paradoxes: strength in weakness, wisdom in folly, glory through shame, felicity through suffering, exaltation through humiliation, life through death, the fortunate fall.[19] Just as the parodic structures in the poem reinforce the dialectic of truth and illusion, operative throughout the plot, the paradoxes implicit in Milton's fable permit the action to proceed more or less simultaneously on at least four different metaphysical (and epistemological) levels—divine, angelic, demonic, and human—and to assume different meanings in proportion to the degree and mode of knowledge appropriate to each. (In actuality, of course, the scheme of cognitive levels is more complex; for the Father surpasses the Son in knowledge as Adam exceeds Eve, and Satan his infernal peers. Moloch and Belial and their companions differ in their ability to understand their predicament; and Sin is aware of facts that neither Satan nor Death has recognized.) These underlying paradoxes not only enhance the ironic element in the narrative, they also provide the occasion for Aristotelian recognitions and reversals, exposing apparent triumph as ultimate defeat and apparent strength and prudence as self-destructive and self-defeating. Finally, since they can be satisfactorily resolved only in the light of divine wisdom, they reinforce the poet's consistent emphasis on Providence.

This juxtaposition of different cognitive levels, or modes of knowledge, makes it possible for Milton to exploit diverse "affects" and literary modes, combining heroic and mock-heroic, tragic and comic elements without inconsistency. Satan, for instance, may be simultaneously absurd (as C. S. Lewis would express it) and sublime (in the idiom of some of his earlier critics). For the average reader, the victorious commander who receives hisses instead of applause after delivering his battle report seems ridiculous, while the same commander in defeat, exhorting his troops to continued warfare against an unconquerable foe, seems equally heroic. In the eyes of God, however, Satan and his rebel angels are clearly ridiculous from the very beginning of their revolt, long before their defeat and expulsion and even before the commencement of battle. Intellectually, we may acknowledge (with Lewis and Williams) the underlying absurdity in the devil's first speeches; but emotionally and aesthetically (for we too are fallen) we react to him as a heroic figure. Even though we recognize its falsity, the portrait strikes us as a heroic rather than a mock-heroic image—as Milton expected it to. Later, with the fuller development of the fable, we can recognize the heroic image for what it is, seeing the inherent absurdity that the deity had perceived from the beginning. By moving from one cognitive level to another, Milton can make his reader respond, affectively as well as intellectually, to the manifold variety of his archangel—a complexity that originates less in the character himself than in the varied perspectives from which he is seen.

Underlying the dialectical conflicts within the poem, the logical distinctions, and the paradoxes is the more fundamental distinction between appearance and reality, secular and divine standards of judgment. The primary struggle in this epic of spiritual combat is epistemological as well as moral; the warfare between good and evil is inextricably interwoven with that between truth and false-hood. Just as Raphael and Michael, Adam's angelic preceptors, mingle legitimate revelation with moral instruction, Satan baits his persuasions to disobedience (essentially a moral transgression) with an epistemological lure, the sweets of forbidden knowledge. The tension between the universal and infallible knowledge of the Creator and the partial and often fallible knowledge of the creature underlies the poetic as well as the logical structure of the plot. Milton's deity is not only the supreme power but also the supreme wisdom. His own judgment constitutes the norm of truth and the determinant of reality. In the epic plot and episodes he not only creates, destroys, and regenerates by his *logos,* his Word, but likewise passes judgment through his Word.

For the resolution of the conflict between truth and falsehood, it is essential that the latter be exposed, that intrinsic evil masquerading as good be stripped of its false pretensions. The sentence of judgment passed on man and the serpent in book 10—and dramatically applied to Satan later in the same book—is a victory of reality over illusion as well as a demonstration of divine justice. A decisive intrusion of divine wisdom into the formal structure of the narrative, it serves not only as rebuke but as rebuttal.

The turning point or hinge of Milton's narrative[20] is an act of moral decision; insofar as it delineates the causes and effects of Adam's sin, the fable itself functions as an ethical exemplum and hence as inductive proof. Although the search for a central theme has largely superseded the quest for a moral, these terms amount to very much the same thing; and it is still debatable whether the implications of Adam's example can be, or were ever intended to be, reduced to a single formula. On this point the neoclassical critics offered useful, but sometimes unreliable, suggestions.

Raphael relates the fall of the angels as a "terrible Example" portraying "the reward / Of disobedience": "firm they might have stood, / Yet fell; remember and fear to transgress" (6.910–12). From Michael's survey of the future history of mankind and the "example" of Christ, Adam similarly learns that it is "best" to love and obey God, to observe his providence and depend solely upon him, and that "suffering for Truths sake / Is fortitude to highest victorie" (12.569–70). Both of these episodes—the narratives of the divine historian and the blessed seer—serve as moral exempla; and Milton's early critics recognized their close relationship, both causal and thematic, with the themes and events of the main plot. Like the episodes, the fable of *Paradise Lost* functions as an ethical exemplum—and again several of the earlier commentators searched assiduously for a single moral. In the opinion of René Le Bossu, the first office of an epic poet was "to find a moral, which his fable is afterwards to illustrate and establish." Johnson observed that this seemed "to have been the process only of Milton; the moral of other poems is incidental and consequent; in Milton's only it is essential and intrinsick. His purpose was the most useful and the most arduous; *to vindicate the ways of God to man;* to shew the reasonableness of religion, and the necessity of obedience to the Divine Law."[21] Addison had been less successful in his search for a moral formula, acknowledging his inability to "find out the particular Moral which is inculcated in *Paradise Lost*." He could not agree with Bossu that "an Epic Writer first of all pitches upon a certain Moral, as the Ground-Work and Foundation of his Poem, and afterwards finds out a Story to it." Nevertheless he believed "that no just Heroic Poem ever was, or can be made from whence one great Moral may not be deduced." The moral of *Paradise Lost*, visibly apparent both in the principal fable and principal episode, was that "*Obedience to the Will of God makes Men happy, and that Disobedience makes the miserable.*" Besides this "great Moral, . . . the Soul of the Fable," moreover, an "Infinity of Under Morals" might be "drawn from the Several Parts of the Poem."[22]

In spite of their reservations concerning Bossu's epic theory, Johnson oversimplified Milton's method of composition and Addison oversimplified the moral inferences to be drawn from his fable.[23] The example of Adam's fall, as Milton portrays it, involves far more than a warning against disobedience.[24] His fallen condition makes it impossible for him or his posterity (including the poet and his readers) to avoid disobeying; yet it also provides the occasion for the operation of grace. A more significant inference to be drawn from the example of the first Adam is the imperative of relying not on one's own righteousness but on divine grace—on the merits of the second Adam and the righteousness of God.

This too is a simplification, however; the ethical and theological implications of Milton's fable—and those of its principal episodes—are too numerous, too complex, and too closely interwoven to be comprehended in a single formula. The poem offers us a unified fable, an image of a single action, which involves a wide variety of themes; it does not offer us (I think) an image of "one great moral" or the demonstration of one central thesis. Perhaps (as Addison remarked on another subject), to look for one is to seek for what Milton never intended.

Although certain dominant themes—the methods of divine providence, the conflict between Christ and Satan, the opposition between good and evil or creation and destruction—are operative throughout the poem, its moral and theological implications are usually progressive, incomplete, and complementary. Emerging from the narrative itself or the reflections of its characters, they illuminate different facets of the poem's moral structure, different aspects of the higher providential design. They become clearer as the narrative proceeds and the plot develops, and as their mutual interrelationships become apparent.

This is also true in the case of Milton's episodes and their thematic relationships with the main plot. The full implications of Raphael's narrative are apparent only in conjunction with that of Michael. It is more than an exemplum of the dire effects of disobedience, although the inferences that the angelic historian draws are both timely and legitimate. Like his admonition against the intemperate thirst for knowledge and his exhortation to contentment ("be lowly wise"), the moral he extracts from the fall of the angels is immediately and primarily relevant to the imminent fall of man; in Milton's theodicy both counsels serve to exonerate divine justice and to place the responsibility for his fall on man himself.

In the larger context of world history, as epitomized in Michael's survey, the themes of the earlier episode acquire additional and clearer significance. Abdiel's role is comparable to that of the "one just man" who recurs periodically in Old Testament history as a type of Christ; from this example, as well as from that of the Redeemer, Adam could have learned the higher fortitude of suffering in the cause of truth. The apocalyptic victory of the Messiah over the rebel angels before the creation of the world parallels the glory of his second advent, his final triumph over the forces of evil at the end of the world; at the same time it offers (to Adam's amazement) a striking contrast to the humility of the first advent, the messianic victory over Sin and Death through ignominy and suffering.

The pattern of destruction and creation[25]—both, significantly, through the *magnalia* of the Son of God—in Raphael's account recurs in the alternating rhythms of destruction and renovation, corruption and regeneration in Michael's prophecy and indeed in the main plot of *Paradise Lost*; like the destruction of the rebel angels and the creation of the world, both the judgment and the regeneration of fallen man are the office of the Son. The degeneration of the angelic nature in the course of the civil war reinforces the patterns of Satan's progressive degeneration in the epic fable and the corruption of human nature after the fall. Yet it also serves as a countertheme to Adam's regeneration, just as the permanent and irrevocable exile of the rebel angels provides a countertheme to the ultimate restoration of man. Milton emphasizes the parallel between the fall of the angels and the fall of man only to introduce a crucial distinction: Adam receives grace and repents, relying on divine mercy; Satan is denied grace and is progressively hardened.[26]

Though the episodes in *Paradise Lost* illuminate each other as well as the events in the fable, they do not always emphasize the same theme or "great moral." As exempla they provide counterthemes and complementary inferences as well as parallels. In a sense they create temporary paradigms, partial and incomplete models, for interpreting the central action in the poem; but these ad hoc patterns are to be gradually revised and corrected as the narrative proceeds. Raphael's narrative of divine and angelic history,[27] for instance, provides a frame of reference for interpreting Michael's more diffuse chronicle of human history as well as the more tightly structured action of the main plot; yet its full meaning emerges only when it is itself reinterpreted in their light.

"*Paradise Lost* is an Epic," acknowledged David Masson.[28] "But it is not, like the Iliad or the Aeneid, a national Epic; nor is it an epic after any other of the known types. It is an epic of the whole human species, an epic of our entire planet, or indeed of the entire astronomical universe." Neither its title nor its opening lines sufficiently indicate "the full nature and extent" of its theme. Even though the whole story bears on one point—man's disobedience and loss of Eden—"it is the vast comprehension of the story, both in space and in time, as leading to this point, that makes [*Paradise Lost*] unique among epics.... It is ... a poetical representation ... of the historical connection between Human Time and Aboriginal or Eternal Infinity, or between our created world and the immeasurable and inconceivable Universe of Pre-human Existence."

The relationship between Milton's poetic design and Renaissance conceptions of world design or world history has engaged numerous critics since Masson. Some of these, like Masson himself, have regarded these cosmic patterns primarily as the larger subject of the epic; they condition its matter rather than its form. Others have stressed the parallels (not uncommon in Renaissance criticism) between the creative art of God and man, and between the structure of nature and the structure of a painting or poem; for these critics, the universe serves not only as the content of Milton's epic, but, more significantly, as a model or paradigm for its structure.[29] Anterior to the order of nature, however, was the ideal model in the mind of the divine artist himself—the internal design subsequently realized in the external design of the natural world. The persistent question—Which of these designs provided the basis for the artist's own internal design or idea?—engaged Renaissance critics of the visual as well as the verbal arts; and this problem is indirectly relevant for Milton's representation of providential or cosmic designs.

As Panofsky points out, such analogies between the roles of divine and human craftsmen (*demiurgoi*) in impressing ideal forms upon matter, and between the archetypal forms in the mind of God and the ideas in the imagination of the poet or painter, were commonplaces in the artistic theory of the Renaissance. Although the majority of critics accepted the principle of ideal imitation, they differed as to the immediate origin of the idea the artist ought to imitate. Did he abstract a norm of beauty from the imperfect particulars of nature? or did he receive it by divine inspiration? What was the precise relationship of his own *disegno interno* to the internal and external designs of the Creator?

In critical debates on these issues Panofsky detected a persistent (though not always consistent) conflict between Aristotelian and Neoplatonic viewpoints. Federico Zuccari (he noted) proceeded from the Aristotelian "premise that that which is to be revealed in a work of art must first be present in the mind of the artist," to a distinction between internal and external design. The former (which "precedes execution and actually is completely independent of it") is possible only because the idea is itself a "spark of the divine mind" and thus enables the artist "to bring forth a new intelligible cosmos" and "to compete with Nature." Etymologizing this term as a divine sign and interpreting *disegno* as *segno di dio in noi*, Zuccari nonetheless differentiated it sharply from the divine design: "in forming this internal Design man is very different from God: God has one single Design, most perfect in substance, containing all things, which is not different from Him, because all that which is in God is God; man, however, forms within himself various designs corresponding to the different things he conceives."

Unlike the design of the divine artist, man's *disegno interno* was an accident and originated in the senses.

On the value of matter, as on the origin of the artist's idea, Renaissance theory was divided along Neoplatonic or Aristotelian lines. Whereas the Aristotelian Zuccari accepted matter as "a thoroughly suitable and unresistant substratum for both the divine and the human idea," Neoplatonic theorists despised matter as "a principle of ugliness and evil." Instead of abstracting the idea of the beautiful from the objects of nature, the Neoplatonic artist must endeavor to overcome the evil disposition of matter (*prava disposi- tione della materia*)—a disposition responsible for the errors and faults in natural phenomena—by creating in his own mind the ideal form intended by the divine Creator, "the *perfetta forma inten- zionale della natura*." The "beautiful in art" resulted not "from a mere synthesis of a scattered yet somehow 'given' multiplicity but from the intellectual grasp of an *eidos* that [could not] be found in reality at all."[30]

For Milton, despite his early interest in Neoplatonism and the occasional charges of Augustinian illuminism that have been advanced against him, there could be little question of directly imitating the ideas in the divine mind. The *Deus absconditus* remained hidden and remote except as he chose to manifest himself in his creation and in the Scriptures or through the inner guidance of the Spirit. Furthermore, there was no inherent depravity in matter, for it was essentially good and had proceeded incorruptible from God himself. Any "depraved disposition" resulted not from nature in its original state but from the fall. The world and its creatures had been created perfect, though neither static nor immutable; Adam and Eve were capable of ascending ultimately to a higher, more spiritual state through continued obedience or of falling through disobedience. The original creation corresponded to its maker's *disegno interno*, his "great Idea," but the poet was compelled to form his own ideas from created nature (the deity's "external design") or from revealed religion. For the book of nature, like the Scriptures themselves, was a manifestation of the Word.

Despite its "vast Design"—comprehending (as Marvell recog- nized) events and localities widely separated in space and time: "*Messiah* Crown'd, God's Reconcil'd Decree, / Rebelling Angels, the Forbidden Tree, / Heav'n, Hell, Earth, Chaos, All"—*Paradise*

Lost is not (strictly speaking) a poetic heterocosm, not a verbal model of the great universe. Although it is, in a sense, a cosmic epic, it is not essentially or primarily an *image* of the cosmos. It is first and foremost the imitation of a single action, structured according to the formal principles of the epic plot, and these principles radically condition the imitation of space and time. In one sense—by no means insignificant for many Renaissance theorists—it resembles the cosmos not simply through its comprehensiveness but paradoxically through its exclusiveness. It achieves formal unity and integrity, symmetry and proportion, inner coherence and order—aesthetic qualities that Renaissance Neoplatonists had extolled in the macrocosm, the art of deity—largely through a judicious regard for the unities. The action of the fable is restricted to one event—man's disobedience and his expulsion from paradise. The effective duration of the action is confined to a period slightly longer than a week. After the introductory councils in heaven and hell, the action is progressively narrowed and (with a few notable exceptions) firmly localized in the happy garden. Although the episodes include events occurring before the creation of the world or after its dissolution, Milton does not allow them to violate the strict unity of his fable. In introducing them, he follows—like Vergil and Tasso—an artificial rather than a natural order.

There is, indeed, a continuing, and deliberate, tension between the comparatively narrow limitations that Milton observes in structuring his principal action and the broader spatial and temporal range[31] he achieves in his episodes or (within the main plot itself) through a careful exploitation of proleptic and retrospective allusion. The poem comprehends (albeit sketchily) a survey and history of the world, but these occur largely outside the main action; they constitute neither the principal subject matter nor the basic pattern of his epic. The primary norm or schema of design is the rigidly conceived pattern of the epic plot—the "idea" of the epic that Milton had abstracted from the epic exemplars of antiquity and from neo-Aristotelian critical theory. The structure of *Paradise Lost* is not modeled on the larger spatial and temporal patterns of world history; it is fashioned after a paradigm of genre.

The comparatively narrow scope of the central action in the poem stands, moreover, in striking contrast to its universal implications.[32] A pilfered apple results in the destruction of a world. The misdemeanor of two individuals incurs a sentence of universal death. The apparent disproportion between the magnitude of the event and its effects, between the instrument and its results, is reinforced by the contrast between the scope of the plot and the scope of the episodes. The radically finite qualities of the main plot—severely limited in action, time, and place—stand in striking contrast to the vast spatial and temporal visions comprehended in the proleptic and retrospective episodes and in the initial scenes in hell and heaven.

The more narrow design of the plot invites comparison with the larger cosmic patterns, then, but it does not mirror them. It can portray them only by breaking them up and introducing the fragments as episodes. They enter the formal structure of the epic design not as intact structures but as broken designs. ("We see in part," Milton might have commented with Saint Paul, "and we prophesy in part.")

Milton's paradise (as many of his critics have recognized) is not merely a lost world, a primeval world; it is an archetypal world—filled (like Spenser's garden of Adonis) with the types and forms of species and exhibiting the radical simplicity and unity of the archetype. It is set apart from our own world not only by the fall, by our own alienation, but by its ideal character; its inhabitants are essentially the norms or ideal forms of natural species. Adam and Eve are our *general* parents; and their condemnation involves the entire human race, just as the curse pronounced on the serpent applies to an entire biological genus. Milton's emphasis is primarily on the universal rather than the particular; and his paradisal realm, for all its burgeoning exuberance and fecundity, is richer in its variety of types than of individuals. Insofar as it comprehends the prototypes of natural species and genera, it is inevitably distinct from (though intimately related to) the creatures of the outside world.

It is also set apart, however, from the greater cosmos and the chaos beyond it—the infinite expanse of space and time—by its finite character. In comparison with the magnitude of Milton's universe and his survey of universal history, paradise and the paradisal life itself seem scarcely more than a point in time and space. The epic's moral schema, in which an action so seemingly insignificant can precipitate universal ruin, enhances its remoteness from our own society and our fallen world. Finally, the plot itself—so severely restricted in characters and events, as in space and time—erects an invisible barrier between the secure confines of unfallen Eden and the "vast design" of Milton's cosmos. In comparison with the apparently limitless reaches of space and time suggested in the episodes and in the preliminary councils in heaven and hell, the fable of *Paradise Lost* is the wall of an enclosed garden.[33]

APPENDIXES

1 A Humanistic Epic
Milton's Debt to Italian Criticism

Among recent studies of Milton's major poetry, its structure, and its relations to epic and tragic tradition, the reader may consult the following books and articles. See also Calvin Huckabay, *John Milton: An Annotated Bibliography, 1929–1968*, rev. ed. (Pittsburgh and Louvain, 1970).

Adams, Robert M. "Contra Hartman: Possible and Impossible Structures of Miltonic Imagery." In *Seventeenth-Century Imagery: Essays on Uses of Figurative Language from Donne to Farquhar*, ed. Earl Miner (Berkeley, 1971), pp. 117–31.
Akagawa, Yutaka. "The Structure of *Paradise Lost*." *Studies in English Literature*, English Literary Society of Japan, 48 (1971): 17–29; 48 (1972): 186–87.
Allen, Don Cameron. *The Harmonious Vision: Studies in Milton's Poetry*. Baltimore, 1954.
Aryanpur, Manoocher. "*Paradise Lost* and the *Odyssey*." *TSLL* 9 (1967): 151–66.
Baker, Stewart Addison. "The Brief Epic: Studies in the Style and Structure of the Genre of *Paradise Regained*." Diss., Yale University, 1971.
Barker, Arthur E. "Structural and Doctrinal Pattern in Milton's Later Poems." In *Essays in English Literature from the Renaissance to the Victorian Age Presented to A.S.P. Woodhouse, 1964*, ed. Millar MacLure and F. W. Watt (Toronto, 1964), pp. 169–94.
———. "Structural Pattern in *Paradise Lost*." *PQ* 28 (1949): 16–30.
Benham, Allan R. "Things Unattempted Yet in Prose or Rime." *MLQ* 14 (1953): 314–47.

144   Appendixes

Blau, Sheridan D. "Milton's Salvational Aesthetic." *JR* 46 (1966): 282–95.
Blondel, Jacques. *Milton poète de la Bible dans le Paradise Perdu. Archives des lettres modernes,* nos. 21–211 (1959).
Bouchard, Donald F. *Milton: A Structural Reading.* London and Montreal, 1974.
Bowra, C. M. *From Virgil to Milton.* London, 1945.
Brand, C. P. *Torquato Tasso: A Study of the Poet and of His Contribution to English Literature.* Cambridge, 1965.
Broadribb, C. W. "Milton and Valerius Flaccus." *N & Q* 175 (1938): 399.
Burden, Dennis H. *The Logical Epic.* London, 1967.
Bush, Douglas. *The Renaissance and English Humanism.* Toronto, 1939.
———. "Virgil and Milton." *CJ* 47 (1952): 203–4.
Colie, Rosalie L. *The Resources of Kind: Genre-Theory in the Renaissance.* Berkeley, Los Angeles, London, 1973.
Condee, Ralph W. "The Formalized Openings of Milton's Epic Poems." *JEGP* 50 (1951): 502–8.
———. "Milton's Dialogue with the Epic: *Paradise Regained* and the Tradition." *YR* 49 (1970): pp. 357–75.
———. "Milton's Theories concerning Epic Poetry: Their Sources and Their Influence on *Paradise Lost.*" Diss., University of Illinois, 1949.
———. *Structure in Milton's Poetry: From the Foundation to the Pinnacles.* University Park: Pennsylvania State University Press, 1974.
Coolidge, John S. "Great Things and Small: The Virgilian Progression." *CL* 17 (1965): 1–23.
Cope, Jackson I. *The Metaphoric Structure of Paradise Lost.* Baltimore, 1962.
Daniells, Roy. *Milton, Mannerism and Baroque.* Toronto, 1963.
Delasanta, Rodney. *The Epic Voice,* De Proprietatibus Litterarum 2. The Hague, 1967.
Di Cesare, Mario A. "Advent'rous Stong: The Texture of Milton's Epic." In *Language and Style in Milton,* ed. Ronald David Emma and John T. Shawcross, pp. 1–29. New York, 1967.
———. "*Paradise Lost* and Epic Tradition." *Milton Studies* 1 (1969): 31–50.
———. *Vida's Christiad and Vergilian Epic.* New York, 1964.
Diekhoff, John S. "The General Education of a Poet: John Milton." *JGE* 14 (1962): 10–21.
Durling, Robert M. *The Figure of the Poet in Renaissance Epic.* Cambridge, Mass., 1965.
Durr, Robert A. "Dramatic Pattern in *Paradise Lost.*" *JAAC* 13 (1955): 520–26.
Eisig, K. T. "Moral Criteria in Renaissance Literary Criticism, with Special Reference to Milton." Master's thesis, University of London, 1952.
Eller, Hans-Peter M. "Light after Light Well Us'd: The Epic Conclusion of *Paradise Lost.*" Diss., University of New Mexico, 1973.
Evans, J. M., *Paradise Lost and the Genesis Tradition.* Oxford, 1968.
Ferry, Anne Davidson. *Milton's Epic Voice: The Narrator in Paradise Lost.* Cambridge, Mass., 1963.

Fisch, Harold. *Jerusalem and Albion: The Hebraic Factor in Seventeenth-Century Literature*. New York, 1964.

Fish, Stanley Eugene. "Discovery as Form in *Paradise Lost*." In *New Essays on Paradise Lost*, ed. Thomas Kranidas, pp. 1–14. Berkeley and Los Angeles, 1969.

———. *Surprised by Sin: The Reader in Paradise Lost*. London and New York, 1967.

Fixler, Michael. "Milton's Passionate Epic." *Milton Studies* 2 (1970): 167–92.

Fletcher, Harris Francis. "Milton's Homer." *JEGP* 38 (1939): 229–32.

Foerster, Donald M. "Homer, Milton, and the American Revolt against Epic Poetry: 1812–1860." *SP* 53 (1956): 75–100.

Ford, P. Jeffrey. "*Paradise Lost* and the Five-Act Epic." Diss., Columbia University, 1966.

Frank, Joseph. "The Unharmonious Vision: Milton as a Baroque Artist." *CLS* 3 (1966): 95–108.

Frye, Roland Mushat. *God, Man, and Satan: Patterns of Christian Thought and Life in Paradise Lost, Pilgrim's Progress, and the Great Theologians*. Princeton, 1960.

Giamatti, A. Bartlett. *The Earthly Paradise and the Renaissance Epic*. Princeton, 1966.

———. "Milton and Fairfax's Tasso." *RLC* 40 (1966): 613–15.

Gilbert, Allan H. "A Parallel between Milton and Boiardo." *Italica* 20 (1943): 132–34.

———. "The Qualities of the Renaissance Epic." *SAQ* 53 (1954): 372–78.

Goode, James. "Milton and Longinus." *TLS* 21 (August 1930): 668.

Gossman, Ann. "The Ring Pattern: Image, Structure, and Theme in *Paradise Lost*." *SP* 68 (1971): 326–39.

Gransden, K. W. "*Paradise Lost* and the *Aeneid*." *EIC* 17 (1967): 281–303.

Gray, J. C. "Emptiness and Fulfillment as Structural Pattern in *Paradise Lost*." *Dalhousie Review* 53 (1973): 78–91.

Greco, Francis G. "Torquato Tasso's Theory of the Epic and Its Influence on Edmund Spenser's *Faerie Queene*." Diss., Duquesne University, 1969.

Greene, Thomas M. *The Descent from Heaven: A Study in Epic Continuity*. New Haven, 1963.

Grose, Christopher Waldo. *Milton's Epic Process: Paradise Lost and Its Miltonic Background*. New Haven and London, 1973, pp. 188–233.

———. "Some Uses of Sensuous Immediacy in *Paradise Lost*." *HLQ* 31 (1968): 211–22.

Gurteen, S. H. V. *The Epic of the Fall of Man*. New York, 1964.

Guss, Donald L. "A Brief Epic: *Paradise Regained*." *SP* 68 (1971): 233–43.

Hägin, Peter. *The Epic Hero and the Decline of Heroic Poetry: A Study of the Neoclassical English Epic with Special Reference to Milton's Paradise Lost*. Bern, 1964.

Hagenbüchle, Roland. *Sündenfall und Wahlfreiheit in Miltons Paradise Lost*. Bern, 1967.

Hamburger, Michael. "The Sublime Art: Notes on Milton and Hölderlin." In *The Living Milton*, ed. Frank Kermode, pp. 141–61, (London, 1960).

Harding, Davis P. *The Club of Hercules: Studies in the Classical Background of Paradise Lost.* Urbana, Ill., 1962.

———. *Milton and the Renaissance Ovid.* Urbana, Ill., 1946.

Hardison, O. B., Jr. *The Enduring Monument: A Study of the Idea of Praise in Renaissance Literary Theory and Practice.* Chapel Hill, N. C., 1962.

Herrick, Marvin T. *The Fusion of Horatian and Aristotelian Literary Criticism, 1531-1555.* Urbana, Ill., 1946.

Hughes, Merritt Y. *Ten Perspectives on Milton.* New Haven and London, 1965.

Huntley, John F. "The Educational, Theological, and Literary Principles of Milton's Poetic Art." Diss., University of Chicago, 1961.

Jonas, Leah. *The Divine Science: The Aesthetic of Some Representative Seventeenth-Century English Poets.* New York, 1940.

Kermode, Frank, ed. *The Living Milton: Essays by Various Hands.* London, 1960; New York, 1961.

Kirkconnell, Watson. *The Celestial Cycle.* Toronto, 1952.

Kranidas, Thomas. *The Fierce Equation: A Study of Milton's Decorum.* The Hague, 1965.

Krieger, Murray. "Jacopo Mazzoni, Repository of Diverse Traditions or Source of a New One?" In *Medieval Epic to the "Epic Theater" of Brecht,* ed. Rosario P. Armato and John M. Spalek, pp. 97–107. Los Angeles, 1968.

Kurth, Burton O. *Milton and Christian Heroism: Biblical Epic Themes and Forms in Seventeenth Century England.* Berkeley, 1959.

Langdon, Ida. *Milton's Theory of Poetry and Fine Art.* New Haven, 1924.

Lewalski, Barbara K. *Milton's Brief Epic: The Genre, Meaning, and Art of Paradise Regained.* Providence, R.I., and London, 1966.

———. "*Paradise Lost* 'Introduced' and 'Structured in Space.'" *MP* 66 (1963): 122–26.

———. "Structure and the Symbolism of Vision in Michael's Prophecy, *Paradise Lost,* Books XI–XII." *PQ* 42 (1963): 25–35.

Low, Anthony. *The Blaze of Noon: A Reading of Samson Agonistes.* New York and London, 1974.

McAdams, James R. "Milton's Epic Synthesis: A Study of the Association of *Paradise Lost* and *Paradise Regained.*" Diss., New York University, 1970.

MacCaffrey, Isabel Gamble. "Structural Patterns in *Paradise Lost,*" in *Paradise Lost as Myth.* Cambridge, Mass., 1959.

McColley, Grant. "The Epic Catalogue of *Paradise Lost.*" *ELH* 4 (1937): 180–91.

———. *Paradise Lost: An Account of Its Growth and Major Origins.* Chicago, 1940.

Mackinnon, Malcolm H. M. "Milton's Theory and Practice of the Epic, Examined in Relation to Italian Renaissance Literary Criticism." Diss., University of Toronto, 1948.

McNamee, Maurice B., S.J. *Honor and the Epic Hero.* New York, 1960.

Miller, Milton, "*Paradise Lost:* The Double Standard." *UTQ* 20 (1951): 183–99.

Mills, Ralph Delano. "The Logic of Milton's Narrative of the Fall: A Reconsideration." Diss., Ohio State University, 1966.

Moag, Joseph Stewart. "Traditional Patterns of Dialogue and Debate in Milton's Poetry." Diss., Northwestern University, 1964.

Morrison, Nan Dansby. "Principles of Structure in *Paradise Lost*." Diss., University of South Carolina, 1967.

Mueller, Martin E. "*Pathos* and *Katharsis* in *Samson Agonistes*." *ELH* 31 (1964): 156–74.

———. "Sixteenth-Century Italian Criticism and Milton's Theory of Catharsis." *SEL* 6 (1966): 139–50.

———. "The Tragic Epic: *Paradise Lost* and the *Iliad*." Diss., Indiana University, 1966.

Myhr, Ivar Lou. "The Evolution and Practice of Milton's Epic Theory." Diss., Vanderbilt University, 1940.

O'Brien, Gordon W. *Renaissance Poetics and the Problem of Power.* Chicago, 1956.

Ogden, H. S. V. "The Principles of Variety and Contrast in Seventeenth Century Aesthetics, and Milton's Poetry." *JHI* 10 (1949): 159–82.

Osgood, Charles Grosvenor. *The Tradition of Virgil.* Princeton, 1930.

Parker, William Riley. *Milton's Debt to Greek Tragedy in Samson Agonistes.* Baltimore and London, 1937.

Patrides, C. A. *Milton and the Christian Tradition.* Oxford, 1966.

Patrides, C. A., ed. *Approaches to Paradise Lost.* York Tercentenary Lectures. London, 1968.

———. *Milton's Epic Poetry: Essays on Paradise Lost and Paradise Regained.* Harmondsworth, Middlesex, 1967.

Prince, F. T. *The Italian Element in Milton's Verse.* Oxford, 1954.

Pujals, Estaban. "Estructura y concepto de *El Paraíso perdido* de Milton." *Atlántida* 5 (1967): 209–19.

Rajan, Balachandra. "Paradise Lost and the Balance of Structures." *UTQ* 41 (1972): 219–26.

———. *Paradise Lost and the Seventeenth Century Reader.* London, 1947.

———. "Simple, Sensuous, and Passionate." *RES* 21 (1945): 289–301.

Rees, Brinley. *Aristotle's Theory and Milton's Practice: Samson Agonistes.* Birmingham, 1971.

———. "'Pathos' in the Poetics of Aristotle." *Greece and Rome* 19 (1972): 1–11.

Reesing, John. *Milton's Poetic Art: A Mask, Lycidas, and Paradise Lost.* Cambridge, Mass., and London, 1968.

Richardson, Janette. "Virgil and Milton Once Again." *CL* 14 (1962): 321–31.

Ricks, Christopher. *Milton's Grand Style.* Oxford, 1963.

Robertson, D. S. "The *Odyssey* and *Paradise Lost*." *TLS* 4 (May 1940): 219, 221.

Rose, Patricia A. "Essentials of Epic Poetry: A Comparative Study of the *Iliad*, the *Chanson de Roland*, and *Paradise Lost*." Master's thesis, Florida State University, 1955.

Rosenblatt, Jason P. "Structural Unity and Temporal Concordance: The War in Heaven in Paradise Lost." *PMLA* 87 (1972): 31–41.

Ross, Malcolm M. *Poetry and Dogma.* New Brunswick, 1954.

Ryken, Leland. "Milton and the Apocalyptic." *HLQ* 31 (1968): 223–38.

Sackton, Alexander H. "Architectonic Structure in *Paradise Regained.*" *UTSE* 33 (1954): 33–45.

Samuel, Irene. *Dante and Milton: The Commedia and Paradise Lost.* Ithaca, N.Y., 1966.

———. "*Paradise Lost* as Mimesis." In *Approaches to Paradise Lost,* ed. C. A. Patrides, pp. 15–29. London, 1968.

———. "*Samson Agonistes* as Tragedy." In *Calm of Mind: Tercentenary Essays on Paradise Regained and Samson Agonistes in Honor of John S. Diekhoff,* ed. Joseph A. Wittreich, Jr., pp. 235–57. Cleveland and London, 1971.

Samuels, Charles Thomas. "The Tragic Vision of *Paradise Lost.*" *University of Kansas City Review* 27 (1960): 65–78.

Sasek, Lawrence A. "Satan and the Epic Hero: Classical and Christian Tradition." Diss., Harvard University, 1953.

Schirmer, W. F. "Die epische Dichtung und John Milton." In *Geschichte der englischen Literatur von den Anfängen bis zur Gegenwart,* pp. 332–41. Halle, 1937.

———. "Das Problem des religiösen Epos im 17. Jahrhundert in England." *Deutsche Vierteljahrschrift* 14 (1936): 60–74.

Scott, William O. "Ramism and Milton's Concept of Poetic Fancy." *PQ* 42 (1963): 183–89.

Seaman, John Eugene. "The Chivalric Cast of Milton's Epic Hero." *ES* 49 (1968): 97–107.

———. "The Epic Art of *Paradise Lost.*" Diss., Stanford University, 1962.

———. "Homeric Parody at the Gates of Milton's Hell." *MLR* 62 (1967): 212–13.

Sedelow, Sally Yeates. "The Narrative Method of *Paradise Lost.*" Diss., Bryn Mawr College, 1960.

Sellin, Paul R. "Milton and Heinsius: Theoretical Homogeneity." In *Medieval Epic to the "Epic Theater" of Brecht,* ed. Rosario P. Armato and John M. Spalek, pp. 125–34. Los Angeles, 1968.

———. "Sources of Milton's Catharsis: A Reconsideration." *JEGP* 60 (1961), pp. 712–30.

Shaw, William. "Milton's Choice of the Epic for *Paradise Lost.*" *ELN* 12 (1974): 15–20.

Shawcross, John T. "The Balanced Structure of *Paradise Lost.*" *SP* 62 (1965): 696–718.

———. "Irony and Tragic Effect: *Samson Agonistes* and the Tragedy of Hope." In *Calm of Mind,* ed. Joseph Anthony Wittreich, Jr., pp. 289–306. Cleveland and London, 1971.

———. "The Son in His Ascendance: A Reading of *Paradise Lost.*" *MLQ* 27 (1966): 388–401.

———. "The Style and Genre of *Paradise Lost.*" In *New Essays on Paradise Lost,* ed. Thomas Kranidas, pp. 15–33. Berkeley, Los Angeles, and London, 1971.

Shumaker, Wayne. "*Paradise Lost* and the Italian Epic Tradition." In

149   Appendixes

Th' Upright Heart and Pure, ed. Amadeus P. Fiore, O.F.M. Pittsburgh, 1967, pp. 87–100.

Sims, James H. "Camoens' *Lusiads* and Milton's *Paradise Lost*: Satan's Voyage to Eden." In *Papers on Milton,* ed. Philip M. Griffith and Lester F. Zimmerman, pp. 36–46. Tulsa, Okla., 1969.

Sirluck, Ernest. *Paradise Lost: A Deliberate Epic.* Cambridge, 1967.

Spencer, T. J. B. "Longinus in English Criticism: Influences before Milton." *RES,* n.s., 8 (1957): 137–43.

–––. "*Paradise Lost:* The Anti-Epic." In *Approaches to Paradise Lost,* ed. C. A. Patrides, pp. 81–98. London, 1968.

Stein, Arnold. *Answerable Style.* Minneapolis, 1953.

–––. *Heroic Knowledge: An Interpretation of Paradise Regained and Samson Agonistes.* Minneapolis, 1957.

Summers, Joseph H. *The Muse's Method.* Cambridge, Mass., and London, 1962.

Swedenberg, H. T., Jr. *The Theory of the Epic in England, 1650–1800.* Berkeley, 1944.

Tasso, Torquato. *Discourses on the Heroic Poem,* trans. with notes by Mariella Cavalchini and Irene Samuel. Oxford, 1973.

Tayler, E. W. "Milton's *Samson:* The Form of Christian Tragedy." *ELR* 3 (1973): 306–21.

Tchakirides, John P. "Epic Prolepsis and Repetition as Structural Devices in Milton's *Paradise Lost.*" Diss., Yale University, 1968.

Thompson, Elbert N. S. *Essays on Milton.* New York, 1967.

Thompson, J. A. K. *Classical Influences on English Poetry.* London, 1951.

Tillyard, E. M. W. *The English Epic and Its Background.* New York, 1954.

Tyson, John Patrick. "The Elements of Aristotelian Tragedy in *Paradise Lost.*" Diss., Tulane University, 1967.

Ulreich, John C., Jr. "The Typological Structure of Milton's Imagery." *Milton Studies* 5 (1973): 67–85.

Waddington, Raymond B. "Melancholy against Melancholy: *Samson Agonistes* as Renaissance Tragedy." In *Calm of Mind,* ed. Joseph Anthony Wittreich, Jr., pp. 259–87. Cleveland and London, 1971.

Watson, J. R. "Divine Providence and the Structure of *Paradise Lost.*" *English Institute Essays* 14 (1964): 148–55.

Weber, Burton Jasper. *The Construction of Paradise Lost.* Carbondale and Edwardsville, Ill.; London and Amsterdam, 1972.

–––. "The Schematic Structure of *Paradise Regained:* A Hypothesis." *PQ* 50 (1971): 553–56.

Whaler, James. *Counterpoint and Symbol.* Copenhagen, 1956.

Whiting, George W. *Milton's Literary Milieu.* Chapel Hill, N.C., 1939.

Williams, Ralph C. *The Theory of the Heroic Epic in Italian Criticism of the Sixteenth Century.* Baltimore, 1917.

Williamson, George. "The Education of Adam." *MP* 61 (1963): 96–109.

–––. *Milton and Others.* Chicago and London, 1965.

Winkler, Hertha. "Das biblisch-religiöse Epos des 17. Jahrhunderts bis zu Miltons *Paradise Lost.*" Diss., Vienna, 1949.

Wittreich, Joseph Anthony, Jr. "'A Poet amongst Poets': Milton and the

Tradition of Prophecy." In *Milton and the Line of Vision*, ed. Joseph Anthony Wittreich, Jr., pp. 97–142. Madison, Wisc., and London, 1975.
———, ed. *The Romantics on Milton*. Cleveland, 1970.
Woodhouse, A. S. P. "Pattern in *Paradise Lost*." *UTQ* 22 (1953): 109–27.
———. "Theme and Pattern in *Paradise Regained*." *UTQ* 25 (1956): 167–82.
———. "Tragic Effect in *Samson Agonistes*." *UTQ* 28 (1959): 205–22.
Yoo, Yeong. *A Study of the Miltonic Epic: Its Poetic Structures from Aesthetic Point of View*. Seoul, Korea, 1968.
Zimmermann, Edward J. "'Light out of Darkness': A Study of the Growth and Structure of Evil in Milton's *Paradise Lost*." Diss., SUNY Buffalo, 1971.

2   Modal Variation in Paradise Lost

In examining Milton's exploitation of pastoral motifs in *Paradise Lost*, Professor Empson[1] has justly emphasized the close associations of the pastoral tradition with the state of innocence. In a more detailed study Professor Knott[2] has reexamined the problem against the background of other epic versions of the pastoral, noting the contrast between the banquet scenes in heaven and in the earthly paradise, and stressing Milton's observance of decorum in his representations of nature and art and in his descriptions of the amenities of Eden, the glory of heaven, and the splendors of Pandaemonium. Knott has also noted the fusion of pastoral and epic traditions in Alexandrian romances (for both Scaliger and Sidney regarded Heliodorus's *Aethiopica* as a model prose epic) and in Sidney's *Arcadia* (a pastoral epic that was also conceived as a heroic poem). Though pastoral elements play a minor, but significant role, in the romantic epics of Ariosto and Spenser, they become more prominent in many of the prose romances and romance epics of the late sixteenth and seventeenth centuries. Professor Giamatti[3] has placed Milton's "happy Garden" in the context of the literary traditions associated with the *locus amoenus* and the gardens of classical myth and Renaissance epic—the Elysian fields, the garden of Alcinous, the garden of the Hesperides, the vegetarian simplicity of the Golden Age, the allegorical gardens of medieval or Renaissance dreamvisions, epic, and romance. Professor D. W. Robertson, Jr.,[4] has explored the medieval traditions associated with the symbolic gardens of Genesis and the Song of Songs. Professor Harry Levin[5] has investigated the literary traditions concerning the Golden Age

1. Empson, pp. 38–39.
2. Knott, *Milton's Pastoral Vision*.
3. A. Bartlett Giamatti, *The Earthly Paradise and the Renaissance Epic* (Princeton, 1966).
4. D. W. Robertson, Jr., *A Preface to Chaucer* (Princeton, 1962).
5. Harry Levin, *The Myth of the Golden Age in the Renaissance* (Bloomington, Ind., 1969).

and the earthly paradise. Professor Stanley Stewart[6] has traced the tradition of the *hortus conclusus* of the Song of Songs in the enclosed gardens of seventeenth-century English poetry. Recent criticism has stressed the symbolic associations of the garden with the contemplative life—the delights of college and cloister, the pleasures of studious leisure and retired meditation—as well as the close association between the wilderness and the temptation ordeal. The solitudes that encourage reflection may also offer occasion for moral trial; and it is in the wilderness that Hercules and Paris, and the protagonists of *Comus, Paradise Lost*, and *Paradise Regained* are exposed to temptation, tried and tested in moral isolation at a spiritual crossroads in an act of *proairesis*.[7]

For the temptation of the shepherd Paris, confronted with a choice between the active, contemplative, and voluptuous lives, see Hallett Smith, *Elizabethan Poetry* (Ann Arbor, 1968), pp. 4–8. For the associations of the pastoral life with the "ideal of the mean estate, content, and *otium*," with the pleasures of love and contemplation, with the life of the Golden Age, and with freedom from the greed and ambition (the "aspiring mind") of princes and courtiers, see pp. 8–18. Observing that the poetic tragedies of the *Mirror for Magistrates* "supported, negatively, the same ideal celebrated by pastoral," Professor Smith notes that the tragic warning in these tales occasionally "concludes with a direct endorsement of the quiet life of content." The pastoral or "satyric" setting of the earthly paradise in Milton's epic is, accordingly, highly appropriate not only for evoking the myth of the Golden Age but also for emphasizing the ideals of content, simplicity and spotless innocence, and freedom from the contagion of ambition and greed—the vices conducive to the tragedy of man as to the tragedy of Satan. In book 4 Milton has shifted his setting from the regal pomp of the *scena tragica* to the sylvan peace of the *scena satyrica*. Introducing the devil into the earthly paradise, he has juxtaposed the tragic (and pseudoheroic) with the pastoral mode, accentuating the contrast between ambition and content, the aspiring and the quiet mind. As elsewhere in the epic, he has utilized contrasting literary modes to emphasize contrasts in *ethos* (character or "moral purpose") and bring ethical concepts into sharper definition and focus through dramatic opposition with their logical contraries.

See Vitruvius, *The Ten Books on Architecture*, trans. Morris Hicky Morgan (New York, 1960), p. 150; "There are three kinds of scenes, one called the tragic, second, the comic, third, the satyric. Their decorations are different and unlike each other in scheme. Tragic scenes are delineated with columns, pediments, statues, and other objects suited to kings; comic scenes exhibit private dwellings, with balconies and views representing rows of windows, after the manner of ordinary dwellings; satyric scenes are decorated with trees, caverns, mountains, and other rustic objects

6. Stanley Stewart, *The Enclosed Garden: The Tradition and the Image in Seventeenth-Century Poetry* (Madison, Wisc., 1966).
7. See Erwin Panofsky, *Hercules am Scheidewege* (Leipzig and Berlin, 1930).

delineated in landscape style." Cf. Vitruvius's remarks on fresco paintings in atriums, peristyles, and other apartments (pp. 210–11): "the ancients required realistic pictures of real things," for a picture is "a representation of a thing which really exists or which can exist: for example, a man, a house, a ship, or anything else from whose definite and actual structure copies resembling it can be taken." In their open rooms the ancients "depicted the facades of scenes in the tragic, comic, or satyric style; and their walks, on account of the great length, they decorated with a variety of landscapes, copying the characteristics of definite spots. In these paintings there are harbours, promontories, seashores, rivers, fountains, straits, fanes, groves, mountains, flocks, shepherds; in some places there are also pictures designed in the grand style, with figures of the gods or detailed mythological episodes, or the battles at Troy, or the wanderings of Ulysses, with landscape backgrounds, and other subjects reproduced on similar principles from real life." Deploring the corruption of taste in his own day, Vitruvius complains that "those subjects which were copied from actual realities" are despised in favor of "fresco paintings of monstrosities, rather than truthful representations of definite things"; the moderns prefer paintings of things that "do not exist and cannot exist and never have existed."

According to the Vitruvian schema, Milton's description of Pandae-monium would belong properly to the *scena tragica* and his description of the earthly paradise to the *scena satyrica*. Vitruvius's emphasis on "realistic pictures of real things" accords with the stress that neo-Aristotelian and neo-Horatian literary theory placed on verisimilitude. Neoclassical theories of painting and poetry would thus tend to reinforce one another. Vitruvius's preference for variety in landscape is paralleled in Renaissance literary and artistic criticism as well as in *Paradise Lost*. His criticism of the monstrous, fantastic, and unrealistic in art is analogous to the objections that neoclassical theorists raised against the artistic styles or modes we would designate as mannerist or baroque; but it also resembles the objections that Renaissance literary critics leveled against the improbable marvels of romance. In *Paradise Lost* the monstrous and fantastic—including the hybrid figures that Horace and Vitruvius dislike—are usually associated specifically with hell, the realm of illusion and depraved nature.

For Cinthio's conception of the satyric setting and for the influence of Vitruvius, see Marvin T. Herrick, *Tragicomedy* (Urbana, Ill., 1962), pp. 11, 169–70; for the Renaissance association between the satyr play and the pastoral, see ibid., passim.

The "happy Garden" had traditionally been interpreted as a type of the Church; and Milton reinforces this analogy with an allusion to the sheepfold of Saint John's Gospel. In leaping over the wall of paradise, Satan combines heroic and biblical decorum; his action is reminiscent of the romantic hero Rodomonte as well as the thief of the biblical parable. As the work of God and nature, the garden of Eden is the archetype of the artificial pleasure-gardens of the fallen world—the gardens of amorous mirth and sensual delight conventional in medieval and Renaissance romance—as well as the meditative retreats of sages and holy men. These are, in a sense, pallid imitations or perverse abuses of the original *hortus deliciarum*, imitating it imperfectly, as art imitates nature. Framed for man's "delightful use," it embodies, moreover, the dual principles of the Horatian aesthetic of joining *utile* and *dulce*, utility and the sweetness of pleasure. It reflects a natural and unfallen poesis, which the artists of the fallen world must endeavor to follow, painfully and imperfectly, in their art.

In its natural arrangement (avoiding the beds and "curious Knots" of "nice Art"), its "various view," its "rural mound," the "mazy error" (or *figura serpentina*) of its brooks, Milton's "happy rural seat" may also (as critics have suggested) reflect Italian tastes in landscape gardening and the preference for natural scenery expressed in Sannazaro's *Arcadia*.

On landscape in *Paradise Lost*, see John R. Knott, Jr., "Symbolic Landscape in *Paradise Lost*," in *Milton Studies* 2 (1970): 37–58; Roy Daniells, "A Happy Rural Seat of Various View," in *Paradise Lost: A Tercentenary Tribute*, ed. Balachandra Rajan (Toronto, 1969), pp. 3–17; J. M. Newton, "A Speculation about Landscape," *CQ* 4 (1969): 273–82. For pastoral in landscape and its associations with naturalness in contrast with art, with simplicity in contrast with ornament, and with the "humble" style, see E. H. Gombrich, *Art and Illusion*, 2d ed. rev. (Princeton, 1961), pp. 378–80; Peter V. Marinelli, *Pastoral* (New York and London, 1971); Emilia Buchwald, "The Earthly Paradise and the Ideal Landscape" (diss., University of Chicago, 1971); Joseph E. Duncan, *Milton's Earthly Paradise* (Minneapolis, 1972).

3   "Those Notes to Tragic"
Epic Fable and the Tragic Illustrious

Paul Sellin has plausibly argued the case for Heinsius's influence on Milton's conception on tragedy. Noting the "theoretical as well as practical influence" of the *De tragoediae constitutione* on seventeenth-century poets and critics—Grotius and Vondel, Opitz and Gryphius, Cats and Revius, Racine and Chapelain and Balzac, Jonson and Dryden—he suggests that Milton's preface to *Samson Agonistes* shows "close theoretical affinity with Heinsius" and that Milton was probably "familiar with the treatise"; see Daniel Heinsius, *On Plot in Tragedy*, trans. Paul R. Sellin and John J. McManmon (Northridge, Calif., 1971), pp. xiv–xv (cited hereafter as Sellin). Just as Milton regards the Greek tragedies as the best "rule" for tragic composition, Heinsius argues that the poet's liberty is not "necessarily confined to those restrictions of philosophy that grammarians prescribe, especially since the best tragic poets antedated precept" (p. 7). In Heinsius's treatise Milton would have found a defense of tragic arguments derived from biblical history (p. 32), a discussion of personifications as dramatis personae (p. 134), and an allusion to the *Christus Patiens*, commonly though erroneously attributed to Nazianzen (p. 130). These were, of course, commonplaces of Renaissance critical theory, and Milton would have encountered them elsewhere. They are interesting, however, as analogues for his own views as reflected in the preface to *Samson*, in *Paradise Lost*, and in his dramatic plans. Also significant for Milton's own art, both in epic and in tragedy, were principles that he would have learned from Aristotle and the Italian commentators but that had also been given lucid and emphatic expression by the Dutch critic: the imitation of "human felicity and adversity" as the "end of tragedy"; the stress on "verisimilar construction and molding of the entire action" (p. 20); the insistence that "the tragic emotions and passions . . . have to come from the very imitation of the action" and that the "end of the tragic poet . . . is not the imitation of manners, but of the actions which those manners derive from" (p. 21).

In Heinsius's work Milton would also have encountered a defense of Lucan's *Pharsalia* as a "complex tragedy" containing "a great and extraordinary peripety" in which "the head of the world suffers beheading," losing life and station and the dignity of burial (p. 127). Heinsius is alluding, of course, to Pompey, the defeated hero of Lucan's epic. The point is interesting not only because *Paradise Lost* is also a complex tragedy in which the "head of the world" is defeated, losing his high station and his immortality, but also (and primarily) because the role of Caesar as victorious conqueror, ambitious destroyer, and heroic villain in the civil wars has frequently been compared with that of Satan in Milton's epic. Moreover, Heinsius's discussion of Sophocles' *Ajax* and Seneca's *Hercules Furens*—emphasizing Ajax's impatience of scorn, his "rage and fury," his shame and suicide, his elevation of soul as "a hero full of rage and magnanimity," and Hercules' unfulfilled threats of suicide (pp. 30–31, 34–35) are not irrelevant to *Samson Agonistes*. The Pythagorean conception of catharsis as a purgation preliminary to the contemplative life "which most closely approximates immortal God" is as relevant to the purification motif in *Comus* as the Aristotelian conception of moderating and tempering the passions through reason is to the concept of catharsis and the motif of purification through trial (recently examined by Professor Gossman) in *Samson* (pp. 11–12).

If Milton was familiar with Heinsius's treatise (as Professor Sellin has argued), he would have found in this work a defense of the tragic poet's liberty to treat a true subject, such as an argument drawn from Scripture. Taking his argument from elsewhere, he adds the disposition "for the most part" himself: "Primo enim, sicut argumentum accipit, ita dispositionem domo adfert ut plurimum, poeta." (On this point it seems necessary to emend the translation in Sellin, p. 32.) Taking his personae from elsewhere, he gives them their character or *ethos* "for the most part" himself: "Secundo, ut personas accipit, ita mores dat ut plurimum personis." He also adds other personae, such as "nurses, messengers, old men, and the like." Finally, a "true action can be verisimilar," except in the case of "things either miraculous or prodigious" (Sellin, p. 32).

Subsequently, in his discussion of episodes, Heinsius again explores the problem of what and how the poet is free to add or invent. Distinguishing between fable and episodes, he defines the former as "a bare imitation of an action" and the latter as "whatever outside that action is added by the poet." Insisting that the episodes must not only "be suitable to the fable" but also "fit neatly and agreeably into the fable," Heinsius assigns them to the complication of the plot but excludes them from the denouement. In Seneca's *Oedipus*, for instance, the denouement contains "nothing that does not subserve the action, nothing irrelevant to the fable." See Sellin, pp. 59–61, 66–67.

It is on the basis of this distinction that Heinsius explains Aristotle's statement that the denouement "should arise out of the plot itself, and not depend on a stage-artifice, as in *Medea,* or in the story of the (arrested) departure of the Greeks in the *Iliad.*" In Aristotle's view, the "artifice must be reserved for matters outside the play—for past events beyond human knowledge, or events yet to come; which require to be foretold or announced; since it is the privilege of the Gods to know everything" (Bywater p. 57). Since Heinsius interprets things "external to the drama" as things pertaining to episode, he adduces the rule: "use contrivance not in the denouement but in complication." Contrivance (i.e., artifice, machine, or *deus ex machina*) can be employed (1) in the prologue, (2) in relating past events that cannot be known by man, and (3) in revealing the future. Aristotle permits the use of contrivance in the denouement if the subject demands it and it cannot be avoided, as in Euripides' *Orestes,* in the *Hercules Oetaeus,* and in *Philoctetes* (Sellin, pp. 63–70).

As a poet or "maker," Milton believed himself to be imitating an action based on biblical history, reconstructing the narrative in such a way as to endow it with organic unity, probability, and affective and exemplary efficacy, rather than chronicling the action as it actually happened or as he believed it to have happened. He was a poet, not a historian or a newspaper reporter or a recording angel. He was fully aware that he was amplifying and restructuring divinely revealed subject matter through his own fictional inventions; and there is no evidence that he believed himself to be adding "historical details" to the Scriptures. On the contrary, he was scrupulously regarding the principles of poetic imitation (as he and many of his contemporaries understood them) and the methods that differentiated the true poet from the true historian. As a poem, *Paradise Lost* is a "thing made," a constructed image. Milton has "made" an imitation fall of man, just as "the poet who was 'maker' of a Fall of Troy . . . made an imitation Fall of Troy." He has constructed an imitation Adam or Eve or Satan, just as an "artist who 'painted Pericles . . . made an imitation Pericles by means of shapes and colours'": see Gilbert Murray's preface in Aristotle, *On the Art of Poetry,* trans. Ingram Bywater (Oxford, 1945), p. 8. Murray further observes that "true Tragedy had always taken its material from the sacred myths, or heroic sagas, which to the classical Greek constituted history"; pp. 12–13. In this respect also there is a significant analogy between Milton's epic and classical tragedy—even though he would not have realized that his argument was actually derived from sacred myth rather than from sacred history.

NOTES

Preface

1. For Aristotle's views on the close affinities between epic and tragedy, see Ingram Bywater, trans., *Aristotle on the Art of Poetry*, (Oxford, 1945), pp. 26, 30–31, 34, 42, 79–85, 92–95. In the epics of Homer, Aristotle finds the prototypes of comedy and tragedy. Just as Homer "was in the serious style the poet of poets, standing alone not only through the literary excellence, but also through the dramatic character of his imitations, so too he was the first to outline for us the general forms of Comedy ... ; his *Margites* ... stands in the same relation to our comedies as the *Iliad* and *Odyssey* to our tragedies" (pp. 30–31). Epic poetry agrees with tragedy insofar as it is "an imitation of serious subjects in a grand kind of verse." It differs from tragedy, however, (1) "in that it is in one kind of verse and in narrative form"; (2) "in its length"; and (3) in its "constituents." Whereas "all the parts of epic are included in Tragedy, ... those of Tragedy are not all of them to be found in the Epic" (p. 34). Thus plot, character, thought, and style (or diction) are common to both genres, but spectacle and melody are denied the epic poet.

The construction of epic stories, Aristotle continues, "should clearly be like that in a drama; they should be based on a single action, one that is a complete whole in itself, with a beginning, middle, and end, so as to enable the work to produce its own proper pleasure with all the organic unity of a living creature" (p. 79). Epic poetry also divides into the "same species as Tragedy; it must be either simple or complex, a story of character or one of suffering." With "the exception of Song and Spectacle," its parts must be the same as those of tragedy, as it "requires Peripeties, Discoveries, and scenes of suffering just like Tragedy." Moreover "the Thought and Diction in it must be good in their way" (p. 81).

Though the marvelous is "certainly required in Tragedy," the epic "affords more opening for the improbable, the chief factor in the marvellous, because in it the agents are not visibly before one" (p. 83).

Finally, Aristotle argues the superiority of tragedy to epic on a variety of grounds. Not only does tragedy contain all the constituents of epic, but it possesses the additional advantage of music and spectacle. Its "reality of presentation" can be experienced, moreover, not only in "the play as acted" but also "in the play as read." It requires "less space for the attainment of its end" and thus produces a "more concentrated" and more pleasurable effect. It possesses greater unity than the epic of "usual" length—"an epic made up of a plurality of actions, in the same way as the *Iliad* and *Odyssey* have many such parts, each one of them in itself of some magnitude." Even though the "structure of the two Homeric poems is as perfect as can be, and the action in them is as nearly as possible one action," tragedy attains "the poetic effect better than the Epic," and is thus "the higher form of art" (pp. 94–95).

1 A Humanistic Epic
Milton's Debt to Italian Criticism

1. Milton also employed an alternative form—"Joannes Miltonus Anglus." See the Columbia edition of his *Works*, 14:2, 18:271.

2. See James Holly Hanford, "The Chronology of Milton's Private Studies," *PMLA* 36 (1921): 251–314.

3. For Renaissance Italian critical theory see, among others, Bernard Weinberg, *A History of Literary Criticism in the Italian Renaissance* (Chicago, 1961); J. E. Spingarn, *A History of Literary Criticism in the Renaissance* (New York, 1899); Allan H. Gilbert, *Literary Criticism, Plato to Dryden* (New York, 1941); Camillo Guerrieri Crocetti, *G. B. Giraldi ed il pensiero critico del sec. XVI* (Milan, 1932); Vernon Hall, Jr., *Renaissance Literary Criticism: A Study of Its Social Content* (New York, 1945); Donald Lemen Clark, *Rhetoric and Poetry in the Renaissance* (New York, 1922); H. B. Charlton, *Castelvetro's Theory of Poetry* (Manchester, 1913); Frederick Morgan Padelford, *Select Translations from Scaliger's Poetics* (New York, 1905). For Milton's poetic theory, see Ida Langdon, *Milton's Theory of Poetry and Fine Art* (New Haven, 1924); F. T. Prince, *The Italian Element in Milton's Verse* (Oxford, 1954); Paul R. Sellin, "Sources of Milton's Catharsis: A Reconsideration," in *Milton Studies in Honor of Harris Francis Fletcher* (Urbana, Ill., 1961), pp. 104–22; Daniel Heinsius, *On Plot in Tragedy*, trans. Paul R. Sellin and John J. McManmon (Northridge, Calif., 1971); Irene Samuel, "*Paradise Lost* as Mimesis," in *Approaches to Paradise Lost*, ed. C. A. Patrides (London, 1968), pp. 15–29; Torquato Tasso, *Discourses on the Heroic Poem*, trans. with notes by Mariella Cavalchini and Irene Samuel (Oxford, 1973). For Renaissance concepts of literary genre and for problems of genre and

literary modes in *Paradise Lost*, see Rosalie L. Colie, *The Resources of Kind: Genre-Theory in the Renaissance* (Berkeley and Los Angeles, 1973); Jörg Kröner, "A Genre Interpretation and Pedagogical Consequences of Milton's *Paradise Lost*," diss., East Texas State University, 1973; Roger B. Rollin, "*Paradise Lost:* 'Tragical–Comical–Historical–Pastoral,' " *Milton Studies* 5 (1973): 3–37; Robert J. Morris, "An Enriching of Art: *Paradise Lost* and the Genre Question," diss., Michigan State University, 1972; Gregory Ziegelmaier, "The Comedy of *Paradise Lost*," *College English* 26 (1965): 516–22; John T. Shawcross, "The Style and Genre of *Paradise Lost*," in *New Essays on Paradise Lost*, ed. Thomas Kranidas (Berkeley and Los Angeles, 1969), pp. 15–33. See also Appendix, chapter 1.

4.   George B. Parks, "The Decline and Fall of the English Renaissance Admiration of Italy," *HLQ* 31 (1968): 341–57; A. Egle, "Milton und Italien" (diss., Freiburg im Breisgau, 1940); Ettore Allodoli, *Giovanni Milton e l'Italia* (Prato, 1907); C. P. Brand, *Torquato Tasso: A Study of the Poet and of His Contribution to English Literature* (Cambridge, 1965).

5.   See *Of Education;* cf. Langdon, p. 225.

6.   For relevant passages in Phillips's *Theatrum Poetarum*, see Allan H. Gilbert, *Literary Criticism*, pp. 672–73: "And therefore it is not a mere historical relation spiced over with a little slight fiction . . . which makes a heroic poem, but it must be rather a brief, obscure, or remote tradition, but of some remarkable piece of story, in which the poet hath an ample field to enlarge by feigning of probable circumstances." In this, as in "proper allegory, invention . . . principally consisteth." The poet's business is "to deliver feigned things as like to truth as may be, that is to say, not too much exceeding apprehension or the belief of what is possible or likely or positively contradictory to the truth of history." For Tasso the poet's first step is to "select a matter capable of receiving the more excellent form that the poet's artifice endeavors to introduce" or impose upon it. (See *Discorsi del Poema Eroico*, in Torquato Tasso, *Prose*, ed. Francesco Flora, [Milan, 1935], p. 341.) "The argument of the most excellent epic should be based on history" (p. 356), and the poet should "avoid feigned arguments" (p. 375). Like Milton, Tasso prefers an argument based on the history of a true religion (i.e., the Judeo-Christian tradition); but unlike Milton he rules out certain scriptural subjects of the highest "authority" on the grounds that they leave the poet too little freedom to invent and to feign. The writer "who did not feign and did not imitate . . . would not be a poet, but a historian" (p. 363). (These reflections did not, however, deter Tasso from writing an epic on the creation, *Il Mondo Creato*.) "Modern histories," Tasso maintains, "deprive the poet of his 'license to feign and to imitate,' " which is particularly necessary to epic poets (p. 364). The history of a very remote period or nation had one distinct advantage; as its events were buried in antiquity (if not oblivion), the poet could "change and reorder and narrate them as he pleased" (p. 363).

7. See A. J. A. Waldock, "The Poet and the Theme," in *Paradise Lost and Its Critics* (Cambridge, 1947), pp. 1–24.

8. Cf. G. A. Wilkes, *The Thesis of Paradise Lost* (Melbourne, 1961), pp. 4–5: "But is *Paradise Lost* accurately described as a poem on the fall of man, with a moral of obedience? ... The subject matter ... is manifestly the 'celestial cycle,' embracing the revolt of the angels and the war in heaven, the narrative of the creation of the world, the temptation and fall of man, the sweep of human history to the flood, and from the flood to the birth of Christ." Though the poem includes all these events it assigns most of them to the characters' episodic accounts of past or future events, instead of describing them directly. Only the temptation and fall of man receives central emphasis in the fable—for this alone is the "subject" of the poem, as Milton employs the term. In the sense that Wilkes often gives this term, it means everything—and consequently nothing.

   Allusions to the *Traité du poème épique* of Réne Le Bossu (published at Paris in 1675) recur throughout Dryden's critical writings. In "The Grounds of Criticism in Tragedy," in *Of Dramatic Poesy and Other Essays*, ed. George Watson (London, 1962), hereafter cited as Watson, he extols Bossu as "the best of modern critics." Citing "the first rule which Bossu prescribes to the writer of an heroic poem"—"to make the moral of the work"—Dryden transfers it to dramatic criticism; in his *Conquest of Granada* he has (he declares) copied Homer's moral, "that union preserves a commonwealth, and discord destroys it." He approves Bossu's suggestions on how to "raise the passion of a judicious audience." With Bossu, he argues that a poet should, if necessary, accommodate historical to ethical truth, emphasizing the virtues of men like the emperors Mauritius and Valentinian and "slurring over" their vices (Watson, 1:246–54). In the preface to St. Evremond's essays, Dryden repeats Bossu's views on the *Aeneid* as imperial propaganda. By "insinuating into the people the piety of their new conqueror," Vergil had assisted Augustus's political designs and his conversion of the Roman commonwealth into a monarchy (Watson, 2:58). In *A Discourse concerning the Original and Progress of Satire*, Dryden maintains that an epic poet "must have exactly studied Homer and Virgil as his patterns, Aristotle and Horace as his guides, and Vida and Bossu as their commentators; with many others, both Italian and French critics" (Watson, 2:96). In *A Parallel of Poetry and Painting* he observes that "Bossu has not given more exact rules for the epic poem, nor Dacier for tragedy" than has du Fresnoy for painting. He accepts Bossu's view that "the moral ... is the first business of the poet, as being the groundwork of his instruction," though he comments (apropos of the unity of time) that Bossu had not yet determined whether "Virgil's action was comprehended in a year, or somewhat more" (Watson, 2:186–93). In his preface to the *Aeneid* he approves Bossu's observation that "Statius ... was ambitious of trying his strength with his master Virgil, as Virgil had before tried his with Homer" (Watson, 2:224). He also credits Bossu (or Segrais) with a critical argument concerning the advantage of epic over tragedy (Watson, 2:233). For Dryden's debt to other literary theorists —Aristotle, Horace, and Quintilian; Scaliger, Heinsius, and Vida; Casaubon, Dacier, Corneille, and Rapin; and Thomas Rymer—see John Dryden, *Selected Criticism,* ed. James Kinsley and George Parfitt (Oxford, 1970), passim.

9. Cf. Watson, 1:248. In the opinion of John Dennis, "it would be an easy matter to prove that none of the Moderns understood the Art of Heroick Poetry, who wrote before *Bossu* took Pains to unravel the Mystery"; *Milton: The Critical Heritage,* ed. John T. Shawcross (New York, 1970), p. 126. Although Addison did not share Bossu's belief "that an epic writer first of all pitches upon a certain moral, as the ground-work and foundation of his poem, and afterwards finds out a story to it," he nevertheless believed "that no just heroic poem ever was, or can be made, from whence one great moral may not be deduced." Elsewhere in his criticism of *Paradise Lost,* Addison alluded to Bossu's authority as epic theorist. Had he chosen to follow "Bossu's method" in his first paper on Milton, Addison would (he declared) have "dated the action" of *Paradise Lost* from the commencement of Raphael's speech in book 5; for Bossu "supposes the action of the *Aeneid,* rather from its immediate beginning in the first book, than from its remote beginning in the second"; Joseph Addison, *Critical Essays from the Spectator,* ed. Donald F. Bond (New York and Oxford, 1970), pp. 121, 169.

10. For Addison's view of the "great Moral" of the poem, cf. Waldock, pp. 6–7, "that Obedience to the Will of God makes men happy, and that Disobedience makes them miserable." For Johnson's conception of the "moral" of *Paradise Lost,* see James Thorpe, *Milton Criticism* (London, 1951), p. 72. "Bossu is of opinion that the poet's first work is to find a *moral,* which his fable is afterwards to illustrate and establish. This seems to have been the process only of Milton; the moral of other poems is incidental and consequent; in Milton's only it is essential and intrinsic. His purpose was the most useful and the more arduous; *to vindicate the ways of God to man,* to shew the reasonableness of religion, and the necessity of obedience to the Divine Law." See Réne Le Bossu, *Treatise of the Epick Poem,* ed. Stuart Curran, Scholars' Facsimiles and Reprints (Gainesville, Fla., 1970).

11. E. M. W. Tillyard, "The Crisis of Paradise Lost," in *Milton: A Collection of Critical Essays,* ed. Louis L. Martz (Englewood Cliffs, N.J., 1966), pp. 159, 166.

12. Wilkes, p. 29.

2 Modal Variation in Paradise Lost

1. For analogies between Satan and Caesar, see William Blisset, "Caesar and Satan," *JHI* 18 (1957): 221–32. For analogies between Satan and

Vergil's Turnus, see Robert M. Boltwood, "Turnus and Satan as Epic Villains," *CJ* 47 (1952): 183-86.
For Milton's use of parody, see John P. Cutts, "The Miserific Vision: A Study of Some of the Basic Structural Imagery of *Paradise Lost*," *EM* 14 (1963): 57-72; and Ernest Schanzer, "Milton's Hell Revisited," *UTQ* 24 (1955): 136-45. For Milton's use of irony, see, among others, Douglas Bush, "Ironic and Ambiguous Allusion in *Paradise Lost*," *JEGP* 60 (1961): 631-40; Robert Walker French, "Verbal Irony in *Paradise Lost*" (diss., Brown University, 1965); James B. Henby, "A Study of Irony in *Paradise Lost*" (diss., Texas Christian University, 1965).
For the psychomachia in Milton's epic, see Priscilla P. St. George, "Psychomachia in Books V and VI of *Paradise Lost*," *MLQ* 27 (1966): 185-96. For the battle in heaven as an "extended metaphor" or as "archetypal pattern," see Arnold Stein, *Answerable Style* (Minneapolis, 1953); C. A. Patrides, "*Paradise Lost* and the Theory of Accommodation," *TSLI* 5 (1963): 58-63; Stella P. Revard, "Milton's Critique of Heroic Warfare in *Paradise Lost* V and VI," *SEL* 5 (1967): 119-39. For metaphoric (and archetypal or mythic) structure in *Paradise Lost*, see Maud Bodkin, *Archetypal Patterns in Poetry* (London, 1934); J. B. Broadbent, *Some Graver Subject* (London, 1960); Christine Brooke-Rose, "Metaphor in *Paradise Lost*," in *Language and Style in Milton*, ed. Ronald David Emma and John T. Shawcross (New York, 1967), pp. 252-303; Cleanth Brooks, "Milton and Critical Re-Estimates," *PMLA* 66 (1951): 1045-54; Jackson I. Cope, *The Metaphoric Structure of Paradise Lost* (Baltimore, 1962); Isabel Gamble MacCaffrey, *Paradise Lost as Myth* (Cambridge, Mass., 1959); Elizabeth Sewell, *The Human Metaphor* (South Bend, Ind., 1964); John T. Shawcross, "A Metaphoric Approach to Reading Milton," *BSUF* 8 (summer 1967): 17-22; idem, "The Metaphor of Inspiration in *Paradise Lost*," in *Th'Upright Heart and Pure*, ed. Amadeus P. Fiore (Pittsburgh, 1967), pp. 75-85; Wayne Shumaker, "*Paradise Lost*: The Mythological Dimension," *Bucknell Review* 10 (1961): 75-86.

2. On Milton's use of the marvelous, see Jacques Blondel, "Le Merveilleux dans le Paradis Miltonien," *EA* 20 (1967): 348-56.

3. For the range of stylistic levels and literary modes in Milton's poetry, see Arnold Stein, *Answerable Style* (Minneapolis, 1953); Hallett Smith, "No Middle Flight," *HLQ* 15 (1952): 159-72; Balachandra Rajan, "The Style of *Paradise Lost*," in *Milton's Epic Poetry*, ed. C. A. Patrides, (Harmondsworth, 1967), pp. 276-97; Thomas Kranidas *The Fierce Equation: A Study of Milton's Decorum* (The Hague, 1965); Geoffrey Hartman, "Milton's Counterplot," *ELH* 25 (1958): 1-12; Martin Mueller, "The Tragic Epic: *Paradise Lost* and the *Iliad*" (diss., Indiana University, 1966); Anthony Low, "No Middle Flight: *Paradise Lost*, I. 14," *Milton Newsletter* 3 (1969): 1-3; Christopher Ricks, *Milton's Grand Style* (Oxford, 1963); William Empson, "Milton and Bentley: The Pastoral of the Innocence of Man and Nature,"

in *Milton: A Collection of Critical Essays*, ed. Louis L. Martz (Englewood Cliffs, N.J., 1966), pp. 19–39; Harold E. Toliver, "Complicity of Voice in *Paradise Lost*," *MLQ* 25 (1964): 153–70; Irene Samuel, "Milton on Comedy and Satire," *HLQ* 35 (1972): 107–30. In "*Paradise Lost:* 'Tragical–Comical–Historical–Pastoral,' " *Milton Studies* 5 (1973): 3–37, Roger B. Rollin analyzes Milton's "encyclopedic drama-epic" in terms of "the theoretic forms of three genres of drama—tragedy, tragicomedy, and history play." The epic poem comprises the tragedy of Satan, the pastoral tragicomedy of Adam and Eve, and the history play of the Son of God. See pp. 7, 22–23 for the application of dramatic critical terms such as protasis, epitasis, catastrophe, and rising or falling action.

4. Cf. the *Dunciad* Variorum, "and (as a fine writer Addison says of *Virgil* in his *Georgics) Tosses about his* Dung *with an air of Majesty*" (*The Poems of Alexander Pope*, ed. John Butt [New Haven, 1970], p. 377). For magnificence in things as well as in words, number (i.e., meter), and thought ("concetto o sentenza"); see Torquato Tasso, *Discorsi del poema eroico*, in *Prose*, ed. Francesco Flora (Milan and Rome, 1935), pp. 469–72. For Scaliger's opinion that the "umiltá di Virgilio ne lo stile sublime, cioè ne l'Eneide, sia differente da quella de la Bucolica in spezia; ma l'altezza de la umiltá de l'Eneide sia diversa non di spezie, ma di modo," see ibid., pp. 472–73. In Tasso's opinion, "Lo stile eroico . . . non è lontano da la gravitá del tragico, né da la vaghezza del lirico; ma avanza l'un e l'altro ne lo splendore d'una meravigliosa maestá" (ibid., p. 474). Tasso maintains that "il temperato e il sublime e l'umile de l'eroico non sia il medesimo con quelli de gli altri poemi; e se fosse pur lecito al poeta usar lo stil dimesso ne l'epopeia, non dee però inchinarsi a quella bassezza ch'è propria de' Comici, come fece l'Ariosto" (ibid., p. 473).

5. Cf. John R. Knott, Jr., *Milton's Pastoral Vision: An Approach to Paradise Lost* (Chicago, 1971); see also Harold E. Toliver, *Pastoral Forms and Attitudes* (Berkeley, 1971).

6. See Michael Lieb, *The Dialectics of Creation* (Amherst, 1970), pp. 32–34, Milton's exploitation of the imagery of flatulence in the Limbo of Vanity episode.

7. For domestic comedy and the principle of decorum in the representation of Eden, see Kranidas, *The Fierce Equation*.

8. Ingram Bywater, trans., *Aristotle on the Art of Poetry* (Oxford, 1945), p. 53.

9. See Knott, "The Pastoral Day in *Paradise Lost*," *MLQ* 29 (1968): 168–82; idem, "The Visit of Raphael," *PQ* 47 (1968): 36–42; idem, *Milton's Pastoral Vision*.

10. See Hallett Smith, *Elizabethan Poetry* (Ann Arbor, 1968), pp. 1–63. For further discussion of pastoral conventions and motifs in Renaissance epic, see Donald Cheney, *Spenser's Image of Nature: Wild Man and Shepherd in "The Faerie Queene"* (New Haven and London, 1966), pp. 1–17, 215–38. See also Margaret E. Dana, "Heroic and

Pastoral: Sidney's Arcadia as Masquerade," *Comparative Literature* 25 (1973): 308–20.

11. Vitruvius, *The Ten Books of Architecture*, trans. Morris Hicky Morgan (New York, 1960), p. 150.
12. Empson, pp. 38–39.
13. Ibid.
14. Hallett Smith, pp. 1–63.

3 "Those Notes to Tragic"
Epic Fable and the Tragic Illustrious

1. G. E. Hadow, ed., *Selections from Dryden* (Oxford, 1908), p. 154.
2. G. Gregory Smith, ed., *The Spectator* (London, 1951), 2:385–86; see no. 297, 9 February 1712.
3. *Paradise Lost*, book 1, "The Argument."
4. Ingram Bywater, trans., *Aristotle on the Art of Poetry* (Oxford, 1945), p. 50.
5. Antonio Minturno, *L'Arte Poetica* (Naples, 1725), pp. 76–77.
6. James Holly Hanford, *A Milton Handbook*, 4th ed. (New York, 1947), p. 185. See also idem, "The Dramatic Element in *Paradise Lost*," *SP* 14 (1917): 178–95; Allan H. Gilbert, "The Cambridge Manuscript and Milton's Plans for an Epic," *SP* 16 (1919): 172–76; Ida Langdon, *Milton's Theory of Poetry and Fine Art* (New Haven, 1924); William R. Parker, "The Trinity Manuscript and Milton's Plans for a Tragedy," *JEGP* 34 (1935): 225–32; idem, *Milton's Debt to Greek Tragedy in "Samson Agonistes"* (Baltimore, 1937).
7. See Arthur O. Lovejoy, "Milton and the Paradox of the Fortunate Fall," *ELH* 4 (1937): 161–79.
8. Milton, *Prose Works* (London: Bohn Library, 1883), 3:473–74.
9. Bywater, pp. 34, 79, 81–84.
10. Torquato Tasso, *Prose*, ed. Francesco Flora (Milan and Rome, 1935), pp. 332–34, 366–69, 418.
11. Minturno, p. 9.
12. Lodovico Castelvetro, *Poetica d'Aristotele Vulgarizzata et Sposta* (Basel, 1576), pp. 276, 527, 548, 696; cf. H. B. Charlton, *Castelvetro's Theory of Poetry* (Manchester, 1913), p. 124.
13. J. E. Spingarn, *Literary Criticism in the Renaissance* (New York, 1925), p. 110.
14. Cf. Milton's definition of magnanimity in the *De Doctrina Christiana* (*Prose Works*, 5:94–95).
15. Bywater, pp. 50–51.
16. Tasso, p. 368.
17. Daniel Heinsius, *De Tragaediae Constitutione* (Leiden: 1643), p. 76.
18. Bywater, p. 50.

19. See S. H. Butcher, *Aristotle's Theory of Poetry and Fine Art*, 3d ed. (London, 1902), pp. 44–45.
20. Cf. Matthew 1:21, 9:2; Romans 5:12, 6:6, 16, 23; Hebrews 10:12; James 1:15; 1 John 1:1, 2:2, 3:4, 5:16, 17.
21. Heinsius, p. 269.
22. Ibid., p. 270.
23. Bywater, p. 50.
24. Castelvetro, p. 283.
25. Jacobus Masenius, *Sarcotis* . . .; *Tum de Heroicâ Poesi Tractatus* (London, 1771), pp. 12–13. In chap. 3 ("An materia Epopoeiae possit esse actio herois, quae virtus non sit, & infelici non minùs, quàm, felici exitu, instar Tragoediae terminari?"), Masenius observes that Aristotle and other preceptors of the art of poetry had failed to raise this question: "Possitne illustris actio infelici exitu, aut contra actio flagitiosa felici, vel etiam infelici exitu terminata, esse Epopoeiae materia?" See also chap. 4, "Quo pacto Epopoeia & Trageodia inter se conveniant & discrepent" (ibid, pp. 17–19).

4 "Miserable of Happy"
Peripeteia in Paradise Lost

1. Ida Langdon, *Milton's Theory of Poetry and Fine Art* (New Haven, 1924); William R. Parker, *Milton's Debt to Greek Tragedy in "Samson Agonistes"* (Baltimore, 1937).
2. E. M. W. Tillyard, *Milton* (London, 1951), p. 343.
3. Johann Vahlen, *Beiträge zu Aristoteles' Poetik*, vol. 2 (Vienna, 1865); Walter Lock, "The Use of *Peripeteia* in Aristotle's *Poetics*," *Classical Review* 9 (1865): 251–53; F. L. Lucas, "The Reverse of Aristotle," *Classical Review* 37 (1923): 98–104; S. H. Butcher, *Aristotle's Theory of Poetry and Fine Art* 3d ed. (London, 1902), pp. 329–30; Ferdinando Albeggiani, *Aristotele: La Poetica* (Florence, 1934), pp. 86–87. Vahlen maintained "that a *peripeteia* is any event where the agent's intention is overruled to produce an effect the exact opposite of his intention" (Lucas, p. 99), and this interpretation influenced a number of later commentators. Lock's avowed purpose (p. 251) was "to emphasize and reinforce the view which was propounded by Vahlen and accepted by Susemihl." Lucas (p. 100) believed that in "the special technical sense" which Aristotle gave the term, *peripeteia* signified " 'the reversal of an agent's intention'; 'a hoist with one's own petard'; 'the issue of action aimed at a result *x*, in the opposite of *x*.' " In Albeggiani's opinion (p. 87), Vahlen's conception of the *peripeteia* was too narrow; "l'interpretazione della peripezia deve essere più comprensiva, poichè essa contiene tanto il cambiamento repentino della situazione, quanto l'ironia del fato per cui esso risulta dalle azioni che sembravano allontanarlo." Although J. Hardy (*Aristote: Poétique* [Paris, 1952], p. 80) criticized the view that "il y a péripétie quand un personnage arrive à une fin ou tombe

dans une situation opposée à celle qu'il attendait," he believed
nevertheless that the term included "une idée de surprise et, semble-
t-il, d'ironie du destin." Other modern commentators have agreed
with Bywater (see *Festschrift Theodor Gomperz*, 1895, pp. 167–72)
in rejecting Vahlen's interpretation. W. Hamilton Fyfe, *Aristotle's
Art of Poetry* (Oxford, 1952), p. 28, identified the *peripeteia* as "a
sudden reversal of fortune's wheel" and observed that though this
term "has often been interpreted to mean the reversal of the agent's
intention, that is, a situation in which the consequence of the hero's
action is the opposite of what he intended," this. "boomerang
device . . . is not the sense in which the word is here used." Similarly,
Alfred Gudeman, *Aristoteles* PERI POIETIKES (Berlin and Leipzig,
1934), p. 220, defined *peripeteia* as "eine besondere Art der *metabolē*,
nämlich der Umschwung des status quo in sein Gegenteil" and explained, "Dass dieser plötzlich oder wider Erwarten vor sich gehen
muss, ist dem Begriff an sich gar nicht immanent, so häufig beides
in praxi vorzukommen pflegt."

4.   John Milton, "Of Education," *Prose Works* (Bohn Library, London,
     1883), 3:473–74.

5.   For the influence of Heinsius's *De Tragoediae Constitutione* (first
     published at Leiden in 1611), see J. E. Spingarn, *A History of Literary
     Criticism in the Renaissance* (New York, 1925), 245–46. See also
     Daniel Heinsius, *On Plot in Tragedy*, trans. Paul R. Sellin and John J.
     McManmon (Northridge, Calif., 1971).

6.   Butcher, p. 330.

7.   Ibid., p. 330. Cf. Albeggiani, pp. 86–87, "l'ironia del fato"; Hardy, p.
     80, "ironie du destin"; Lucas, p. 102, "The *peripeteia* is the working
     of that irony of Fate which makes life a tragedy of errors, so that we
     become the authors of our own undoing"; D. S. Margoliouth, *The
     Poetics of Aristotle* (London, 1911), pp. 174–75, "The Irony of Fate is
     the transformation of an experience into its contrary."

8.   Ingram Bywater, trans., *Aristotle on the Art of Poetry* (Oxford,
     1945), p. 46.

9.   Lodovico Castelvetro, *Poetica d'Aristotele Vulgarizzata et Sposta*
     (Basel, 1576), p. 237.

10. Daniel Heinsius, trans., *Aristotelis de Poetica*, printed with *De
     Tragoediae Constitutione* (Leiden, 1643), p. 262.

11. Butcher, p. 39.

12. Castelvetro, p. 242.

13. Bywater, p. 46.

14. Castelvetro, p. 238.

15. Heinsius, p. 262.

16. Torquato Tasso, *Discorsi del Poema Eroico*, in *Prose*, ed. Francesco
     Flora (Milan and Rome, 1935), p. 414. Cf. ibid., p. 335, "il
     rivolgimento, che peripezia prima dissero i Greci, la quale è una
     mutazione da la buona ne la rea fortuna, o da la rea ne la buona."

17. Ibid., p. 414. Jacopo Mazzoni likewise regarded the *peripeteia* as a
    change of state ("mutatione di stato"); see his *Della Difesa della
    Commedia di Dante* (Cesena, 1587), p. 658, and his *Discorso in
    Difesa della Commedia del Divino Poeta Dante*, ed. Mario Rossi
    (Cittá di Castello, 1898), pp. 80–83.

18. Heinsius, p. 51.

19. Castelvetro, p. 243.

20. Ibid., p. 238.

21. Ibid., pp. 240–41.

22. Ibid., p. 242.

23. Ibid., p. 239, "Adunque la favola ugale è quella, che, servando
    per tutta lei uno medesimo tenore di miseria, o di felicita, non riceve
    alcuna mutatione di fortuna. . . . Et la favola disugale è quella,
    che ha mutatione di stato felice in misero, o per lo contrario di misero
    in felice."

24. Butcher, p. 329.

25. Milton, *The Reason of Church Government*, in *Prose Works*, 2:479.

26. *The Spectator*, ed. G. Gregory Smith (London and New York, 1951),
    p. 385, no. 297, Saturday, 9 February 1712; see also James E. Thorpe,
    ed., *Milton Criticism: Selections from Four Centuries* (London,
    1951).

27. *The Spectator*, ed. Smith, p. 385.

28. *Nascimbaeni Nascimbaenii, in . . . Sex Primos Aeneidos Libros . . .
    Explanatio* (Basel, 1596), printed with *L. Hortensii Montfortii Enar-
    rationes . . . in XII. Libros . . . Aeneidos.*

29. Milton, *The Christian Doctrine*, in *Prose Works*, 4:220, "The Provi-
    dence of God as regards mankind, relates to man either in his state of
    rectitude, or since his fall." For the relationship of the theology of
    Paradise Lost to that of the *De Doctrina*, see Maurice Kelley, *This
    Great Argument* (Princeton, 1941).

30. Castelvetro, p. 534.

31. Tillyard, "The Crisis of *Paradise Lost*," in *Studies in Milton* (London,
    1951), p. 44.

32. Ibid., p. 10.

33. Bywater, p. 45.

34. Antonio Minturno, *L'Arte Poetica* (Naples, 1725), p. 42.

35. Ibid., pp. 42–43.

36. Castelvetro, pp. 243–44.

37. Ibid., pp. 239–40. "Favola interna è quella, che ha le cagioni della
    mutatione dello stato di misero in felice, o per lo contrario di felice in
    misero procedenti dalle cose dentro dalla favola ordinate a contrario
    fine." "La favola forestiera risponde all'nterna in questo, che dove
    nella'nterna le cagioni della mutatione dello stato procedono dalle
    cose dentro dalla favola ordinate a contrario fine, in lei le cagioni
    della mutatione dello stato procedono da cose di fuori ordinate a

questo fine, o almeno non ordinate a fine contrario." Castelvetro subsequently declares, however (ibid., p. 243), that "alcune cose della favola forestiera ... sono ordinate a contrario fine."

38. Ibid., p. 242.

39. Ibid., p. 243; cf. p. 242.

40. Ibid., p. 243. Castelvetro also cites (ibid., pp. 239–40) Aristotle's example of the messenger in *Oedipus Rex* and an instance in Ariosto's *Orlando Furioso*, "dove è introdotto un discreto villano volere consolare Orlando, che era turbato, col racconto dell'amore di Medoro, & d'Angelica. & con quel medesimo racconto gli accresce tanto il dolore, che egli diviene matto, & furioso."

41. Ibid., p. 243.

42. *De hist. anim.* 8. 2. 590b.13. Cf. Butcher, p. 330; Margoliouth, p. 174; Hardy, p. 80; Lucas, p. 100. Margoliouth calls this "an admirable example of the Irony of Fate. . . . 'The Polypus devours the Karabos, the Karabos the Conger, and the Conger the Polypus.' The experience of the Polypus, pursuit and eating, is by law of nature transformed into the contrary, being pursued and being eaten." Lucas similarly regards it as "the hoist with one's own petard, the return of the boomerang—the eater is eaten by its food's food."

43. Heinsius, p. 51.

44. Ibid., p. 53.

45. Ibid., p. 52.

46. Ibid., p. 261.

47. Nascimbaenus. Cf. Castelvetro, p. 528, on *peripeteia* in the *Iliad*, despite Aristotle's conception of this work as "epopea simplice": "io vi riconosco molte mutatione, & rivolgimenti, vincendo hora i Troiani, & hora i Greci."

48. G. Gregory Smith, ed., *Elizabethan Critical Essays* (London, 1950), 2:216.

49. Milton, *Prose Works*, 4:200–206.

50. Ibid., 3:474.

51. Ibid., 4:284.

52. Ibid., 4:253. "The Providence of God as regards the fall of man, is observable in the sin of man, and the misery consequent upon it, as well as in his restoration." Cf. ibid., 4:47, "It was ... man as a being who was to fall of his own accord, that was the matter or object of predestination; for that manifestation of divine grace and mercy which God designed as the ultimate purpose of predestination, presupposes the existence of sin and misery in man, originating in himself alone."

53. Ibid., 4:319. "The renovation of man is that change whereby he who was before under the curse, and obnoxious to the divine wrath, is brought into a state of grace."

54. Ibid., 4:332, "The effects of regeneration are repentance and faith."

5 "Eyes True Op'ning"
Recognition in *Paradise Lost*

1. Ingram Bywater, trans, *Aristotle on the Art of Poetry* (Oxford, 1945), p. 38. For the Greek text, see S. H. Butcher, *Aristotle's Theory of Poetry and Fine Art* (London, 1902).
2. Torquato Tasso, *Discorsi del Poema Eroico*, in *Prose*, ed. Francesco Flora (Milan and Rome, 1935), p. 391.
3. See *The Reason of Church Government* (John Milton, *Prose Works* [Bohn Library, London, 1883], 2:478); *Of Education* (ibid., 3:473–74); *A Second Defence of the English People* (ibid., 1:299); and the preface to *Samson Agonistes*. For a fuller discussion of Milton's poetic theory, see Ida Langdon, *Milton's Theory of Poetry and Fine Art* (New Haven, 1924).
4. Bywater, pp. 47, 38, 46, 81.
5. Ibid., p. 47.
6. Merritt Y. Hughes, ed., *Paradise Regained* (New York, 1937), p. 531n; cf. Langdon, *Milton's Theory of Poetry and Fine Art*.
7. Bywater, p. 47.
8. *Dan. Heinsii de Tragediae Constitutione* (Leiden, 1643), p. 58.
9. Bywater, pp. 47–48.
10. Ibid., pp. 53–55.
11. For Milton's use of the rhetorical figure *traductio* or "the *turn*" in this passage, see W. K. Wimsatt, Jr., *The Verbal Icon* (New York, 1958), p. 211.
12. Bywater, p. 47.
13. *Prose Works*, 4:264–65, "And this death took place not only on the very day, but at the very moment of the fall. They who are delivered from it are said to be *regenerated*, to be *born again*, and to be *created afresh*."
14. Ibid., p. 343.
15. Ibid.
16. Ibid. Italics mine.
17. See Milton's chapter "Of Justification," ibid., pp. 349–58.
18. Ibid., pp. 319, 329–30.
19. *Biblia Sacra . . . Scholiis Illustrati ab Immanuele Tremellio & Francisco Junio* (Hanoviae, 1624), p. 352. Tremellius rendered this text as follows: "Et induite novum qui renovatur in agnitionem juxta imaginem ejus qui creavit ipsum." Beza translated it thus: "Et induti sitis novo illo, qui renovatur in agnitionem congruentem imagini ejus qui ipsum condidit." Cf. the notes on *renovatur* ("Novitas vitae in agnitione hominem ad Dei conditoris imaginem [id est, ad totius animae rectitudinem] transformante posita est") and on *agnitionem* ("Loquitur de agnitione efficaci"). For Milton's use of the Junius-Tremellius Bible in his *De Doctrina*, see Maurice Kelley, *This Great Argument* (Princeton, 1941), passim. For the theological term *agnitio*

Christi, see Melanchthon's *Loci Theologici, Corpus Reformatorum* (Brunswick, 1854), vol. 21, col. 681.

20. Heinsius, passim; cf. Heinsius's translation of Aristotle's *Poetics* in the same volume. In the *Discorsi del Poema Eroico,* Tasso uses the term *agnizione.* Castelvetro, Minturno, and Mazzoni, on the other hand, prefer to render the Aristotelian *anagnorisis* as *riconoscenza* or *riconoscimento.*

21. Bywater, p. 47. Cf. Heinsius, pp. 263–64; Antonio Minturno, *L'Arte Poetica* (Naples, 1725), p. 43; Lodovico Castelvetro, *Poetica d'Aristotele Vulgarizzata et Sposta* (Basel, 1576), pp. 238, 247, 249, 251–52.

22. Castelvetro, pp. 248–49.

23. Tasso, p. 414.

24. Castelvetro, p. 250.

25. Ibid., p. 253.

26. In her valuable essay, "The Regaining of Paradise," in *The Prison and the Pinnacle,* ed. Balachandra Rajan (Toronto, 1972), pp. 111–34, Irene Samuel argues against the view (expressed by Calton in the eighteenth century) that in *Paradise Regained,* book 4, lines 560–61, "Christ declares himself to be the God and Lord of the Tempter" and that this passage constitutes an Aristotelian *anagnorisis* or discovery. As she correctly points out, Calton distorts the sense of Scripture (Deuteronomy 6:16; Matthew 4:7; and Luke 4:12) as Reformation commentators usually interpreted it. What "smites Satan with amazement" is (she suggests) "precisely that the man, whose special nature as 'Son of God' he has so insidiously tried to make the ground of his defeat, takes his stand *not* on his special nature at all, but on his common bond with all humanity."

The Christ of Milton's epic is not (as she justly emphasizes) asserting his divinity—an interpretation contrary not only to Reformation interpretations but also to most modern explanations of the biblical account of this temptation. On the contrary, he is successfully resisting the temptation to presumption. This is an exercise of his humility and his faith in his Father, a test of his full reliance on divine providence and paternal care. The hero's faith, moreover, is promptly vindicated—paradoxically by the fulfillment of the very text that Satan had quoted and Christ had refused to test. Immediately ("strait") after Satan's fall, the angels do in fact intervene to protect the Son from danger, rescuing him "From his uneasie station" and lifting him ("upbore") through the "blithe Air."

In the *De Doctrina,* Milton distinguishes four contraries or opposites of *fiducia* ("trust in God" considered as "an effect of love, and as a part of internal worship, whereby we wholly repose on him"): (1) "distrust of God," (2) "overweening presumption," (3) "carnal reliance," and (4) "trust in idols." Though the temptations in *Paradise Regained* are too complex to be comprehended in a single schema or formula (and the critic may, in fact, legitimately distinguish several overlapping patterns or schemas), it is significant that each of the three temptations emphasizes one of these contraries: the first, distrust of God; the second, carnal reliance; and the third, presumption. Milton's hero thus provides a pattern of heroic trust, the *fiducia in Deo* that the ordinary wayfaring or warfaring Christian—the *miles Christianus* of less exalted rank—must emulate in a less eminent degree and on a lesser scale. The power that miraculously sustains him in his perilous eminence (and subsequently delivers him) is the Father's power, the object of his trust and reliance. The miracle follows a demonstration of faith, serving as divine testimony to the Son's filial obedience and constancy. The miracle that strikes Satan with amazement is a divine action, operated by the Father in and through the Son; and, insofar as Satan can recognize the divine agency as such, it is a discovery and an *anagnorisis.*

6 "Scene of Suffering"
Critical Background

1. On rhetoric and poetic in the Renaissance, see J. W. H. Atkins, *Literary Criticism in Antiquity* (Cambridge, 1934); idem, *English Literary Criticism: the Renaissance* (London, 1947); idem, *English Literary Criticism: Seventeenth and Eighteenth Centuries* (London, 1951); J. E. Spingarn, *A History of Literary Criticism in the Renaissance,* 2d ed. (New York, 1954); C. S. Baldwin, *Medieval Rhetoric and Poetic* (New York, 1928); idem, *Renaissance Literary Theory and Practice* (New York, 1939); Thomas Kranidas, *The Fierce Equation* (The Hague, 1965); Wilbur Samuel Howell, *Logic and Rhetoric in England, 1500–1700* (Princeton, 1956); Rosemond Tuve, *Elizabethan and Metaphysical Imagery* (Chicago, 1947); O. B. Hardison, Jr., *The Enduring Monument* (Chapel Hill, N.C., 1962); idem, "The Orator and the Poet: The Dilemma of Humanist Literature," *Medieval and Renaissance Studies,* 1 (1971):33–34; Christopher Grose, "Milton on Ramist Similitude," in *Seventeenth Century Imagery,* ed. Earl Miner (Berkeley, 1971), pp. 103–16; idem, "Some Uses of Sensuous Immediacy in *Paradise Lost,*" *HLQ* 31 (1968): 211–22; John S. Major, "Milton's View of Rhetoric," *SP* 64 (1967): 685–711; Karl R. Wallace, *Francis Bacon on Communication and Rhetoric* (Chapel Hill, N.C., 1943); idem, *Francis Bacon on the Nature of Man* (Urbana, Ill, 1967); Joseph Antony Wittreich, Jr., "Milton's Idea of the Orator," *Milton Quarterly* 6 (1972): 38–40; Bernard Weinberg, ed., *Trattati di poetica e retorica del Cinquecento* (Bari, 1970–72); idem, *A History of Literary Criticism in the Italian Renaissance* (Chicago, 1961); Jerrold E. Seigel, *Rhetoric and Philosophy in Renaissance Humanism* (Princeton, 1968).

2. For Heinsius's reorganization of the chapters in the *Poetics* and his conception of pathos as "practically the most important part of the fable," see Daniel Heinsius, *On Plot in Tragedy,* trans. Paul R. Sellin and John J. McManmon (Northridge, Calif., 1971), pp. 159–60. According to Heinsius's interpretation of Aristotle, *pathos* (like

anagnorisis and *peripeteia* is "to be sought from the plot itself," and Aristotle is showing "what sort of arrangement of the fable produces emotion." Just as *pathos* "springs from plot, so it is aroused to the utmost by a turn of good fortune into adversity, or the other way around." See also Maggi's discussion of the kind of action arousing pity and fear, the superior affective power of tragic deeds premeditated by members of the same family in comparison with similar injuries premeditated by enemies (cf. chap. 14 of the *Poetics*), and Aristotle's discussion of pity and fear in the second book of the *Rhetoric*. According to Maggi, "actiones hostiles adversus hostes . . . nihil, quod misericordia dignum sit, ostendunt, nisi causa perturbationis illius, id est ratione necis, quae spectatur, aut vulnerum. si enim inimicus inimicum perimat, egregium existimatur. . . . Relinquitur igitur tertium membrum; cùm scilicet inter amicos crudele quid agitur: ut cùm frater fratrem, vel mater filium, aut filius matrem intermit, aut interempturus esset, vel aliquid aliud atrox facere moliatur. ex hac constitutione terror, ac misericordia fabulis comparatur." In Pazzi's translation, "Perturbationes verò ipsae, quando evenerint inter necessarios, veluti si frater fratrem filius patrem, mater filium, filius matrem vel necet, vel necaturus sit, aut etiam tale quid facinus patret, patraturusve sit, captandae sunt." See *Vicentii Madii Brixiani et Bartholomaei Lombardi Veronensis in Aristotelis Librum de Poetica Communes Explanationes* (Venice, 1550), reprinted in *Poetiken des Cinquecento*, ed. Bernhard Fabian (Munich, 1969), pp. 163–64. For a discussion of Pazzi's text, the explanations by Maggi and Lombardi, and Maggi's annotations, see Bernard Weinberg, *A History of Literary Criticism in the Italian Renaissance* (Chicago, 1961), pp. 406–18.

3. For the problem of catharsis in *Samson Agonistes*, see, among others, John Arthos, "Milton and the Passions: A Study of *Samson Agonistes*," *MP* 69 (1972): 209–21; Paul R. Sellin, "Sources of Milton's Catharsis: A Reconsideration," *JEGP* 60 (1961): 712–30; A. S. P. Woodhouse, "Tragic Effect in *Samson Agonistes*," *UTQ* 28 (1959): 205–22; Irene Samuel, "*Samson Agonistes* as Tragedy," in *Calm of Mind*, ed. Joseph Anthony Wittreich, Jr. (Cleveland and London, 1971), pp. 235–57; Martin E. Mueller, "*Pathos* and *Katharsis* in *Samson Agonistes*," *ELH* 31 (1964): 156–74; Sherman H. Hawkins, "Samson's Catharsis," in *Milton Studies* (Pittsburgh, 1970), 2:211–30.

4. In commenting on Aristotle's *pathos*, Bywater notes "the variety of senses attaching to" this term. In common speech it "often involves the idea of great suffering, and has the concrete sense of a great trouble or affliction of body or mind." Though "apart from the theatre the terms *pathos* (suffering) and *praxis* (action) are natural opposites," Aristotle's definition of the term as an action of a certain kind probably reflects established theatrical usage. Like *anagnorisis* and *peripeteia*, the *pathos* is "one of the incidents of the play and as such part of the *praxis* or action"; Aristotle, *On the Art of Poetry*, trans. Ingram Bywater (Oxford, 1909), p. 204. In Bywater's opinion,

the word *periōduniai* "signifies bodily agnonies" whereas *hosa toiauta* ("and the like") includes "the less physical forms of pain," such as the spiritual torment of Oedipus. Bywater argues that in *Oedipus Rex* (the "perfect model" of tragedy for Aristotle) the *pathos* is the "mental anguish of Oedipus much more than the physical horror of his self-inflicted blindness" (ibid., p. 205). This edition will henceforth be cited as Bywater, *Aristotle's Poetics*. A brief edition of Bywater's translation was published at Oxford in 1920 with a preface by Gilbert Murray under the title *Aristotle on the Art of Poetry*. This edition (frequently reprinted since) will be cited simply as Bywater. In *Comic Theory in the Sixteenth Century* (Urbana, Ill., 1964), pp. 69–70, Marvin T. Herrick observes that Quintilian divides the emotions into two classes—pathos ("the more violent emotions") and ethos ("calm and gentle" emotions) and associates the former with tragedy and the latter with comedy; cf. pp. 146, 155.

5. Bywater, p. 48.

6. Torquato Tasso, *Prose*, ed. Francesco Flora (Milan and Rome, 1935), p. 417.

7. In analyzing Aristotle's definition of *pathos*, Else maintains that "the pathos is not limited to complex plots" and that its function is "not to intensify the tragic emotions but to provide a base-point . . . to which they can attach themselves." In his opinion, the *pathos* is "the fatal or painful event—the 'thing suffered'—around which the action, simple or complex revolves, and without which it would lack not merely intense emotional quality but the basic emotional potential" (Gerald F. Else, *Aristotle's Poetics: The Argument* [Cambridge, Mass., 1963], p. 356). Else challenges the "universal" belief that Aristotle's phrase *en tōi phanerōi* refers to "deaths, etc. on stage" on several grounds— the rarity of onstage deaths in Greek tragedy; the fact that wounds (like deaths) are reported rather than "enacted before the public"; the fact that Aristotle "allows the *pathos* to be only intended, not performed"; the fact that the *pathos* "may actually take place, but not in the play itself, as in the *Oedipus*"; and Aristotle's insistence that the tragic effect is not dependent on stage representation (pp. 357–58; cf. pp. 366, 414–15, 438, 450–51). In Else's opinion, the phrase *en tōi phanerōi* is simply a "generic characterization of the events in question" rather than a "requirement that they must be performed where an audience can see them." Aristotle is "contrasting the *pathos* with peripety and recognition," which are essentially "invisible events" and "take place in the realm of the mind." Death, pain, and wounds serve as "the postulated physical correlate of the moral or mental events which transpire as peripety and recognition."

8. Bywater, p. 64.

9. Ibid., p. 46.

10. Ibid., p. 49.

11. Ibid., p. 81.

12. For the four kinds of tragedy and for the textual emendation underlying Bywater's interpretation of the fourth species as a tragedy of spectacle, see Bywater, *Aristotle's Poetics*, pp. 248–51. In Bywater's view, each of the four species of tragedy arises "through the prominence in it of one of the several elements in a play. Nevertheless all of these elements are necessary for a perfect tragedy, and "none can be neglected with impunity." If *peripeteia* and *anagnorisis* are "the whole thing," the play is complex. If the "element of *pathos* is especially prominent, it is *pathētikē;* if it is mainly a portrait of character, it is *ēthikē;* and if it depends largely on the 'spectacle,' it is 'spectacular.' " For the four species of epic, see p. 311.

 In Else's version, the fourth species of tragedy is the "episodic," such as *Phorcides, Prometheus,* and "all the actions in Hades"; Else, pp. 522–23. He regards as "not fully satisfactory" the suggestion that Aristotle's "pathetic" tragedy is the "kind which is dominated by the *pathos* or tragic deed," and his "ethical" tragedy "the kind which is dominated by 'character.' " In his opinion, the "pathetic" species is defined not only in terms of "the dominance of the *pathos*" but also in terms of the complex and moral species; "as against 'complex' it suggests a simple plot-structure, and as against 'moral' it connotes an unhappy ending." Like Heinsius, Else suggests the possibility of "a one-to-three scheme" (i.e., the complex plot as opposed to the "simple plots" of moral, pathetic, and episodic tragedy); but, unlike Heinsius, he believes that this schema would be "carrying our analysis too far." Instead, he argues that, whereas the simple and complex categories are mutually exclusive, the pathetic and moral (and possibly the episodic) species could also be associated with a complex plot-structure (pp. 524–33). For the four species of epic, see pp. 594–601.

13. S. H. Butcher, *Aristotle's Theory of Poetry and Fine Art* (London, 1902), pp. 66–67.

14. Madius, pp. 146–47.

15. Ibid., pp. 193–96.

16. *Petri Victorii Commentarii, In primum librum Aristotelis de Arte Poetarum* (Florence, 1560, HEH #226708), pp. 111–12, 176–77.

17. *Francisci Robortelli Utinensis in librum Aristotelis de Arte Poetica Explicationes* (Florence, 1548, HEH, #239579), pp. 116–17, 150–51, 154, 210–11.

18. *Annotationi di M. Alessandro Piccolomini, nel libro della Poetica d'Aristotele; con la traduttione del medesimo libro, in lingua volgare* (Venice, 1575, HEH #221311), pp. 174–75, 255–56, 377, 386.

19. *Poetica d'Aristotele vulgarizzata, et sposta per Lodovico Castelvetro. Riveduta, & ammendata* (Basel, 1576, HEH #380612), pp. 253–56, 267.

20. *Poetica Aristotelis ab Antonio Riccobono latine conversa: Eiusdem Riccoboni paraphrasis in poeticam Aristotelis* (Padua, 1587, HEH #425310); see text, pp. 14, 21–22, 32, 34; paraphrase, pp. 53, 58–60.

21. Tasso, *Prose*, ed. *Flora, p. 417*.
22. Sellin, *On Plot in Tragedy*, p. 44.
23. Ibid., p. 47.
24. Bywater, p. 52.
25. Sellin, *On Plot in Tragedy*, p. 51.
26. Ibid., p. 62.
27. See Horace, *Ars Poetica*, in Allan H. Gilbert, ed., *Literary Criticism,
     Plato to Dryden* (Detroit, 1962), pp. 133–34; Aristotle, *Rhetoric*,
     book 2, chap. 5 (on fear) and chap. 8 (on pity), trans. Theodore
     Buckley (London, 1850).
28. For Aristotle's emphasis on the primary importance of the plot
     (*mythos*) as the "arrangement" or "structure of the events" (*synthesis
     or systasis tōn pragmatōn*), see Else, pp. 237–38, 242–44, 261–63;
     Butcher, pp. 284, 346–47. For Aristotle's "structuralist" view of
     tragedy, and the subordination of structure to function (i.e., emo-
     tional effect), see Else, pp. 328, 353, 366, 442–43, 538.

7   "Scene of Suffering"
Passion in *Paradise Lost* and
Samson Agonistes

1. *Francisci Robortelli Utinensis in librum Aristotelis de Arte Poetica
    Explicationes* (Florence, 1548, HEH #239579).
2. *Poetica Aristotelis ab Antonio Riccobono latine conversa: Eiusdam
    Riccobini paraphrasis in poeticam Aristotelis* (Padua, 1587, HEH
    #425310), p. 34.
3. Ingram Bywater, trans., *Aristotle on the Art of Poetry* (Oxford,
    1945), p. 45.
4. Riccoboni, p. 53.
5. Merritt Y. Hughes, *Paradise Regained* (New York, 1937), p. 636; see
    also Annabel M. Patterson, *Hermogenes and the Renaissance: Seven
    Ideas of Style* (Princeton, 1970).
6. Theodore Buckley, trans., *Aristotle's Treatise on Rhetoric* (Bohn's
    Classical Library: London, 1850), pp. 121–27.
7. Buckley, pp. 136–40.
8. Robortello, p. 154. According to Aristotle, "Perturbationes verò
    ipsae, quando evenerint inter necessarios, veluti si fratrer [*sic*] frat-
    rem, filius patrem, mater filium, filius matrem vel necet, vel necatu-
    rus sit, aut etiam tale quid facinus patret, patraturusve sit, captandae
    sunt." In commenting on this text, Robortello attempts to explain
    how and why atrocious acts among closely related persons arouse the
    tragic emotions (p. 154): "respondeo utrumque in his inesse propter
    consanguinitatem, cuius ius, cum maximum sanctissimumque sit à
    natura ipsa sancitum inter homines, nefas videtur esse violare. Quòd
    si quando contingit ut violetur, atrox videtur factum, atque legibus na-
    turae repugnare. Eorum igitur calamitatem, qui odio aliquo impulsi,

coniunctionem consanguinitatis derimunt; contemptoque omni iure naturali, se ipsos perimunt; non commiseramur modo, sed & caedem intuentes illorum inhorrescimus, quòd non sine Deorum ira talia patrari posse existimamus; qui homines improbos ulcisci pro sua aequitate dum volunt; efficiunt saepe, ut praeteritorum scelerum, quae ab avis, proavisque fuerint admissa; nepotes poenas luant; atque furore exagitati seipsos perimant." Citing Horace's *Odes and Epodes* on Rome's legacy of ancestral crime and her inherited guilt of fraternal slaughter, Robortello observes that "Huiusmodi igitur facta atrocia, ob hanc causam animis iniiciunt terrorem. Et atrocia quidem sunt . . . ipsis consanguineis inter se, reliquis verò qui ipsos norunt de facie, atque amicitiae aliquo vinculo cum illis coniuncti sunt; commiserabilia, & horribilia."

9. Cf. Michael West, "The *Consolatio* in Milton's Funeral Elegies," *HLQ* 24 (1971): 233–49; see also A. S. P. Woodhouse, "Tragic Effect in *Samson Agonistes*," *UTQ* 28 (1959): 205–22.

10. Ann Gossman, "Milton's Samson as the Tragic Hero Purified by Trial," *JEGP* 61 (1962): 528–41; idem, "Samson, Job and the Exercise of Saints," *ES* 45 (1964): 212–24; Martin Mueller, "*Pathos* and *Katharsis* in *Samson Agonistes*," *ELH* 31 (1964): 156–74.

11. Cf. William R. Parker, *Milton's Debt to Greek Tragedy in "Samson Agonistes"*; J. C. Maxwell, "Milton's Samson and Sophocles' Heracles," *PQ* 33 (1954): 90–91; F. Michael Krouse, *Milton's Samson and the Christian Tradition* (Princeton, 1949); James Holly Hanford, *A Milton Handbook*, 4th ed. (New York, 1946).

12. See *TLS*, 8 February 1968, p. 134; Michael Fixler, "Milton's Passionate Epic," *Milton Studies* 1 (1969): 167–92. Like the *Aeneid*, *Paradise Lost* is partly modeled on both the *Iliad* and the *Odyssey*—epics that Aristotle classified as pathetic and ethical respectively—though in fact the latter poem stresses the hero's sufferings as well as his heroic prudence and concludes with the tragic reversal in the sudden and unexpected slaughter of the insolent and hubristic suitors.

13. Quoting Aristotle's *Ethics* on the "kind of man" who, erring unawares, "does not merit the name of a good man because he has trespassed against what is right," but who does not merit that of a wicked person either since he offends . . . unintentionally," Heinsius stresses the parallel between poetic and civil justice. The tragic poet and the legislator have "regard for the same thing" in imposing or remitting penalties, for both "distinguish crimes according to whether something was done deliberately or involuntarily"; Daniel Heinsius, *On Plot in Tragedy*, trans. Paul R. Sellin and John J. McManmon (Northridge, Calif., 1971), p. 50. The three requirements for the tragic person (as Heinsius interprets Aristotle) are (1) that he "exceed neither in vice nor virtue"; (2) that his adversity result not from wickedness but from lack of knowledge, from ignorance or mistake; and (3) that "he should previously have been of the highest station, whereby the greater calamity will simultaneously increase the terror and pity"; Sellin, *On Plot in Tragedy*, p. 51.

In the infliction or remission of punishments, Milton as tragic poet is imitating the judgments of the divine "legislator"; his poetic justice is an image of divine justice. The issue, however, is not one of voluntary or involuntary transgression; Adam and Eve are free agents, "Authors to themselves in all / Both what they judge and what they choose," and "they themselves ordain'd thir fall." The fundamental distinction for distributive justice is between autosuggestion and external suggestion:

> The first sort by their own suggestion fell,
> Self-tempted, self-deprav'd: Man falls deceiv'd
> By the other first: Man therefore shall find grace,
> The other none.
>
> [3.129–32]

Of Heinsius's (and Aristotle's) three requirements for the tragic hero, only the third ("highest station") is strictly applicable to the protagonists of *Paradise Lost*; and in *Samson* this consideration is one of the sources of tragic effect in the parodos:

> O mirror of our fickle state,
> Since man on earth unparallel'd!
> By how much from the top of wondrous glory,
> Strongest of mortal men,
> To lowest pitch of abject fortune thou art fall'n.

The first and second conditions are only partially relevant to Milton's epic. Created perfect, Adam and Eve are not depraved, though their transgression results in depravity; they are not vicious until they voluntarily disobey. Since they bear the divine image in its pristine perfection, they "exceed ... in virtue," even though this is innate and natural virtue rather than virtue as a habit acquired and tested through exercise. Though virtuous, they are still, in large part, inexperienced in virtue. Since they have been fully and repeatedly warned of the consequences of disobedience, they do not sin through ignorance, but rather through desire for forbidden knowledge by forbidden means. Though Eve is beguiled by the serpent, Adam is not deceived, but overcome with female charm. Neither Samson's fall nor that of Adam and Eve is a case of "undeserved misfortune." See Bywater, pp. 49–51.

There are analogies, but also differences, between Samson's ruin and that of Adam. Though both are overcome by female charm and fall through weakness rather than depravity, Adam has been created perfect. Samson, on the other hand, excels in strength but not in wisdom. Nevertheless, both are fully responsible for their own actions. Although Samson has committed an "error of judgment" in trusting Dalila, he has not transgressed in utter ignorance. He has had ample experience already of her treacherous character—and of the faithlessness of his earlier Philistine bride—but his eyes have been blinded by passion. Heroic constancy, magnanimity, and the better fortitude of patience have (ironically) been subverted by a concubine on her own condign battlefield.

The tragedy of the Philistines, finally, like that of the suitors in the *Odyssey*, may inspire terror and horror, but it is not calculated to arouse pity. It is an execution of justice rather than an "undeserved misfortune"; and it approximates a pattern that Aristotle had specifically rejected as unsuitable for tragedy—the pattern of "an extremely bad man ... seen falling from happiness to misery"; see Bywater, pp. 49–51.

14. Bywater, p. 46.
15. Ibid., p. 47.
16. Marvin T. Herrick, *Comic Theory in the Sixteenth Century* (Urbana, Ill., 1964), pp. 69–70.
17. Despite extensive analysis, the *commos* of Milton's tragedy still presents certain unresolved problems. Aristotle had defined this term as *threnos koinos chorou kai (tōn) apo skēnēs:* "a lamentation sung by chorus and actor in concert"; Bywater, p. 49; S. H. Butcher, *Aristotle's Theory of Poetry and Fine Art* (London, 1902), p. 42. How far this definition actually fits the concluding lines of *Samson* is debatable. As Parker correctly observes, lines 1660–1707 (which several commentators had identified as a *commos*) are sung by chorus and semichoruses alone. Moreover, the choral ode preceding Manoa's speech "is anything but a dirge." Parker himself attempts to resolve the problem by including Manoa's speech and the final chorus in the *commos* (i.e., the entire passage from line 1660 to the end of the play); *Milton's Debt to Greek Tragedy*, pp. 103–9. If we accept Parker's interpretation, we must regard Milton's *commos* as radically different both in form and in content from the *commoi* that Sir Richard Jebb had identified in Sophocles' *Oedipus Rex*, lines 649–97, 1297–1368; cf. Jebb's edition (Cambridge, 1920), pp. xxvi–xxvii, xxxii–xxxiv. In the first *commos* of Sophocles' drama, there are frequent responses not only between Oedipus and the chorus but between Oedipus and Creon and between the chorus and Jocasta. The second *commos* immediately follows the second messenger's account of Oedipus's self-inflicted blindness and consists of a continuous dialogue between the blind king and the chorus. It begins (perhaps significantly) with a reference to the hero's visible *pathos:* "O dreadful anguish (*pathos*) for men to see!" In Aeschylus's *Seven against Thebes*, the *commos* (lines 860–940) consists entirely of a choral ode chanted after the dead bodies of Eteocles and Polynices have been brought on stage; and it is immediately followed by the stichomythic dirge or *threnos* recited by Antigone and Ismene (lines 941–95); see the edition of this play by A. W. Verall and M. A. Bayfield (London, 1901), p. xxix.

Though Milton's alleged *commos* occurs precisely at the point where one might expect a *commos* to occur—that is, immediately after the messenger's account of the "horrid spectacle" concluding in the report of Samson's death—it appears to differ both in form and in content from the kind of joint lament that Aristotle had described and that modern classical scholars have identified in Greek tragedy. The variation itself, however, is significant; for it appears to underline the kind of providential reversal of expectation implicit in the entire action of the play. The hero's suffering or *pathos* proves a source of consolation. Manoa finds therein nothing that warrants lamentation or the tears and breast-beating of the traditional *threnos*. On the contrary, it is an occasion not for passion but for reassurance and tranquility of mind: "what may *quiet* us in a death so noble." Rightly understood, the *pathos* becomes an argument for consolation, an instrument of catharsis. The apparent irregularity of Milton's *commos* provides the final irony in a drama notable for its ironic reversals of expectation. The point of the formal *threnos* or choral lament is that there is no cause for lamentation: "nothing but well and fair." Milton has skillfully undercut the tragic dirge, just as he has (on other occasions) undercut the Sicilian pastoral, the court masque, and the heroic epic.

In form (though not in content) the lyric interchanges between Samson and the chorus in lines 541-57 bear a closer resemblance to the traditional *commos* than does the dialogue between Manoa and the chorus in the final section of the play. These lyric passages, however, are devoted primarily to the hero's former temperance rather than to his sufferings.

Elsewhere in the drama, the expression of intense grief may approach the quality of lyric; but these are, for the most part, individual rather that joint lamentations. Though they are not the only laments in the tragedy, they are notable both for their length and for their lyric intensity; and for the sake of a convenient nomenclature we may refer to them as *threnoi*. Milton usually underlines their nature and significance as threnodies through terms like "bemoan" or "bewail." The three principal threnodies of this sort are Samson's initial complaint over the miseries of his condition, blindness and bondage (lines 64-110); the chorus's lament over his bondage and "lost sight" (lines 151-75); and his bitter expression of the torments of the mind (lines 606-51).

18. Kester Svendsen, *Milton and Science* (Cambridge, 1956); Sherman Hawkins, "Samson's Catharsis," in *Milton Studies* (Pittsburgh, 1970), 2:211-30.

8   Epic and Tragic Affects
Miracle and the Epic Marvelous

1. Torquato Tasso, *Prose*, ed. Francesco Flora (Milan and Rome, 1935), pp. 331-34, 379. Italics mine.

2. Ingram Bywater, trans., *Aristotle on the Art of Poetry* (Oxford, 1951), pp. 83-84.

3. *Discorso di Giacopo Mazzoni in Difensa della "Commedia" del Divino Poeta Dante*, ed. Mario Rossi (Città di Castello, 1898), pp. 95-96.

4. *L'Arte Poetica del Signor Antonio Minturno* (Naples, 1725), p. 41.

5. Lodovico Castelvetro, *Poetica d'Aristotele Vulgarizzata et Sposta* (Bacol, 1576), p. 518.

6. *The Prose Works of John Milton* (Bohn's Standard Library, London, 1883), 3: 473–74. See Ida Langdon, *Milton's Theory of Poetry and Fine Art* (New Haven, 1924) and Milton's *Reason of Church Government* (*Prose Works*, 2: 479).

7. Tasso, p. 361.

8. Castelvetro, p. 228.

9. Milton, *Prose Works*, 4:289–96.

10. Tasso, p. 333.

11. Minturno, p. 41.

12. Castelvetro, p. 552. Cf. *Aeneid*, 12, lines 693, 704, 730, 742, 758–61.

13. Castelvetro, p. 513.

14. Cf. ibid., p. 612, on the marvelous in "l'uccisione de drudi di Penelope."

15. Cf. ibid., p. 253.

16. Tasso, pp. 333–34.

17. Ibid., p. 334.

18. Bywater, p. 45.

19. Daniel Heinsius, trans., *Aristotelis De Poëtica* (Leiden, 1643), p. 261, "haec ipsa maxime admirationem movent, sed praecipue cum praeter expectationem alterum alterius est causa."

20. Bywater, pp. 45–46. Cf. Heinsius, p. 261, "ea maxime admiratione digna videntur, quae non absque causa fiere existimantur."

21. Minturno, p. 40. Cf. Bywater, p. 46.

22. Mazzoni, p. 96, "l'*Odissea* ... è come piu piena del maraviglioso, per havere il riconoscimento, sul quale non è dubbio che tutto il mirabile della poetica favola si fonda."

23. Bywater, p. 84; cf. Castelvetro, pp. 553–54.

24. Mazzoni, pp. 83–86.

25. Tasso, pp. 361–62.

26. Milton, *Prose Works*, 3:474.

27. Ibid., 4:212; cf. Columbia Edition, 15:94–95. See Maurice Kelley, "Milton and Miracles," *MLN* 53 (1938): 170–72.

28. Bartholomaeus Keckermannus, *Systema SS. Theologiae* (Hanover, 1611), pp. 465–66.

29. *Christianae Theologiae Compendium ... Authore Iohanne Wollebio* (Amsterdam, 1633), p. 57. See Maurice Kelley, "Milton's Debt to Wolleb's *Compendium Theologiae Christianae*," *PMLA* 50 (1935): 156–65; T. S. K. Scott-Craig, "Milton's Use of Wolleb and Ames," *MLN* 55 (1940): 403–7; and my note, "Milton and Wolleb Again," *Harvard Theological Review* 53 (1960): 155–56.

30. *Operum Theologicorum D. Hieronymi Zanchii* (Geneva, 1611), vol. 3, cols. 192–95. According to Zanchius's definition (col. 192), "*Miraculum* ... est externum ac visible, verum & simpliciter mira-

bile factum: ad optimos fines, atque inprimis ad salutem hominum, &
ad Dei gloriam promovendam editum."

31. Saint Thomas Aquinas, *Super Epistolas S. Pauli Lectura*, ed. P.
Raphael Cai (Rome and Turin, 1953), 2:201.

32. Idem, *Summa Theologiae*, ed. Petrus Carmello (Rome and Turin,
1948), part 1, Q. 110, A. 4 and Q. 114, A. 4.

33. In Milton's hands, this lying wonder is the central link in the chain of
Satan's argument; the false miracle supposedly effected in the serpent
is presented as proof that the tree can accomplish a similar miracle in
the case of Eve. This exploitation of the miraculous subjects her faith,
as well as her obedience to trial. Significantly, Zanchius maintains
(col. 195) that God permits the demons to perform false miracles in
order to try the faith and patience of the elect. Moreover, as a devil
cannot "open the eyes of the blind" (John 10:21), there is a certain
degree of irony in the promise (based on Genesis 3:5) that "your Eyes
that . . . are but dim, shall perfetly be then Op'n'd and clear'd"
(9.706–8).

34. Milton, *Prose Works*, 4:212; Columbia Edition, vol. 15, pp. 94–97.

Epilogue   Plot as Paradigm
Epic Design and Divine Idea

1. Ingram Bywater, trans., *Aristotle on the Art of Poetry*, (Oxford,
1945), pp. 40–41.

2. John Dryden, *Of Dramatic Poesy and Other Critical Essays*, ed.
George Watson (London and New York, 1962), 2:84.

3. John T. Shawcross, ed., *Milton: The Critical Heritage*, (New York,
1970), p. 114.

4. Shawcross, pp. 128–29.

5. Shawcross, p. 256.

6. E. L. McAdam, Jr., and George Milne, eds., *A Johnson Reader*, (New
York, 1964), pp. 410–21.

7. R. M. Cummings, ed., *Spenser: The Critical Heritage* (New York,
1971), pp. 16, 203, 206, 222, 260, 332.

8. James Thorpe, ed., *Milton Criticism: Selections from Four Centuries*,
(New York, 1969), pp. 23–25.

9. McAdam and Milne, pp. 410–21.

10. Watson, 2:84.

11. Shawcross, p. 256.

12. Thorpe, pp. 48–49. For the relation between epic and tragic structure
in Paradise Lost, see Martin Mueller, "The Tragic Epic: *Paradise Lost*
and the *Iliad*," diss., Indiana University, 1966; Charles Thomas
Samuels, "The Tragic Vision of *Paradise Lost*," *University of Kansas
City Review* 27 (1960): 65–78; T. S. K. Scott-Craig, "Miltonic
Tragedy and Christian Vision," in *The Tragic Vision and the*

Christian Faith, ed. Nathan A. Scott, Jr. (New York, 1957), pp. 99–122; John Patrick Tyson, "The Elements of Aristotelian Tragedy in *Paradise Lost,*" diss., Tulane University, 1967; Herbert Weisinger, *Tragedy and the Paradox of the Fortunate Fall* (London, 1969).

13. See Arthur E. Barker, "Structural Pattern in *Paradise Lost,*" in *Milton: Modern Essays in Criticism,* ed. Arthur E. Barker (New York, 1965), pp. 336–41, for analysis of *Paradise Lost* in terms of five-act dramatic structure and the structural implications of Milton's shift from a ten-book to a twelve-book epic. In *Milton's Poetic Art: A Mask, Lycidas, and Paradise Lost* (Cambridge, Mass., 1968), John Reesing also considers the structural implications of Milton's twelve-book pattern. See also Robert A. Durr, "Dramatic Pattern in *Paradise Lost,*" *JAAC* 13 (1955): 520–26; J. H. Hanford, "The Dramatic Element in *Paradise Lost,*" in *John Milton, Poet and Humanist* (Cleveland, 1966), pp. 224–43; P. Jeffrey Ford, "*Paradise Lost* and the Five-Act Epic," diss., Columbia University, 1966; Gerald D. Grow, "*Paradise Lost* and the Renaissance Drama: Milton's Theme of Fall and Its Dramatic Counterpart in Marlowe, Shakespeare, Jonson, and Middleton," diss., Yale University, 1969.

14. Bywater, p. 95.

15. Bywater, p. 34.

16. This parallel should not be pressed too far, however. Despite Lucan's sympathy for Pompey and his veneration for Cato, Caesar remains the protagonist for the *Pharsalia;* Adam, not Satan, remains the protagonist for *Paradise Lost.* Nonetheless, where Adam merely chooses, Satan vigorously acts. Insofar as Milton's epic is truly the imitation of an action, its pseudohero plays a principal, albeit incomplete, role in the organization of the plot.

   For Satan's role in the formal structure of Milton's plot, see Calvin Huckabay, "Satan and the Narrative Structure of *Paradise Lost:* Some Observations," *Studia Neophilologica* 33 (1961): 96–102; Putnam F. Jones, "Satan and the Narrative Structure of *Paradise Lost,*" in *If by Your Art* (Pittsburgh, 1948), pp. 15–26. In Jones's view, the structure of Milton's narrative was largely responsible for the Satanist controversy; Huckabay, in turn, emphasized the central position of man in the poem in spite of Satan's dominance in the early books.

17. The relationship between divine decree and epic action in *Paradise Lost* is conditioned largely by the poet's emphasis on man's free will and by the demands of his subject. The initiative in the epic enterprise logically belongs to the powers of hell. Though this pattern was scarcely appropriate for the epic model favored by the majority of Renaissance critics—a heroic enterprise ordained and aided by heaven and executed by a paragon of heroic virtue—it was not uncommon in poetry centered (like Satan's own enterprise) on direct opposition to the divine will. In arguments like the massacre of the innocents or the Gunpowder Plot, the initiative rests with the devil. In epics devoted to evils of civil war, the initiative belongs to the forces of

discord, demonic or human. The warfare in the later books of the *Aeneid*—a rebellion against a divine decree, though neither Amata nor Turnus recognizes it as such—is incited by an infernal Fury at Juno's behest. This was the natural, indeed inevitable, pattern for Milton to follow in *Paradise Lost*, where the Adversary alone provokes rebellion against a divine decree, instigating the revolt of the angels as well as man's rebellion.

18.   Cf. Dennis H. Burden, *The Logical Epic: A Study of the Argument of Paradise Lost* (London, 1967); Ross C. Brackney, " 'By Fallacy Surpris'd:' Logic and the Miltonic Hero," diss., Stanford University, 1970.

19.   See Rosalie L. Colie, *Paradoxia Epidemica: The Renaissance Tradition of Paradox* (Princeton, 1966); idem, "Time and Eternity: Paradox and Structure in *Paradise Lost*," *Journal of the Warburg and Courtauld Institutes* 23 (1960): 127–38; Arthur Lovejoy, "Milton and the Paradox of the Fortunate Fall," *ELH* 4 (1937): 161–79; William H. Marshall, "*Paradise Lost: Felix Culpa* and the Problem of Structure," in *Milton: Modern Essays in Criticism*, ed. Arthur E. Barker (New York, 1965), pp. 336–41; William Madsen, "The Fortunate Fall in *Paradise Lost*," *MLN* 74 (1959): 103–5; Clarence C. Green, "The Paradox of the Fall in *Paradise Lost*," *MLN* 53 (1938): 557–71; John E. Parish, "Standing Prostrate: The Paradox in *Paradise Lost*, X, 1099, and XI, 1," *English Miscellany* 15 (1964): 89–101; David V. Harrington, "A Defense of the *Felix Culpa* in *Paradise Lost*," *Cresset* 28 (1965): 12–14; Earl Miner, "*Felix Culpa* and the Redemptive Order of *Paradise Lost*," *PQ* 47 (1968): 43–54; Enno Klammer, "The Fallacy of the *Felix Culpa* in Milton's *Paradise Lost*," *Cresset* 23 (1960): 13–14; Corinne E. Kauffman, "Adam in Paradox," *Arlington Quarterly* 1 (1968): 111–17; John E. Seaman, *The Moral Paradox of Paradise Lost* (The Hague, 1971); John C. Ulreich, Jr., "A Paradise Within: The Fortunate Fall in *Paradise Lost*," *Journal of the History of Ideas* 32 (1971): 351–66; J. C. Gray, "Paradox in *Paradise Lost*," *Milton Quarterly* 7 (1973): 76–82.

For the parodic structure of *Paradise Lost*, see John P. Cutts, "The Miserific Vision: A Study of Some of the Basic Structural Imagery of *Paradise Lost*," *English Miscellany* 14 (1963): 57–72; Mother Mary Christopher Pecheux, "O Foul Descent: Satan and the Serpent Form," *SP* 62 (1965): 188–96. See also the recent discussion of parodic structure in Milton's poetry by Balachandra Rajan, "The Cunning Resemblance," in *Milton Studies* (Pittsburgh, 1975), 7:29–48. For Milton's parody of epic conventions, see Stella P. Revard, "Milton's Critique of Heroic Warfare in *Paradise Lost* V and VI," *SEL* 7 (1967): 119–39; Arnold Stein, "Milton's War in Heaven—An Extended Metaphor," *ELH* 18 (1951): 201–20; John E. Seaman, "Homeric Parody at the Gates of Milton's Hell," *MLR* 62 (1967): 212–13. William J. Knightley, "The Perfidy of the Devils' Council," *University of Mississippi Studies in English* 5 (1964): 9–14, stresses the close analogies between the works of Christ and Satan in Milton's epic.

20. For discussion of the center or crisis of Milton's plot, see Douglas Knight, "The Dramatic Center of *Paradise Lost*," *South Atlantic Quaterly* 63 (1964): 44–59; E. M. W. Tillyard, "The Crisis of *Paradise Lost*," in *Studies in Milton* (London, 1951); Millicent Bell, "The Fallacy of the Fall in *Paradise Lost*," *PMLA* 68 (1953): 863–83; H. S. V. Ogden, "The Crisis of *Paradise Lost* Reconsidered," *PQ* 36 (1957): 1–19; Joseph H. Summers, "*Paradise Lost*: The Pattern at the Center," in *The Muse's Method: An Introduction to Paradise Lost* (Cambridge, Mass., and London, 1962); John T. Shawcross, "The Son in His Ascendance: A Reading of *Paradise Lost*," *MLQ* 27 (1966): 388–401; William B. Hunter, Jr., "The Center of *Paradise Lost*," *ELN* 7 (1969): 32–34.

21. McAdam and Milne, p. 411.

22. Shawcross, p. 219.

23. The critical hazards involved in the search for a central thesis or moral are more clearly evident in Dryden's remarks on Bossu's theory than in Addison and Johnson. "The first rule which Bossu prescribes to the writer of an heroic poem . . . is to make the moral of the work, that is to lay down to yourself what that precept of morality shall be, which you would insinuate into the people." Homer's moral was "that union preserves a commonwealth, and discord destroys it; Sophocles, in his *Oedipus*, that no man is to be accounted happy before his death. 'Tis the moral that directs the whole action of the play to one centre, which confirms the truth of it to our experience." (Watson, 1:248; cf. idem, 2:186).

24. Cf. Merritt Y. Hughes, "Beyond Disobedience," in *Approaches to Paradise Lost*, ed. C. A. Patrides (London, 1968), pp. 181–98.

25. Cf. Michael Lieb, *The Dialectics of Creation: Patterns of Birth and Regeneration in Paradise Lost* (Amherst, Mass., 1970); Stanley Eugene Fish, *Surprised by Sin: The Reader in Paradise Lost* (London and New York, 1967), p. 49.

26. Though Raphael is aware not only that Adam will fall but that he will receive conditional pardon, the angel scrupulously conceals this knowledge. His duty as ambassador is to warn a potential rebel, not to offer amnesty or consolation in advance. At the moment, the crucial issue for Adam, as formerly for Satan, is obedience or disobedience to a divine edict. After man's fall the terms will be different, as Michael's prophecy will demonstrate; the essential issue will be the merits of Christ's obedience, the acceptance or rejection of grace. In order to enhance the efficacy of Michael's consolation, and to achieve a final *peripeteia* at the very conclusion of the plot, Milton leaves Adam in ignorance of his future redemption until virtually the last lines of the poem. The protevangelium, the first annunciation of a future redeemer, is couched in dark and mysterious terms that Adam does not yet comprehend. Although he is partly regenerated, he does not yet recognize the agent of his regeneration; he does not yet realize that he is being clothed in the Son's own "Robe of

righteousness." Milton deliberately keeps his epic protagonist in the dark in order to arouse, in the end, the characteristic epic "affect" of wonder.

27. To a limited degree Raphael's histories of the angelic war and the creation of the world resemble miniature epics or divine poems. Each is centered on a single action and celebrates an exploit accomplished single-handedly by the Messiah in obedience to a divine decree. Although they portray contrary actions, creation and destruction, both depict the Messiah's imposition of divine order upon confusion.

28. David Masson, ed., *The Poetical Works of John Milton* (London, 1903), 2:26–27.

29. For an excellent discussion of the analogy between divine and human art, the theory of correspondences, and "cosmic patterns" in the works of Spenser and other Renaissance poets, see the chapter "Poem as Literary Microcosm," in S. K. Heninger, Jr., *Touches of Sweet Harmony: Pythagorean Cosmology and Renaissance Poetics* (San Marino, California, 1974), pp. 364–97. For mathematical or numerological patterns in Milton's epic, see Gunnar Qvarnström, *The Enchanted Palace: Some Structural Aspects of Paradise Lost* (Stockholm, 1967); Maren-Sofie Røstvig, *The Hidden Sense and Other Essays* (Oslo and New York, 1963), pp. 1–112; idem, "Renaissance Numerology: Acrostics or Criticism?" *Essays in Criticism* 16 (1966): 6–21. Though M. M. Mahood did not employ the numerological method, her observations on the "exact correspondence" between Milton's "world-picture" and the shape and movement of his epic (the two principal aspects of its form) emphasized its mathematical structure: "The shape of *Paradise Lost* as a poem coincides so justly with the concentric spheres of Milton's cosmography that it might be called geometric; and the movements of various bodies in this cosmos are repeated in the work's dynamic form." In her opinion, the *Aeneid* supplied the "pattern," and the Book of Genesis the "design" of the poem, but the "form of the epic" was "entirely organic by reason of its dependence on Milton's own thought" (Mahood, *Poetry and Humanism* [New York, 1970], p. 177).

30. Erwin Panofsky, *Idea: A Concept in Art Theory*, trans., Joseph J. S. Peake (Columbia, S.C., 1968), pp. 85–95.

31. For the representation of time and space in *Paradise Lost*, and their relation to the structure of the poem, see Jackson I. Cope, "Time and Space as Miltonic Symbol," *ELH* 26 (1959): 497–531; idem, *The Metaphoric Structure of Paradise Lost* (Baltimore, 1962); Albert R. Cirillo, "Noon-Midnight and the Temporal Structure of *Paradise Lost*," *ELH* 29 (1962): 372–95; Walter C. Curry, "Some Travels of Milton's Satan and the Road to Hell," *PQ* 29 (1950): pp. 225–35; Roy Daniells, *Milton, Mannerism and Baroque* (Toronto, 1963).

32. As Helen Gardner comments, "The plucking of the apple is not in itself imaginatively powerful; its power over us springs from its very triviality; the meaning and the consequences are so much greater than

the image of a hand stretched out to pluck the fruit"; Gardner, "Milton's 'Satan' and the Theme of Damnation in Elizabethan Tragedy," in Barker, p. 209. See also the chapters on "The Universe of *Paradise Lost*" and "The Cosmic Theme" in Helen Gardner, *A Reading of Paradise Lost* (Oxford, 1965), pp. 29–75.

33. For the motif of the *hortus conclusus* in the Renaissance, see Stanley Stewart, *The Enclosed Garden: The Tradition and the Image in Seventeenth-Century Poetry* (Madison, Wisc., 1966).

INDEX

Vettori, P., 76, 80, 86–87
Vitruvius, 25, 151–52
Voltaire, 122, 124
Vossius, Gerard Jan, 3

Waldock, A. J. A., 10

Weinberg, Bernard, 172
Wilkes, G. A., 10, 160
Wolleb, J., 116–17

Zanchius, Hieronymus, 116, 180
Zuccari, Federico, 137–38